T0319118

The Political Value of Time

Waiting periods and deadlines are so ubiquitous that we often take them for granted. Yet they form a critical part of any democratic architecture. When a precise moment or amount of time is given political importance, we ought to understand why this is so. *The Political Value of Time* explores the idea of time within democratic theory and practice. Elizabeth F. Cohen demonstrates how political procedures use quantities of time to confer and deny citizenship rights. Using specific dates and deadlines, states carve boundaries around a citizenry. As time is assigned a form of political value, it is deployed to transact over rights. Cohen concludes with a normative analysis of the ways in which the devaluation of some people's political time constitutes a widely overlooked form of injustice. This book shows readers how and why they need to think about time if they want to understand politics.

Elizabeth F. Cohen is Associate Professor of Political Science at the Maxwell School of Citizenship and Public Affairs at Syracuse University. She is the author of *Semi-Citizenship in Democratic Politics* (Cambridge University Press, 2009), and her scholarship has featured in *Citizenship Studies, Perspectives on Politics*, and *Ethics and International Affairs*. In addition, she publishes op-eds in newspapers, including the *Washington Post* and *Politico*.

The Political Value of Time

Citizenship, Duration, and Democratic Justice

ELIZABETH F. COHEN

CAMBRIDGE
UNIVERSITY PRESS

CAMBRIDGE
UNIVERSITY PRESS

University Printing House, Cambridge CB2 8BS, United Kingdom

One Liberty Plaza, 20th Floor, New York, NY 10006, USA

477 Williamstown Road, Port Melbourne, VIC 3207, Australia

314–321, 3rd Floor, Plot 3, Splendor Forum, Jasola District Centre, New Delhi – 110025, India

79 Anson Road, #06–04/06, Singapore 079906

Cambridge University Press is part of the University of Cambridge.

It furthers the University's mission by disseminating knowledge in the pursuit of education, learning, and research at the highest international levels of excellence.

www.cambridge.org
Information on this title: www.cambridge.org/9781108419833
DOI: 10.1017/9781108304283

First published 2018

A catalogue record for this publication is available from the British Library.

ISBN 978-1-108-41983-3 Hardback
ISBN 978-1-108-41225-4 Paperback

Cambridge University Press has no responsibility for the persistence or accuracy of URLs for external or third-party internet websites referred to in this publication and does not guarantee that any content on such websites is, or will remain, accurate or appropriate.

For my father, Ira J. Cohen, who supplies our family with an abundance of mirth, merriment, and metaphors.

Contents

Acknowledgements   *page* viii

1   Introduction   1
2   The Sovereign Temporal Borders around Nation-States,
    Populations, and Citizenries   29
3   Democracy, Duration, and Lived Consent   62
4   Time's Political Value   97
5   The Political Economy of Time   120
6   Conclusion   153

Bibliography   164
Index   178

Acknowledgements

Any acknowledgment I write must begin where my story begins, with my grandfather, Chaim Feiner's quiet heroism. But for the fact of his strength and courage, our family would not exist. Much of his life was lived without security or basic necessities, let alone the formal education for which he yearned. Yet he left the world a legacy of grandchildren with doctorates and great-grandchildren poised for more. His biography is a defiant rebuke to those who believe they can extinguish a person's existence. The persecuted only come back smarter and stronger.

Portions of this book were workshopped at the Departments of Political Science at Yale University, Princeton University, Stanford University, Columbia University, New York University, Johns Hopkins University, Temple University, Swarthmore College, and the law schools at Duke University, Cornell University, and Temple University.

While I was working on this project I received generous support from the Russell Sage Foundation, the National Endowment for the Humanities, the Mellon Foundation, and New York University. I also acknowledge the Dean's Office at the Maxwell School of Syracuse University and the Campbell Public Affairs Institute for their support.

My graduate school mentors at Yale, Rogers Smith, Ian Shapiro, and John McCormick, remain important influences on my work. I am thankful to now count them as colleagues and friends.

Along the way I have received extremely generous feedback from Hans Oberdiek, Benjamin Berger, Josh Ober, Lennie Feldman, Jeffrey Isaac, Corey Brettschneider, Peter Breiner, Melissa Schwartzberg, David Owen, Rainer Baubock, Erin Chung, Peter Spiro, Adam Cox, Michael Jones Correa, Andy Sabl, Dan Tichenor, Jan-Werner Muller, Stephen Macedo,

Heath Davis, Sarah Song, Melissa Lane, Hiroshi Motomura, Sanford Levinson, Ayten Gündoğdu, Joe Carens, Paul Frymer, Jennifer London, Turkuler Isiksel, Paulina Ochoa Espejo, Seyla Benhabib, Karthick Ramakrishnan, Kenneth Baynes, Glyn Morgan, and Heidi Swarts.

I was fortunate to receive early encouragement for this project from my editor at Cambridge University Press, Robert Dreesen, and excellent support from the Cambridge production team. I also thank the anonymous reviewers who provided incisive feedback on the manuscript.

For his patient and energetic research assistance, I thank Philip Perez. Three other former students, Jenn Kinney, Lindsey Kingston, and Chris Morley, have been top-notch co-authors and incredibly supportive of this project in its earliest stages. They are sterling people who mentor me way more than I ever mentored them.

At the Russell Sage Foundation, where I spent a year as a visiting scholar, I found a welcoming and rich academic cohort. Sheldon Danziger, Suzanne Nichols, Aixa Cintron, and the staff of the Information Services make the foundation an incredibly welcoming place. While there, I was fortunate to become friends with Mona Lynch, Susan Silbey, Sean Reardon, Karl Jacoby, Ann Morning, Susan Stokes, Jay McCann, and Tom Palfrey. Aliya Saperstein became a dear friend with whom I shared both harrowing and triumphant moments as well as some incredible meals.

Janelle Wong and Dara Strolovitch were among the first people I met when I got to Yale and all these years later they remain the most stalwart of friends.

At Syracuse I have become acquainted with the liveliest friends I could imagine having. Over the years I have benefited from Keith Bybee's razor sharp intellect and wit. Tom and Meredith Perreault have bolstered my spirits and kept me well fed. Long therapeutic conversations with Sarah Pralle have provided precious insight and empathy.

Wherever I find myself, Cyril Ghosh is the smartest, most loyal, loving, gently critical, and honest friend I could imagine having. Dave Reischman opened the boathouse to me and made it a haven and a home.

My small but mighty family is the greatest piece of luck anyone has ever had. I grew up with two parents who were each other's intellectual equal and who assumed I would join their conversation as soon as I learned to talk. They have always managed to both challenge and sustain me. The older I get, the more I recognize what a boon it has been to grow up with a mother for whom no institution was too powerful to take down, no person too well regarded to question, and no science too complex to master. Everyone should grow up knowing a woman who doesn't understand what it means to be quieted or intimidated.

From the moment that I began work on this book I have known that the project was unusually enjoyable and that the fun I was having derived from a singular way of thinking modeled for me by my father. An average afternoon with him will involve clever wordplay, deep erudition, and kaleidoscopic metaphors with multiple meanings. As generations of his undergraduate and graduate students will attest, the combination is magical. Without its influence, I would have not come upon the ideas I have developed in this book or had all the lasting satisfaction that comes along with having written it. The best thing I have to offer by way of thanks is the book itself, and so I dedicate it to him with boundless love and admiration.

Introduction

Time is widely recognized as one of the most precious and finite resources required for the accomplishment of human purposes. Within the domain of the political, time is required for almost any exercise of liberty that people seek to protect through the enforcement of social contracts, constitutions, and laws. Time is therefore inextricable from the realization of any vision of political justice.

All political subjects encounter myriad ways in which their time is structured, valued, appropriated, or freed by the state. In the United States, we wait to turn 18 to acquire political voice and full representation. Then we wait again, to turn 62 or 66, when we can retire from work and receive retirement benefits, if we wish. People file taxes on April 15; redistricting hinges on decennial censuses; and prosecutors specify when crimes were committed to determine whether statutes of limitation have expired. Around us, convicted criminals are punished with prison sentences of varying durations, legal permanent residents refrain from traveling for long periods of time as they seek to naturalize, and election cycles run their course only to begin anew. Despite the significance of time for the satisfaction of people's ends, the legitimate power of the state to command the time of its subjects and set a political schedule is not generally contested.

Scientifically measured durational time – clock and calendar time[1] – is one of the most common units of value used for transactions over power

---

[1] Sociologists of time distinguish scientifically measured time from other ways of thinking about time – for example cyclical time, natural time, sacred time, ecological time, and so on. See Eviatar Zerubavel, "The Standardization of Time: A Sociohistorical Perspective," *American Journal of Sociology* 88, no. 1(1982); Barbara Adam, *Time Watch: The Social Analysis of Time* (Chichester, UK: Wiley, 2013); Barbara Adam, *Time and Social Theory* (Chichester, UK: Wiley, 2013); E.P. Thompson, "Time, Work–Discipline, and Industrial Capitalism," *Past & Present* 38 (1967). Scientifically measured durational time is distinctly linear and closely identified with modernity. I also want to stress that for the purposes of this book time does not refer to historical context but instead to durations measured by clocks and calendars.

and rights in democracies. Durational time is a prerequisite for the acquisition and exercise of many rights in liberal democracies. Prison sentences, naturalization procedures, social welfare benefits eligibility, abortion restrictions, and probationary periods are only a few of the most prominent examples of laws and policies that confer or deny rights and political status based on formulae that include precise durations of time. Deadlines and waiting periods of both momentous and trivial importance abound in modern life. We expect military service to be measured primarily in precisely measured tours of duty, political terms to end after elections, and different offices to be associated with different length terms. We insist on cooling-off periods during negotiations, former officeholders must refrain from doing work such as lobbying for a specific period of time after they leave office, and a member of the US military is required to seek a waiver before assuming a political position in a president's cabinet prior to the elapse of seven years.[2] A full enumeration of the temporal political procedures one encounters throughout the course of a lifespan could easily dwarf the word count of this chapter – possibly the whole book.

In fact, it is virtually impossible to find a realm of politics in which the deployment of scientifically measured durational time does not figure prominently. From the constitutive elements of politics, such as the moment at which sovereignty commences, to true procedural minutiae, such as the period of time that police officers are instructed to wait before giving a statement after a shooting, time is bound deeply and inextricably to the exercise of power.[3]

The Political Value of Time proceeds with the following goal: to examine how and why durational time has become such a critical part of the architecture of every democratic state. As American political development (APD) and public policy scholars have long noted, time is an "essential constitutive dimension of politics."[4] Culture and politics are "indelibly (even if obscurely) marked with the signature of time."[5]

---

[2] Joe Gould and Leo Shane III, "U.S. Congress Passes Waiver for Mattis to Lead Pentagon," *Defense News* (Jan. 13, 2017), www.defensenews.com/articles/us-congress-passes-waiver-for-mattis-to-lead-pentagon
[3] Jaeah Lee, "Why Cops Are Told to Keep Quiet after a Shooting: The Controversial Science between the 48-Hour Rule," *Mother Jones* (Aug. 12, 2015), www.motherjones.com/politics/2015/08/why-do-police-departments-delay-interviewing-officers-involved-shootings
[4] Karen Orren and Stephen Skowronek, *The Search for American Political Development* (Cambridge University Press, 2004), 75.
[5] Margaret R. Somers, "Where Is Sociology after the Historic Turn? Knowledge Cultures, Narrativity, and Historical Epistemologies," in *The Historic Turn in the Human Sciences*, ed. Terrence J. McDonald (University of Michigan Press, 1996), 54.

Consequently, law and policy are "deeply embedded with ideas about time that deserve our attention."[6] Yet, despite the nearly universal experience of having one's time valued or devalued by the state, time's ubiquity in politics, and widespread social scientific interest in temporality, durational time has not received much attention within political theories of legitimacy or justice. We implicitly accept that a state can and does legitimately command the time of its subjects. However, our sense of why this is so or what it means for a state to make illegitimate claims on the time of democratic citizens is relatively inchoate.

No comprehensive explanation for the role of durational time in procedural democracy has yet been elaborated. Political science has much to gain from developing a concept of political time.[7] When a precise date or duration of time is given explicit importance in a political procedure we ought to ask why this is so. We must also scrutinize the consequences of such procedures in order to see whether the use of time in policies and laws has normative implications for those affected by them.

This book brings into relief the importance of scientifically measured durational time in the architecture and practice of liberal democratic politics. It also elaborates an explanation for why time figures so prominently in transactions over the acquisition and exercise of citizenship rights and political power. The guiding set of questions for this endeavor are: how does durational time come to structure and distribute political power? Why is durational time so frequently inserted into political procedures for granting, denying, and exercising rights? How can we evaluate the normative effects of the ways that states command the time of their citizens?

Briefly put: the book advances the claim that scientifically measured durational time is assigned political value within every liberal democracy. Political time – moments, dates, ages, and durations of time that have been

---

[6] Rebecca R. French, "Time in the Law," *University of Colorado Law Review* 72 (2001): 672.

[7] Here I must distinguish my usage of the phrase "political time" from that of Stephen Skowronek's. In *The Politics Presidents Make* and *Presidential Leadership in Political Time* Skowronek deploys "political time" in reference to the context in which presidents make decisions. See Stephen Skowronek, *The Politics Presidents Make: Leadership from John Adams to Bill Clinton* (Cambridge, MA: Harvard University Press, 1993); Stephen Skowronek, *Presidential Leadership in Political Time: Reprise and Reappraisal* (University Press of Kansas, 2008). Whereas Skowronek's political context has to do with existing ideologies and relationships of power, this book treats political time as the actual dates and quantities of time used by the state in its capacity as sovereign.

accorded value by the state – is a valuable good that is frequently used to transact over power. Time's political value is based on beliefs about durational time's role in a set of processes that are themselves integral to democratic politics. These beliefs need not be either shared by all or be demonstrably true in order for time to take on political value. In fact, one of the conclusions reached in the book is that imperfect overlap of beliefs about the meaning of time sustains important political compromises that could not otherwise be reached. The valuing of time in politics transforms time into a political good that is used when states and political subjects transact over power. Formulae for assigning or retracting all kinds of rights often include a temporal component. This book focuses attention on the subject of how precise durations of time come to have value in politics and it examines some of the implications of treating time as a political good. Of particular importance will be making room in theories of justice for robust understandings of temporal justice. This book offers an original means for diagnosing temporal injustices that develop from temporal political procedures in which similarly situated persons' time is not treated as having similar value.

Compared to many other political goods whose normativity is intuitively evident both to individuals and in the context of the state, the role of durational and calendrical time in politics is not obviously normative. In fact, time can easily appear almost natural when compared to the normativity of something like rules about who is eligible to vote or to receive formal representation. Unlike property, work, representation, or many other widely recognized political goods, time is not routinely thought of as a good that is created and governed in the context of the state. This may be why time isn't the subject of much work on social justice even though any scheme of distributive and democratic justice requires its authors to make many decisions about the time of individual members.

While it is easy to take for granted that people wait to acquire many rights or that elections happen on a predictable schedule, the durations of time that compose such schedules are deliberately designed structures of a political system and are laden with normative meaning. Waiting periods and schedules are predicated on the fact that time has political value. Understanding the sources and nature of this value is essential to making sense of political decisions that make claims on or even just structure people's time.

It is particularly important to identify and understand the relationship between political time and social justice. Racialized incarceration practices, delayed naturalization, and obstructionist abortion waiting periods[8] are all instances in which select people's time is appropriated as a means of denying them rights that others enjoy. Economists have a conceptual framework for such discussions: if these were workers whose time spent working was not being remunerated an economist could say this is wage theft. But these are members of a polity and it is their political time that is being undervalued or taken from them. They experience a form of time theft with profound consequences for which political scientists have little conceptual language. A carceral system that misappropriates the time of entire classes of people delegitimizes a democratic state. So too do lengthy naturalization queues that deny rightful citizens an array of rights for the duration of their wait. Political science needs analyses of how time operates in all realms of politics in order to recommend judicious decisions about temporal rules and normative guidelines for how to treat the political time of individuals in a fair and egalitarian fashion. The goal of this endeavor is not to treat time as some sort of political master variable that is more important than any other variable. Instead, it is to show how durational time is integrated into political procedures and how it interacts with other, better understood, political goods. This will allow comparisons of normative expectations about time with political practices and the drawing of conclusions about how citizens' time is and ought to be treated by the state.

OUTLINE OF THE BOOK

Four substantive discussions constitute the bulk of the material presented in this book. Chapter 2 lays the groundwork for the core arguments of the book by describing how and why calendrical time is woven into the fabric of sovereign states. States are constituted with boundaries inscribed in time. These temporal boundaries form around the margins of states at the moments when states are founded. Often the composition of the citizenry is dictated by connection (or lack thereof) between the land and people at that precise moment in time. The existence of temporal boundaries reminds us that rights derive not just from *who* we are and *where* we are but also from *when* we are. The temporal boundaries that circumscribe states are as stark and significant as the territorial boundaries on which so

---

[8] Jenny Kutner, "Louisiana Is Imposing a 3-Day 'Reflection' Period on Women Seeking Abortions," *Mic* (May 23, 2016), https://mic.com/articles/144150/louisiana-will-force-women-to-spend-three-days-thinking-about-if-they-want-abortions#.THpgCu9nr

much current scholarship focuses.⁹ Temporal boundaries also form
within states, crisscrossing the interior of a polity. For example, curfews
determine who can move freely at which times, visas create temporal
boundaries dictating which non-citizens can stay in a country for how
long, and deadlines of all sorts impose boundaries on citizens' choices and
opportunities.

The fact that time is an inextricable part of political foundation means
that temporality will inevitably bear on any normative assessment of
a state or particular regime. Different types of temporal boundaries have
different normative valences. Among the most significant kinds of temporal boundaries I observe three main types: single moment fixed deadlines; countdown deadlines; and recurring deadlines. Examples of the first
are fixed single dates, such as those associated with "zero option
countries,"¹⁰ *Calvin's Case*,¹¹ and the French Republican Calendar
(FRC). In these instances, one moment in time serves as an impermeable
boundary. A constitution or a single law can impose a date before or after
which one's legal status is entirely different. The second involves count-
downs of the sort one might experience with a visa expiration or a statute
of limitations. The third includes recurring deadlines such as an election or
reapportionment. Each has a different logic and relationship to democratic norms and political justice more generally. Single moments such as
those of state formation aren't particularly democratic whereas deadlines
that recur open up the possibility for making and remaking decisions in
ways that approximate democratic consent. Recurring deadlines, such as
elections, are less arbitrary than deadlines that occur only once, such as

---

⁹ See Anna Stilz, *Liberal Loyalty: Freedom, Obligation, and the State* (Princeton University
Press, 2009); Arash Abizadeh, "On the Demos and Its Kin: Nationalism, Democracy, and
the Boundary Problem," *American Political Science Review* 106, no. 4 (2012);
Sarah Song, "The Significance of Territorial Presence and the Rights of Immigrants," in
Migration in Political Theory: The Ethics of Movement and Membership, eds. Sarah Fine
and Lea Ypi (Oxford University Press, 2014); David Miller, "Territorial Rights: Concept
and Justification," *Political Studies* 60, no. 2 (2012); Paulina Ochoa Espejo, "Taking
Place Seriously: Territorial Presence and the Rights of Immigrants," *Journal of Political
Philosophy* 24, no. 1 (2016).
¹⁰ The term "zero option" refers to a legal expression (usually a constitutional provision)
that identifies a specific date upon which a form of legal sovereignty commences.
The dissolution of empires such as the Soviet Union into constituent parts, and the
conclusion of military conflicts, such as World War II, are examples of events that often
trigger the need for zero-option rules as countries reconstitute themselves.
¹¹ Chapter 2 explores the common law precedent *Calvin's Case* as a paradigmatic instance
of using a zero-option date to determine who is or is not a full political subject. *Calvin
v. Smith*, 77 Eng. Rep. 377 (KB 1608).

those associated with state formation, allowing for alterations to be made to power arrangements that are decided at one moment in time and reconsidered at a later moment in time. Such deadlines are less vulnerable to pathologies of bounded rationality, in which the very existence of a deadline alters the frame of mind and behavior of decision-makers.[12]

Chapter 3 builds on the idea of recurring deadlines to develop a discussion of the significance of duration to democracy. Deadlines that recur carve out durations of time and mark them as significant. The importance of duration extends to the very core of democratic politics. Woven into justifications of the many formulae that confer, deny, and structure rights are long-standing and widely held beliefs about the connection between durational time and process. Because all processes unfold in durations of time, the latter is an inextricable part of process. Processes of particular practical and normative importance to participatory self-government ensure an enduring connection between durational time, democratic theory, and political procedures. These can be processes of character development, relationship building, consent, learning, deliberation, thought, judgment, etc. In fact, as this chapter demonstrates, time is essential to the processes that develop almost all characteristics, relationships, experiences, forms of knowledge, and other qualities that political systems deem essential to democratic citizenship.

Acknowledging the relationship between time and political processes clears the ground required to introduce one of the central arguments of the book: that durational time is assigned value in politics. Time acquires a very specific form of value in democratic politics. Through its connection to processes that are themselves valuable to democratic politics, time becomes a democratic good. Here the term good is used as economists might, to refer to something that meets people's needs, and also as a political theorist might, to indicate that goods acquire their form of value from within human society. Time is a good with an array of uses within a polity and the particular value it is assigned is derived from within any given society.

The chapter briefly examines the thought of select ancient and modern democratic theorists who speak to the relationship between time and democracy. While both ancient and modern democratic theorists note the importance of time for self-rule, modern democratic theorists and practitioners seize on this, making durational time and the temporal

---

[12] Herbert A. Simon, "Theories of Bounded Rationality," in *Decision and Organization*, eds. C.B. McGuire and Roy Radner (London/Amsterdam: North-Holland, 1972).

structure of democratic decision-making central to their institutional pre-scriptions for eliciting democratic consent. Using as a center of gravity Condorcet's detailed procedural descriptions for how to create demo-cratic consent and make decisions, the chapter reveals a close relationship between durational time and consent. This relationship is borne out in the first established form of modern consensual politics: US citizenship. Court rulings and legislative debates from the early republic closely mirror Condorcet's ideas, very explicitly linking durational time to legitimate consent as well as the processes through which people come to be entitled to rights. In short, time is integral to consent and liberal democracies come to use precise durations of time as proxies for consent. Using time as a proxy for consent enables these states to enact decision-making proce-dures that can be called consensual even when politics is being conducted on a mass scale and without assurances of full deliberative participation. The passage of a set period of time during which people have the oppor-tunity to engage in the activities that produce consent is critical to legit-imizing consent. I term this "lived consent."

But why time? Why not some other good? To address this question, Chapter 4 more closely examines the reasons that time becomes so impor-tant in political procedures. Time's political value is both instrumental and representational. Time's instrumental value comes from its relation-ship to process as described above. Time also acquires political value because it can represent, or serve as a proxy for, the same characteristics, relationships, and experiences that are deemed essential to a person's entitlement to rights. Governing a democratic state poses the challenge of expressing numerous intangibles such as relationships, obligations, and characteristics, in concrete terms. Loyalty or civic virtue may be desirable prerequisites for citizenship, but agreeing on precisely how they are embodied is difficult. States need concrete demarcations and identifiers for a vast array of vague concepts. Time works elegantly as a means to translate intangibles like loyalty and civic virtue into precisely measured political terms. A duration of time can stand in for an entire complex of processes that culminate in civic ties among compatriots, fitness for citi-zenship, or loyalty. Equally, durations of time represent the processes that punish, reform, and redeem criminals. The duration of that sentence will be an important proxy for the process of punishment and/or rehabilita-tion, neither of which readily lends itself to quantitative measurement. Various political actors may even disagree about which of the possible purposes of punishment ought to be the goal of a prison sentence. Once established, however, it matters less whether one thinks the prison sentence is intended to punish or to rehabilitate – as long as the duration of the sentence is acceptable to all parties.

The chapter details five overlapping reasons that time is such a widely used proxy in politics, particularly in liberal democracies. First, time takes on a distinct meaning in any society. Some conception of time is generally attached to a group's deepest normative traditions.[13] Of particular note is the fact that shared temporal context, facilitated by the regularization of clock time, was crucial to the founding of the modern nation-state.[14] No surprise, then, that time is so important to sovereignty and subjectivity.

Second, time can be subjected to systematically scientific treatment by law and political practice. Scientifically measured time offers a rational way of organizing decision-making and other core political processes. As Ian Hacking has chronicled, quantitative measurement proliferated in modernity as a means of channeling probability in the service of under-standing and reducing risk.[15] Martha Nussbaum reminds us, "The denumerable is the definite, the graspable, therefore also the poten-tially tellable, controllable; what cannot be numbered remains vague and unbounded, evading human grasp."[16] Quantitative means of administra-tion maximize forms of efficiency and uniformity prized by bureaucratic states charged with governing large and often diverse populations.[17] If one were to replace the many temporal measures of fitness for citizenship – adequate deliberation, reflection, and other elements of democracy – with qualitative measures of the same processes, politics in liberal democratic states of any size would grind to a halt. It would also be stripped of the guise of neutrality that quantitative measures confer and that liberal democracies prize. Imagine how challenging and dubious a venture pun-ishment would become in a context that required qualitative sentences for each crime.

---

[13] Simon, "Theories of Bounded Rationality."

[14] Writing about the effect of the French Revolution on European identity, Peter Fritzsche proposes a dualist thesis about European identity in which shared context and differ-entiation were produced by the "specific temporal identity not unlike the feeling of generation, and separated or decoupled... from their forebears two or three generations earlier." *Stranded in the Present: Modern Time and the Melancholy of History* (Cambridge, MA: Harvard University Press, 2004), 54.

[15] *The Taming of Chance* (Cambridge University Press, 1990).

[16] *The Fragility of Goodness: Luck and Ethics in Greek Tragedy and Philosophy* (Cambridge University Press, 2001), vol. II, 107.

[17] James C. Scott, *Seeing Like a State: How Certain Schemes to Improve the Human Condition Have Failed* (New Haven, CT: Yale University Press, 1998).

The fact that time can be quantified in scientific terms makes it easy to assume it is a universal and neutral proxy. This assumption is critical for liberal states. There are other attributes of time that feed into these assumptions. Time is experienced by all political subjects in a way that gives it a guise of universality. If we do not scrutinize time, it can seem like it stands outside of law, politics, and social facts. Time may seem natural, either in natural law theory, because God created time, as Augustine described, or in positive law, because time is an artifact of scientific laws over which sovereigns can claim to have no control. Everyone exists in time and everyone understands this about themselves and others. Clock and calendar time can thus seem universal and neutrally scientific. Time can also be applied to almost any kind of action or relationship. We use it to identify common law marriages, maturity, civic knowledge, and many other things. Time can therefore appear to be simultaneously universal and particular.

Third, because clock and calendar time are widely regarded as universal and neutrally scientific, temporal laws and policies can convey the appearance of being more egalitarian and less partial than other traditional means of making claims to political standing. Clock and calendar time are rational forms of time. Unlike something like social time, a highly particular and embedded form of time produced by social practices and not expressed quantitatively, scientifically measured time is taken to be a phenomenon governed by laws of physics and science rather than social norms or political decisions.[18]

Time can therefore be taken to be an egalitarian measure or proxy in politics because everyone has time. In contrast to something like money or aristocratic birth, clock-time is often assumed to be held in equal quantities by all. Furthermore, we do not transfer time intergenerationally, from parents to children, as we do property, money, and other forms of privilege. The clock ticks and calendar days pass at the same rate regardless of someone's social class, status, birth, or other personal characteristics. In theory, other goods such as money, property, lineage, and work could be used as criteria for the acquisition of rights. But it is highly unusual for democratic states to allow the purchase of naturalization or payments in exchange for commuting a prison sentence.

---

[18] On the connection between numbers and rationality for the purposes of commensuration, see Wendy Nelson Espeland and Michael Sauder, *Engines of Anxiety: Academic Rankings, Reputation, and Accountability* (New York: Russell Sage Foundation, 2016).

Using scientifically measured time as a proxy also allows political procedures to give the appearance of sidestepping the kinds of partiality that manifest themselves when qualitative standards have to be created. In general, quantitative measures are treated as more objective than their qualitative counterparts.[19] When devices rather than humans appear to control the measurement this effect is magnified. Clocks and calendars exhibit no independent bias. Compared to a qualitative test, a temporal standard for whether a person is mature or has enough civic ties for citizenship seems impartial. Qualitative tests for maturity, integration, prisoner rehabilitation, etc. would necessarily be highly subjective. By contrast, allowing a clock or a calendar to determine someone's fate removes potentially biased, flawed, or arbitrary discretion from the most visible part of a procedure. Compared to the task of developing a test that could be administered to people to see if they are mature enough to exercise the franchise or consent to sex, imposing an age of consent or maturity appears relatively impartial.

Time's appearance of egalitarianism and impartiality gives it special appeal in liberal democracies, which require criteria for the acquisition of rights that treat similarly situated persons in similar fashion. But actually fulfilling expectations of egalitarianism and impartiality is a weighty normative burden for temporal procedures and rules. At the same time that these rules must be egalitarian and impartial, they must also accommodate differences in various people's entitlement to rights. Not everyone will be qualified to exercise all of the rights of democratic citizenship. Someone who has not fully experienced processes such as character development or learning (e.g. a child or person designated as not legally competent) will not qualify for a full set of rights. In other words: a deficiency in someone's qualification for rights derives from that person's disparate experiences of processes. This inference – that temporal rules imply judgments about whether someone has experienced character development, learning, or other important processes – matters greatly when deciding whether temporal rules actually are egalitarian and impartial. I return to the analysis of when temporal rules do and do not fulfill claims of egalitarianism and impartiality in Chapter 5.

That time can appear simultaneously situated and neutral or abstract is a final reason that durational time is so often used as a proxy in transactions over rights. Despite not appearing like a social or political construct,

---

[19] Theodore M. Porter, *Trust in Numbers: The Pursuit of Objectivity in Science and Public Life* (Princeton University Press, 1996).

time is very readily incorporated into political structures and adapted to different schema. Few other goods have the potential to be applied to politics in both highly specific and in general ways.

Chapter 5 delves into the kinds of political arrangements that result from using a numeric measure to represent processes, relationships, and traits. This chapter proceeds in two parts: the first evaluates the strengths and weaknesses of the kind of commensuration that is enacted when time is used as a proxy in the ways discussed in Chapter 4; the second identifies and discusses instances in which temporal rules and laws instantiate unfair and inegalitarian outcomes.

Quantitative measures of qualitative traits facilitate forms of political arithmetic in which time functions as a medium of political exchange – a good with value that is used to transact over power.[20] Such arithmetical exchange allows political actors in liberal democracies to transact over rights, creating what I call a political economy of time. This argument draws a heuristic analogy between how time functions in politics and the role that time fulfills for Marx. Time is a pivotal concept for Marx, performing the constant function of commensurating the work done by workers and the compensation that they receive. Work, which could be measured in various forms of effort, productivity, or output, is commonly measured in quantitative units of time. This makes it possible to also compensate workers in precise quantities of money that correspond to precise durations of time.

The analogy to Marx's idea of value is solely heuristic and what is important is not whether readers agree that time is treated in politics exactly as it is treated in the economy. It is not. The goal is simply to highlight time as a unit of commensuration in politics. Commensuration, in this context, is the transformation of qualities into quantities. It is an essential practice in large liberal democratic states. In the political economy of time, durations of time allow large modern states to commensurate otherwise incommensurable norms and values. Once durations of time have been assigned value and treated as means for commensuration, these durations can be incorporated into political formulae for fundamental political procedures. The formulae mix quantitative and qualitative

---

[20] This book will not be the first to use a heterodox understanding of the concept, "medium of exchange." Luhmann and Parsons, among others, have also done so. See Niklas Luhmann, *Social Systems* (Stanford University Press, 1995); Talcott Parsons, "On the Concept of Political Power," *Proceedings of the American Philosophical Society* 107, no. 3 (1963).

variables. Prison sentences follow formulae in which one's age, past criminal record, and class of criminality, yield a punishment: the duration of time one must spend incarcerated. Similarly, naturalization is granted through a formula that includes a set period of residence along with good moral character, an examination of one's civic knowledge, and an oath. Because quantification admits distinctions of small and large degrees, as well as the inclusion of other variables, these formulae are almost infinitely adjustable. There is room for modification both within the calculation of the temporal variable (for example, non-citizens who marry US citizens as well as non-citizen members of the military get two years knocked off the otherwise mandatory probationary period) and alongside the temporal variable (for example, solitary confinement can enhance the severity of a prison sentence).

While a political economy of time is highly compatible with modern liberal democratic states, even ancient moral philosophers observed a predisposition toward commensuration as a means of stabilizing political judgment. What is measurable is commensurable and what is commensurable is comprehensible and communicable. That which is not measurable is unspecifiable, chaotic, and threatening.[21] Time, which is experienced by all, subject to precise measurements that can be expressed mathematically, and has a valence of scientific clarity and precision, circumvents the uncertainty and threat of the unmeasurable. This makes time an ideal unit of commensuration. Martha Nussbaum and Rosalind Hursthouse write of the indeterminacy people would experience without such units when trying to value and evaluate.[22] They describe the imperative to approach scientifically that which creates uncertainty. A science of measurement is the antidote to such uncertainty because it imposes order and rules.[23] In *Euthyphro*, Socrates sees that:

the art of science of weighing, counting, and measuring . . . has made human beings capable of taking things quite different in kind and comparing them with respect to some property in which they are interested.[24]

Socrates points to this as a way of resolving moral conflict. The drive to quantify and systematize precedes the existence of the state but gains momentum once the state develops. Socrates' insight becomes only more apt in large-scale pluralist politics. The political formulae referenced

[21] Martha C. Nussbaum and Rosalind Hursthouse, "Plato on Commensurability and Desire," *Proceedings of the Aristotelian Society, Supplementary Volumes* 58 (1984): 57.
[22] Nussbaum and Hursthouse, "Plato on Commensurability and Desire," 57.   [23] Ibid.
[24] Nussbaum, *Fragility of Goodness*, 106.

earlier are efficient ways of combining multiple variables and measures in the procedures that govern the conferral, denial, and exercise of rights.

Without commensuration, qualitative judgments would have to be made every time someone sought political recognition as an adult or wanted to apply for unemployment benefits, for example. To some people's minds, these qualitative judgments might even hold great appeal as fairer or more accurate means of evaluation. And, in certain cases, as in naturalization, qualitative judgments such as an interview are included with quantitative and temporal metrics. But it is difficult to imagine that all of the instances in which time is invoked in transactions over political power could be revamped to use solely qualitative judgment. This is not just because qualitative judgments would be inefficient and difficult to compare to one another, although efficiency and fairness do matter. Commensuration also allows participants in transactions over power to compromise when they experience deep normative disagreement. Because time can mean different things to different people (for example, the naturalization probationary period might stand for proof of loyalty in some people's minds while in others' it might represent the development of civic ties), it allows a society to gloss over its differences and come to agreements about how to transact over power. The political economy of time allows for transactions over power that are, in the language of Cass Sunstein, "incompletely theorized agreements." Commensuration procedures provide a context in which fierce contests over norms and values can be averted with minimal sacrifices by the participants. In other words, they "make it possible to obtain agreement where agreement is necessary, and to make it unnecessary to obtain agreement where agreement is impossible."[25] If a quantifiable good such as time has meaning, but that meaning is never specified, this makes it a perfect medium for commensuration in a political system where contestation is a given. Its relationship to compromise means that commensuration is absolutely essential, not just to the state, but to liberal democracies in which divergent parties need to compromise in order to govern themselves together.

This chapter also surveys arguments about the normative pitfalls of commensuration, some of which were first lodged by ancient philosophers and others of which are modern. Here the book transitions from an analysis of how and why time plays the role it does in politics to

---

[25] "Incompletely Theorized Agreements in Constitutional Law," *Social Research* 74, no. 1 (2007).

a normative discussion of how to use these insights to understand temporal injustice. It also gestures at questions about the political legitimacy of democratic states that misappropriate the time of their citizens.

Commensuration is widely vilified by democratic theorists for being reductive and damaging to social meanings. In this view, the true value of something such as deliberation cannot actually be translated into a temporal measure. Furthermore, commensuration tends to elide the distinct features of different goods and activities by representing complex goods using interchangeable measures. In general, this is a persuasive argument against commensuration in spheres of politics that invoke discrete fundamental values and first principles. However, time presents a challenge to the idea that all commensuration is reductive. Because time has already been shown to be associated with a rich array of social and political meanings, it stands apart from other quantitative measures of qualitative processes. Time is better situated to represent distinct meanings even when the representations replace qualitative goods with a quantitative measure.

Despite this, the political economy of time still holds the potential for damaging and unjust outcomes. Like many goods, people's time is appropriated, valued, and governed by the state. The time of political subjects must be governed according to an accepted set of normative principles, just as would be expected for any good to which rights attach. We need to know if people's time is being valued fairly and appropriately in all contexts. To understand the political inequality engendered by temporal injustice one must understand how people's time is being treated by political actors and procedures. Returning to the comparison with Marx's description of time, labor, and commensuration: we can no more understand how capitalism works in the absence of analyses of wage labor than we can understand how a political system works – particularly a democracy – without analyses of how the political time of its subjects is treated.

Unfairness enters into political procedures that invoke time when the time of differently situated persons is treated as if these persons were similarly situated. Not all people have the same quantity or quality of time. People are of different ages, have different life expectancies, and experience different forms of exigency. The clocks of an affluent and a poor person will operate identically but the way in which either person must "spend" their time is a product of social class and circumstances that are not themselves often figured into temporal rules. The time poverty experienced by a poor person who must work excessive hours to make ends meet is different than the time poverty of a professional woman who shoulders a gendered division of labor in the private sphere which in turn contrasts with the constraints faced by a middle-aged man experiencing age discrimination. A five-year prison term may be a life sentence for someone with a terminal illness and even six months of incarceration could permanently derail the life trajectory of a very young person.

These are grave consequences of laws, policies, and practices that do not account adequately for difference and treat people as if they all have the same relationship to time. However, in the political economy of time, there is ample evidence that the reverse – the treatment of similarly situated persons as if their time has different value – is even more problematic. We can often identify instances of injustice and deeply illiberal state practices by observing cases in which the time of similarly situated persons is not treated as having similar value. A person who has to wait vastly longer than a similarly situated peer in order to gain the rights of citizenship is experiencing an injustice. Here the inference made earlier about the relationship between important democratic processes such as character development and learning resurface. Chapters 3 and 4 reveal that the political value of time derives from time's connection to processes, for example character development, relationship building, education, and reflection that are important to politics. Implicit in the differential valuing of similarly situated people is the message that some people – those whose time is devalued – are incapable of, or immune to, the political processes for which time is a proxy. For example, when some people receive longer sentences for the same crimes, these people are implicitly being treated as if the process of punishment operates less effectively for them than for others. Indeed, this is close to the stated intent of sentencing guidelines that punish likely repeat offenders – to determine which criminals' characters are the most deficient and incorrigible.[26] The preceding inference is true whether punishment is intended to rehabilitate, exact retribution, deter, or be restorative. Incarcerating some people for longer periods of time than others convicted of similar crimes implies that the people with longer sentences require more rehabilitation, owe society a large debt, or pose a greater threat than their peers with briefer sentences.

---

[26] Peter B. Hoffman, "Twenty Years of Operational Use of a Risk Prediction Instrument: The United States Parole Commission's Salient Factor Score," *Journal of Criminal Justice* 22, no. 6 (1994).

Just as the unremunerated or undervalued time of workers becomes the vehicle for their economic exploitation in Marx, the unrewarded or undervalued time of political subjects becomes the vehicle for their political domination. A person who has to wait longer than others for liberty or any citizenship rights is vulnerable to all manner of downstream consequences after their time is devalued. When an individual or group's time is undervalued or devalued by politics they experience something akin to a political version of exploitation. They lose rights and political power that other similarly situated people acquire and exercise in time.

The differential treatment of similarly situated persons' time is an outcome, in part, of the application of market logic to political procedures that govern rights and status. Commensuration that occurs in the political economy of time bears the imprint of market logic. As is the case when market logic governs any good, it is possible to undervalue or overvalue some people's political time. People whose political time is undervalued will suffer not just momentary effects, but also downstream consequences long after the initial point at which they have been deprived of rights and status. These effects are often extended from individual cases to groups. So it goes when states implement rules that, for example, curtail how long people have to fulfill the documentary requirements to vote or extend a state of emergency. The effects of these rules are not felt identically across the board and the consequences can transform both individual lives and politics more generally.

Fortunately, time can sometimes also be used as a means of rectifying injustices. A fascinating game theoretic intervention into discussions of how to circumvent majoritarian tyranny involves the idea of "vote storage," in which voters are permitted to use a set number of votes over time rather than one per election.[27] Minority coalitions can organize to defeat majorities during elections of particular importance. This principle essentially takes the idea of a protected majority–minority district, which is spatial, and makes it temporal. Vote storage allows members of minority groups to use time as a means of compensating for one of the enduring weaknesses of a democracy: its inability to consistently protect the political interests and voices of numeric and structural minorities. Similarly, true filibusters allow a numeric minority to use time as a means of overcoming their relatively weak political position. And early or

---

[27] Alessandra Casella, Thomas Palfrey, and Raymond G. Reizman, "Minorities and Storable Votes," *Quarterly Journal of Political Science* 3, no. 2 (2005).

extended voting is often regarded as a means to circumvent the obstacles that vulnerable groups face when trying to exercise their franchise rights.[28] Those obstacles include temporal obstruction such as long voting queues[29] and an absence of provisions like a national election day holiday for people with burdensome work schedules.

Thus, the connection of time and political justice has wide-reaching implications. Claims of this scope warrant not only carefully composed reasoning but also enough context to situate the argument alongside related thought on the subject of time in politics. To that end, the second half of this introductory chapter offers a compact overview of existing thought on the connections between time and politics. Because the literature on time is voluminous and spans many disciplines I have made every effort to focus on the most salient contributions in the social sciences and humanities.

TIME IN THE SOCIAL SCIENCES

In a famous 1922 exchange at Société Française de Philosophie, Henri Bergson asserted the inadequacy of Albert Einstein's definition of time, ultimately ensuring that the famous physicist never received a Nobel Prize for his work on relativity.[30] Their interaction draws attention to a period when philosophy could speak truth to the power of hard science and the world would snap to attention. It also makes evident that there is a long and rich intellectual tradition of scrutinizing the concept of time. Durational time has figured prominently in every subfield of the social sciences and political philosophy. Beginning with Durkheim in 1915, social scientists and legal theorists ceased to assume that time is a natural and unproblematic background fact and began studying time in social and political life. Scholarship on political economy and time has focused on work time,[31]

---

[28] Paul Gronke et al., "Convenience Voting," *Annual Review of Political Science* 11 (2008).

[29] Ronald J. Krotoszynski, Jr., "A Poll Tax by Another Name," *New York Times: Opinion* (Nov. 14, 2016), www.nytimes.com/2016/11/14/opinion/a-poll-tax-by-another-name.html?_r=1

[30] The Nobel that Einstein received was for his work in theoretical physics, specifically his discovery of the law of the photoelectric effect. Paul Rabinow, *Marking Time: On the Anthropology of the Contemporary* (Princeton University Press, 2009), ch. 1.

[31] Dan Clawson and Naomi Gerstel, *Unequal Time: Gender, Class, and Family in Employment Schedules* (New York: Russell Sage Foundation, 2014); Thompson, "Time, Work–Discipline, and Industrial Capitalism"; Jerry A. Jacobs and Kathleen Gerson, "Overworked Individuals, or Overworked Families? Explaining Trends in Work, Leisure, and Family Time," *Work and Occupations* 28, no. 1 (2001).

leisure time,[32] and interactions of time with variables such as gender.[33] There is now widespread awareness of capitalism's structuring effects on the time of workers,[34] wage theft,[35] and an array of temporal artifacts of the market economy, particularly as it pertains to globalization.[36]

In political science, time has been focal to studies of institutional development and periodization, particularly in the context of APD, much of which derives its basic premises from Durkheim's theories about evolutionary complexity.[37] Of special interest have been the relationships of processes that unfold over long periods of time, path dependence, the effects of ordering and sequences on causality,[38] and electoral timing.[39] Questions of how specific moments in time set processes in

---

[32] Robert E. Goodin et al., *Discretionary Time: A New Measure of Freedom* (Cambridge University Press, 2008); Robert E. Goodin et al., "The Time–Pressure Illusion: Discretionary Time vs. Free Time," *Social Indicators Research* 73, no. 1 (2005); John Urry, "Time, Leisure, and Social Identity," *Time & Society* 3, no. 2 (1994).

[33] Laura Sanchez and Elizabeth Thomson, "Becoming Mothers and Fathers: Parenthood, Gender, and the Division of Labor," *Gender & Society* 11, no. 6 (1997); Linda C. Sayer, "Gender, Time, and Inequality: Trends in Women's and Men's Paid Work, Unpaid Work, and Free Time," *Social Forces* 84, no. 1 (2005); Michael Bittman and Judy Wajcman, "The Rush Hour: The Character of Leisure Time and Gender Equality," *Social Forces* 79, no. 1 (2000); Tracey Warren, "Class and Gender-Based Working Time? Time Poverty and the Division of Domestic Labor," *Sociology* 37, no. 4 (2003); Theodore N. Greenstein, "Economic Dependence, Gender, and the Division of Labor in the Home: A Replication and Extension," *Journal of Marriage and Family* 62, no. 2 (2000).

[34] Thomas M. Beers, "Flexible Schedules and Shift Work: Replacing the '9-to-5' Workday?" *Monthly Labor Review* 123 (2000); David Harvey, "Time–Space Compression and the Postmodern Condition," in *Modernity: Critical Concepts in Sociology*, ed. Malcolm Waters (London: Routledge, 1999), vol. IV.

[35] Kim Bobo, *Wage Theft in America: Why Millions of Americans Are Not Getting Paid – And What We Can Do about It* (New York: The New Press, 2011); Ruth Milkman et al., Wage Theft and Workplace Violations in Los Angeles (Los Angeles, CA: Institute for Research on Labor and Employment, 2010).

[36] Bob Jessop, "Time and Space in the Globalization of Capital and Their Implications for State Power," in *Rethinking Marxism* 14, *no.* 1 (2002): 103–5.

[37] Paul Pierson, *Politics in Time: History, Institutions, and Social Analysis* (Princeton University Press, 2004).

[38] Skowronek, *Politics Presidents Make*, 546; Karen Orren and Stephen Skowronek, "Order and Time in Institutional Study: A Brief for the Historical Approach," in *Political Science in History: Research Programs and Political Traditions*, ed. James Farr et al. (Cambridge University Press, 1995), 296; Liaquat Ali Khan, "Jurodynamics of Islamic Law," *Rutgers Law Review* 61 (2008); Andrew S. McFarland, "Interest Groups and Political Time: Cycles in America," *British Journal of Political Science* 21, no. 3 (1991): 257.

[39] Dennis F. Thompson, "Democracy in Time: Popular Sovereignty and Temporal Representation," *Constellations* 12, no. 2 (2005): 245–61; Jessica E. Boscarino, Rogan T. Kersh, and Jeffrey M. Stonecash, "Congressional Intrusion to Specify Specific Voting Dates for National Office," *Publius* 38, no. 1 (2008): 137–51.

motion, with attention to the pace and speed of politics, have also garnered the attention of the field.[40]

Political scientists have developed hypotheses about the temporal predis-
positions of legislatures, executives, and judiciaries, especially in light of
recent interest in executive emergency powers.[41] While it makes sense that
APD scholars have treated time as a dimension in their search for patterns and
causality in politics, one of the premises of this book is that conceptual and
normative analyses point toward treating time as a political good as well.

Since Durkheim wrote, social theorists have devoted extensive attention to
an array of subjects. The most fundamental contributions to this literature
have discussed types of time – from differences between cyclical and linear
time[42] – to the ways that different types of time can be understood.[43]
Philosophers and social theorists have explored the value of time in Marxist
theory and specified the terms in which time is used to transform labor into
value.[44] Structuration theory incorporates time into concepts such as
time–space distanciation and the compression of time in modernity.[45]
Hartmut Rosa has developed a nuanced theory of acceleration and the
compression of time.[46] Legal philosophers have offered general applications
of time studies to legal thought.[47] They have also contributed scholarship that

[40] William E. Scheuerman, *Liberal Democracy and the Social Acceleration of Time*
(Baltimore, MD and London: Johns Hopkins University Press, 2004); Hartmut Rosa,
"Social Acceleration: Ethical and Political Consequences of a Desynchronized
High-Speed Society," *Constellations* 10, no. 1 (2003); *High-Speed Society: Social
Acceleration, Power, and Modernity*, eds. Hartmut Rosa and William E. Scheuerman
(University Park, PA: Pennsylvania State University Press, 2009).
[41] Leonard C. Feldman, "The Banality of Emergency: On the Time and Space of 'Political
Necessity,'" in *Sovereignty, Emergency, Legality*, ed. Austin Sarat (Cambridge University
Press, 2010); William E. Scheuerman, "Emergency Powers," *Annual Review of Law and
Social Science* 2 (2006).
[42] Ronald Aminzade, "Historical Sociology and Time," *Sociological Methods and Research*
20, no. 4 (1992).
[43] Eviatar Zerubavel, *Time Maps: Collective Memory and the Social Shape of the Past*
(University of Chicago Press, 2012); Barbara Adam, *Time* (Cambridge, UK: Polity,
2004), 33.
[44] Shannon Stimson, "Rethinking the State: Perspective on the Legibility and Reproduction
of Political Societies," *Political Theory* 28, no. 6 (2000).
[45] Anthony Giddens, *The Consequences of Modernity* (Cambridge, UK: Polity, 1990): 97.
[46] *Social Acceleration: A New Theory of Modernity* (Columbia University Press, 2013).
[47] Carol J. Greenhouse, "Just in Time: Temporality and the Cultural Legitimation of Law,"
Yale Law Journal 98, no. 8 (1989); Carol J. Greenhouse, *A Moment's Notice: Time
Politics Across Cultures* (Ithaca, NY: Cornell University Press, 1996); Rebecca R. French,
"Time in the Law," *University of Colorado Law Review* 72 (2001); Ali Liaquat Khan,
"Jurodynamics of Islamic Law," *Rutgers Law Review* 61 (2008); Rosalyn Higgins,
"Time and the Law: International Perspectives on an Old Problem," *International and*

discusses time in the history of political thought, and in particular within the social contract tradition.[48] Political and legal theorists have also chronicled the relationship of time and emergency powers as well as the way that law has absorbed capitalist industrial premises about time[49] and the importance of leisure time to freedom.[50]

Perhaps of any relevant discipline, historians have made time a focal point of academic inquiry. The Annales School's introduction of the *longue durée* forced scholars of history to identify and consider the implications of focusing on events rather than structure and evolution that occurs in small increments over extended periods of time.[51] And historiography, following the path-breaking work by Reinhart Koselleck, has taken up the topic of temporality and national identity.[52] For many thinkers who focus on the subject of time, transformations of political subjectivity that occur when geographic borders are crossed or reworked necessarily draw attention to time. They inscribe temporal borders based on when they occur, how long they last, and other circumstances of such processes. Thomas R. Allen has made a recent pivotal contribution bridging historical work on time with a documentary account of "the importance of accurate time measurement to the establishment of a coherent national identity."[53] And William Max Nelson documents how the measurement of time evinced an attempt to colonize the nation's future in revolutionary France. Nelson provides an analysis of the philosophical

Comparative Law Quarterly 46, no. 3 (1997); Alison L. LaCroix, "Temporal Imperialism," *University of Pennsylvania Law Review* 158 (2010); Lior Barshack, "Time and the Constitution," *International Journal of Constitutional Law* 7, no. 4 (2009).

[48] Jose Brunner, "Modern Times: Law, Temporality and Happiness in Hobbes, Locke and Bentham," *Theoretical Inquiries in Law* 8, no. 1 (2007).

[49] Todd D. Rakoff, *A Time for Every Purpose: Law and the Balance of Life* (Cambridge, MA: Harvard University Press, 2002), 57.

[50] Jeff Noonan, "Free Time as a Necessary Condition of Free Life," *Contemporary Political Theory* 8, no. 4 (2009): 377–93.

[51] Fernand Braudel, *On History*, trans. Sarah Matthews (University of Chicago Press, 1980), 3.

[52] Some have paid special attention to how the figure of the émigré – someone who is between one citizenry and another – illustrates fundamental beliefs of a society about rupture and continuity in time. See Fritzsche, *Stranded in the Present*, esp. ch. 2, "Strangers." Koselleck makes the apt observation that Augustine's doctrine of the two worlds was produced after witnessing "the streams of refugees [that] poured into North Africa from Rome after its conquest by Alaric in 410." Reinhart Koselleck, *The Practice of Conceptual History: Timing History, Space Concepts*, trans. Todd Samuel Presner (Stanford University Press, 2002). Furthermore, Commynes, Machiavelli, and Guicciardini all wrote in exile (ibid.).

[53] Thomas M. Allen, *A Republic in Time: Temporality and Social Imagination in Nineteenth-Century America* (University of North Carolina Press, 2008).

underpinnings of the calendrical system imposed following the French Revolution, demonstrating that different ways of measuring time correspond to different relationships to the past, the future, and (especially) the precise conditions under which progress and regeneration can occur.[54] More generally, scholars of the history of time and timekeeping have paved a way for political theorists to think about the topic of political time.[55]

Within the subfield of historical political thought, J.G.A. Pocock's encyclopedic *The Machiavellian Moment* has dominated discussions of time.[56] Pocock details the Polybian cycles that foretold a lifespan of ascent and inevitable political decline for early republics. Political innovation came to be seen as inherently unstable and therefore fraught with danger.[57] More recently, democratic theorists have grappled with the temporal problem of "infinite regress," in which the legitimacy of a democracy cannot be established without reference to a prior set of legitimate rules under which the present order was established. Thus, Paulina Ochoa Espejo argues for examining time as conceived by Bergson and filtered through the thought of Arendt and Ortega as a means of evading the problem of infinite regress and grounding a legitimate popular sovereignty. Her conception of time is one in which "[d]emocratic legitimacy cannot arise from the people themselves, it is always authorized from an unspecifiable temporal standpoint, one that is not measured in years."[58] Lindahl, drawing on Benveniste,[59] makes a related point, saying that the "historical time of a collective" is "irreducible to dated time."[60] Prior to the moment of establishment there is no

[54] Nelson, William Max "The Weapon of Time: Constructing the Future in France, 1750 to Year I" (PhD diss., University of California, Los Angeles, 2006). See esp. ch. 4, 218–69.

[55] David S. Landes, *Revolution in Time: Clocks and Making of the Modern World* (Cambridge, MA: Belknap Press of Harvard University Press, 2000); Vanessa Ogle, *The Global Transformation of Time: 1870–1950* (Cambridge, MA: Harvard University Press, 2015).

[56] In ancient thought, "Time was the inescapable condition of particular existence." John Greville Agard Pocock, *The Machiavellian Moment: Florentine Political Thought and the Atlantic Republican Tradition* (Princeton University Press, 2009), 22.

[57] "By the institutionalization of civic virtue, the republic or polis maintains its own stability in time and develops the human raw material composing it toward that political life which is the end of man." Pocock, *Machiavellian Moment*, 183.

[58] Paulina Ochoa Espejo, "The Time of Popular Sovereignty: Political Theology and the Democratic State" (PhD diss., Johns Hopkins University, 2006), 106.

[59] Emile Benveniste, "Le langage et l'expérience humaine," in *Problèmes du langage*, ed. Emile Benveniste (Paris: Gallimard, 1966).

[60] Hans Lindahl, "Breaking Promises to Keep Them: Immigration and the Bounds of Distributive Justice," in *A Right to Inclusion and Exclusion? Normative Fault Lines of*

"people" and hence there can be no such thing as popular sovereignty. If there is no popular sovereignty, any rules that come about in this moment cannot be democratically legitimate. However, this imposition is necessary for the establishment of rules and procedures through which future democratic decisions can be reached. Jed Rubenfeld argues against a related vulnerability: that of presentism, in which speech-modeled and "presentist" forms of legitimation displace thicker, historically rooted, written models of constituting politics.[61] Michelman and Habermas frame the problem as a contradiction, or tension, between political norms and practices.[62]

Temporal justice has also been examined by contemporary political theorists in studies of workplace fairness, inequalities of discretionary time, and autonomy, all of which adversely affect people's opportunities to self-govern[63] Concerns about how the pace of politics advantages some over others also invoke claims of political justice.[64] Following a long period in which standard pluralists dominated these discussions, agonistic democratic theorists have redirected our attention to the connection between agency and temporality.[65] This dialogue developed alongside psychoanalytic insights that incorporate gendered fears of mortality into explanations for prevalent practices of states and nations.[66]

Within the subfield of democratic theory, which is often less abstract than studies of social justice, the concrete influence of time has been sidelined by many scholars. Work on the knowledge and cognitive capabilities of citizens makes very direct reference to the importance of diachronic analysis and the fact that intelligence is distributed spatially and temporally within a citizenry but defers analysis of the ways in which citizenries learn.[67] The wisdom of the crowd might refer to the wisdom of

---

the EU's Area of Freedom, Security and Justice, ed. Hans Lindahl (Oxford: Hart, 2009), 149.

[61] See Jed Rubenfeld, *Freedom and Time: A Theory of Constitutional Self-Government* (New Haven, CT: Yale University Press, 2001), esp. ch. 6.

[62] Frank Michelman, "Morality, Identity, and Constitutional Patriotism," *University of Colorado Law Review* 76 (1998): 399–427; Jürgen Habermas, "Constitutional Democracy: A Contradictory Union of Contradictory Principles?" *Political Theory* 29, no. 6 (2001): 766 (trans. William Rehg).

[63] Robert E. Goodin, "Temporal Justice," *Journal of Social Policy* 39, no. 1 (2010).

[64] William E. Connolly, *Neuropolitics: Thinking, Culture, Speed* (University of Minnesota Press, 2002), vol. XXIII.

[65] William E. Connolly, *A World of Becoming* (Durham, NC: Duke University Press, 2011).

[66] Jacqueline Stevens, *States without Nations: Citizenship for Mortals* (Columbia University Press, 2010).

[67] Hélène Landemore, *Democratic Reason: Politics, Collective Intelligence, and the Rule of the Many* (Princeton University Press, 2013), 20.

a group deliberating and deciding together but it might also refer to the wisdom of an equal number of people who exist at different times and accumulate wisdom over time. Like epistemic democratic theorists, many empirical scholars of democracy, for whom the precisely measurable quality of durational time surely holds great research appeal, have not yet mined the rich ore of questions related to time. For example, Paul Pierson notes the fact that rational choice theory has stumbled because of its inattention and perhaps inability to capture the phenomenon of duration.[68] And Schedler and Santiso's "invitation"[69] for political scientists and public policy scholars to think more about time has been taken up only episodically, primarily in the contest of EU and European governance.[70]

It is not entirely clear why most contemporary theorists of political and social justice talk about procedural justice in ways that rarely contemplate time. They refer to distributive patterns, structural inequality, or liberty, to name a few of the most central axes of justice. Following Rawls, twentieth-century theorists make arguments about fair procedures and just outcomes, referring to a set of goods that have value and the methods that exist for prioritizing and ensuring access to those goods. These goods are generally recognized as acquiring their value from within the social systems that seek to distribute them.[71] From the arguments that philosophers make about political justice we get discussions about political procedures and outcomes that focus on such fundamental subjects as distribution, democratic representation, and identity. However, time is integrally important to each of these subjects, structuring how long one may receive distributive benefits such as unemployment or cash assistance, the schedule of reapportionment for congressional districts, and the length

---

[68] Paul Pierson, *Politics in Time: History, Institutions, and Social Analysis* (Princeton University Press, 2004), 9.

[69] Javier Santiso and Andreas Schedler, "Democracy and Time: An Invitation," *International Political Science Review* 19, no. 1 (1998).

[70] Jan-Hinrik Meyer-Sahling, "Time and European Governance: An Inventory," *Archive of European Integration* (paper presented at the Biennial Conference of the European Studies Association, Panel "The Temporality of Europeanisation and Enlargement," Montreal, Canada, May 17–20, 2007); Klaus H. Goetz and Jan-Hinrik Meyer-Sahling, "Political Time in the EU: Dimensions, Perspectives, Theories," *Journal of European Public Policy* 16, no. 2 (2009); Klaus H. Goetz, "How Does the EU Tick? Five Propositions on Political Time," *Journal of European Public Policy* 16, no. 2 (2009); Klaus H. Goetz and Jan-Hinrik Meyer-Sahling, "The EU Timescape: From Notion to Research Agenda," *Journal of European Public Policy* 16, no. 2 (2009).

[71] Michael Walzer, *Spheres of Justice: A Defense of Pluralism and Equality* (New York: Basic Books, 1983).

of time a resident has to wait before becoming a full citizen. Rawls gives a nod to intergenerational justice but, like many of his peers, does not include any substantive discussion of how a state should treat the time of its citizens. In other cases, time is invoked by theorists of justice uncritically, as Michael Sandel does when he advocates for the principle of "waiting one's turn" instead of allowing people to purchase access to things for which one ordinarily waits (face time with legislators, tickets to publicly sponsored events, citizenship). Sandel never explains why it is fairer and better that people spend their time rather than their money to obtain these goods and opportunities.

It is clear that a great deal of work remains to be done on the positive and normative roles played by time in politics. While debates about novelty, historicized time, and even the politics of exception are not unrelated to the subject at hand, none directly deals with the phenomena identified by this book: namely, the facts that time is used to carve sovereign boundaries around citizenries, as a means for measuring qualitative attributes of citizens, and for political exchange value through which amounts of time are demanded of individuals in exchange for rights.

A FEW CAVEATS

The type of political time discussed in this book is scientifically measured durational time. It is not cyclical time, generational time, ecological time, natural time, social time, or any of the other myriad forms of time that social scientists and historians have identified and which coexist with scientifically measured time. Scientifically measured durational time is discrete from, although it can overlap with, these other forms of time, as is evident in the case of the ways in which time can be used by a state to demarcate itself from a state that preceded it or from other nation-states and other social or political forms.

Next, although this is not a work grounded in close readings of ancient theory, Aristotle's distinction between *kairos* and *chronos* may make legible the subject of the book for some readers. Whereas *kairos* is a specific moment in which things are possible and in which opportunities must be seized, *chronos* is quantitatively measured time of a non-contextualized nature.[72] Often people use the word "time" to mean the

---

[72] Melissa S. Lane, *Method and Politics in Plato's Statesman* (Cambridge University Press, 1998).

context in which an event may or did take place.[73] Temporality becomes a reference to circumstances. For the purposes of this book, time does not refer to historical context. Time refers to precise durations measured by clocks and calendars. Social science methodologists have also distinguished duration from tempo, acceleration, and sequencing, as a part of a larger project that clarifies causal and predictive processes.[74] Despite their significance to studying political processes, none of the two latter ways of studying time feature prominently in this book and tempo receives only brief treatment. The phenomenon of valuing time identified in this book is an artifact of durational time. References to tempo, acceleration, and sequencing are subsidiary to the larger idea that time is a means of commensuration in politics.

The emphasis on duration is not intended to imply that duration is more significant than other ways of thinking about time or other political variables. The argument of the book is that scientifically measured durational time is a highly significant and underexplored political good. It is a pervasive means of representing processes, characteristics, relationships, and other things that have political value. But the pervasiveness of temporal measures does not mean that time is somehow more important than other political goods, nor are temporal measures better, fairer, or in any other way superlative. My strenuous case for thinking about time through the lens of power and political transaction is made only on behalf of expanding analyses to include this way of thinking about time. Making the argument that time is underappreciated as a political good, or that it has a singular role in politics, should not be construed to mean that time is more important than other political goods.

Third, the forms of duration with which this book is most concerned are those that are specified in political procedures. Here I make a distinction between officially sanctioned and structured periods like probations, deadlines, age limits, and specific waiting periods that apply to entire classes of persons and the kinds of indefinite waiting that result from scarcity, delays, stalling, and arbitrary obstruction. Although there are occasions on which the two types of temporal experiences can merge, have similar motivations, or have similar outcomes, they also diverge in

---

[73] This is how scholars classify Skowronek's approach. Graham G. Dodds and Stephen Skowronek, "Presidential Leadership in Political Time: Reprise and Reappraisal," *Canadian Journal of Political Science* 41, no. 4 (2008).

[74] Anna Grzymala Busse, "Time Will Tell? Temporality and the Analysis of Causal Mechanisms and Processes," *Comparative Political Studies* 44, no. 9 (2010): 1289.

important ways. I have chosen to address only durations of time that are planned and dictated by law and policy rather than those that are the outcome of other decisions. I delve into the politics of waiting, delays, queues, and other types of waiting elsewhere.[75]

Finally, in the book I identify various temporal rules and formulae. Temporal formulae in politics are ubiquitous. In order to be able to connect the analysis of each chapter, particularly Chapters 3–5, I refer repeatedly to only a subset of these formulae, particularly the age of maturity that divides children from full adult citizens, the probationary period that non-citizens must wait before naturalizing, and prison sentences. This is not because the arguments of the book only apply to these three examples, as should be evident from this introductory chapter. It is only for the sake of clarity and consistency that I refrain from repeatedly mentioning abortion waiting periods, retirement ages, and the multitude of other instances in which time structures democratic politics.

CONCLUSION

This book is a study of a phenomenon that hides in plain sight: the valuation of time by the state as a means of representing and commensurating politically important processes. As laws about voting ages, retirement, naturalization, and incarceration suggest, time has political value that is generally determined by the state from within a political system. The fact that time is inevitably a part of every person's life and therefore inevitably a part of all politics does not mean the ways in which it is a part of politics and the role it plays in political justice can be taken for granted. It is quite often the case that political procedures invoking time could be (and sometimes are) performed without using time. When a duration of time is given explicit importance in a political procedure that could be structured on a non-temporal basis we need to know why time has been selected for that role.

The chapters that follow examine the relationship between scientifically measured time and democratic politics with the goal of understanding how and why liberal democratic states come to measure people's fitness or entitlement to hold basic rights using precise quantities of scientifically measured time. Using moments and durations of time to represent that which would otherwise be difficult to represent is common. The reasons for the ubiquity of this practice can be time's quantifiability,

---

[75] See unpublished manuscript on file with author.

which is practical, and the degree to which time is integral to the very idea of the nation-state. However, they also incorporate widely held intuitions that clocks and calendars are detached and fair decision-makers. When pressed, many of these intuitions fail to yield much assurance that time actually is impartial, egalitarian, or fair. It is also difficult to envision an alternative to temporal measures, so embedded are they in every stage of the exercise of power. We rely on temporal measures to facilitate compromises among conflicting values and to make political procedures proceed efficiently.

The book's conclusions address the question of identifying which kinds of temporal practices are fair and comport with the fundamental normative framework of a liberal democracy. While standards for just laws and policies will vary based on the attributes of any given polity, a few generalizations can be made. Most of these derive from the premise that, as with other goods, we expect the time of similarly situated persons to be treated in a similar fashion by the state. When there is a glaring disparity in how the time of otherwise similarly situated people is valued it is likely that an illiberal and undemocratic practice exists. For these reasons, ongoing scrutiny of practices in which states command the time of their citizens is as integral to assessing the justness of a polity as is scrutiny of distribution, representation, and other common subjects of normative inquiry. If we want to understand political justice, we need to look closely at practices relating to political time as well as the normative consequences of the innumerable laws and policies that rely on time. A state should provide very good reasons for asking people to wait for things, for the precise length of time that they wait, and for the order in which they receive that for which they wait. In order to provide these reasons, it must first be clear how and why time takes on normative weight in a liberal democracy. The chapter that follows begins this project by examining the relationship between time and sovereignty.

2

The Sovereign Temporal Borders around Nation-States, Populations, and Citizenries

INTRODUCTION

The problem of boundaries in democratic theory is generally taken to be a question of either territoriality, inclusion in the *demos*, or some permutation of both. While critical theorists have recognized that borders themselves are complex and multifaceted, the role of time has taken a back seat to other relevant political processes. Recent work on the boundary problem has made arguments in favor of regarding territorial presence as prerequisite to democratic inclusion.[1] Much of this work was spurred by discussion of Robert Goodin's "all affected principle" that explodes the notion of a territorial *demos* in favor of a *demos* of shared interests, decisions, and consequences.[2] Many of the new territorialists also respond to Arash Abizadeh's more confined claims about the "unbounded demos" and the rights of anyone coerced by the constitution of a bounded *demos* to participate in procedures that impose those boundaries.[3]

Implied in any of these or related theories about political boundaries is some kind of schedule of political decision-making in which a point of commencement is followed by regularly scheduled deliberations and voting. In other words, a temporal component is included in each and every discussion of the boundaries around sovereign states and *demoi*.

The connection of time and political boundaries is illustrated by an obscure but non-trivial fact: prior to the twentieth century, it is believed that the word deadline referred not to a moment past which an assignment

---

[1] Sarah Song, "The Significance of Territorial Presence and the Rights of Immigrants," in *Migration in Political Theory: The Ethics of Movement and Membership*, eds. Sarah Fine and Lea Ypi (Oxford University Press, 2014); Paulina Ochoa Espejo, "People, Territory, and Legitimacy in Democratic States," *American Journal of Political Science* 58, no. 2 (2014): 466–78.

[2] Robert Goodin, "Enfranchising All Affected Interests, and Its Alternatives," *Philosophy & Public Affairs* 35, no. 2 (2007): 40–68.

[3] "On the Demos and Its Kin: Nationalism, Democracy, and the Boundary Problem," *American Political Science Review* 106, no. 4 (2012): 867–82; Goodin, "Enfranchising All Affected Interests, and Its Alternatives," 40–68.

29

or task would be considered "late" but to the line around a military prison beyond which anyone attempting to escape would be shot. Deadlines demarcated a specific territory. The more modern usage of the word, to refer to a time limit, conceals two features of its prior definitions: its denotation of a territorial boundary and its connection to state power. But those features nonetheless remain integral to the political experience of deadlines. Time and territory are both implicated in the creation of political boundaries.

Most constitutions refer to a point in time, usually a specific day of a specific year, at which they take effect. Before that time sovereignty may have been differently constituted or not constituted at all. Many other forms of temporal boundaries also exist. Quarantines, curfews, dates of establishment, statutes of limitations, and myriad other kinds of temporal boundaries are all imposed by states to limit and direct the power that people and groups have to move, reside, act, and claim or exercise rights. They have in common a boundary-keeping function that marks out the beginning and end of political regimes, and, within those regimes, structure claims of fundamental rights including free movement and political participation. They are ordinary and yet integral features of politics that merit systematic interrogation by political theorists. Yet many fundamental rights and statuses are contingent on meeting political deadlines. Ignoring their significance is generally the privilege of those who fall on the more fortunate side of such boundaries. It therefore bears asking: what is the relationship between temporal boundaries and political justice?

The invisibility of temporal boundaries belies the immense influence they have on the structure and distribution of political power. Time is an important political variable that can be manipulated to achieve greater or lesser degrees of inclusion in the population. Temporal boundaries separate in from out, enfranchised from disenfranchised, and rights-bearing from rightless. We cannot see or feel a date on a calendar, or a deadline on a schedule, in the same way that we might be able to see armed guards standing in a row or feel razor wire installed in the ground. But the date and the deadline can divide people and political power at least as effectively as the armed guard or the fence. Temporal boundaries may sometimes be more heavily policed and governed than geographic boundaries. Even a rudimentary system of documentation can precisely identify when someone arrives or departs from a territory. So, creating a deadline for departure or adjustment of status can be negotiated within a political system whereas moving a territorial boundary will require the assent of at least one other independent sovereign state.

This chapter will discuss how calendrical time is integral to the establishment and maintenance of four pivotal types of political boundaries including: sovereign borders around nation-states; the boundaries between the populations of different nation-states; boundaries within the interior of nation-states that restrict free movement of parts of the population; and, finally, boundaries that divide rights-bearing persons from non-rights-bearing persons.

Through this analysis there emerge three different ways of designing the temporal boundaries that form the most prominent strands in the temporal web that structures political power. They are: fixed single boundaries that refer to a single point in time, countdown boundaries such as statutes of limitation, and recurring boundaries such as a decennial census. Identifying different types of temporal borders and analyzing their relationship to democratic norms grounds arguments about the normative consequences of choosing one or another form of temporal boundary and measurement. These arguments help us judge how inclusive and democratic is any law or policy that imposes a temporal boundary. The concluding section of the chapter provides a normative analysis of how well each type of temporal boundary accommodates core democratic norms. It makes the case that fixed single temporal boundaries are well suited to non-consensual realms of politics, such as the establishment of a sovereign state, but are less suitable for the implementation of democratic norms, because they are often highly arbitrary. Countdown boundaries have greater potential for being normatively justifiable by democratic standards because they carve out more temporal space within which claims may be made. Recurring temporal boundaries hold the most potential to accord with core tenets of democratic theory because they offer the strongest promises of the greatest number of opportunities for inclusion and participation.

BOUNDARIES

The temporal boundaries discussed in this chapter have in common the fact that they use time to demarcate the spaces within which powers and rights may or may not be exercised. Sociologists have long been cognizant of the processes implied in the marking of time. All events exist in relation to other events, and their historical meaning is situated in a "structural position" with relation to other events.[4] To the sociologist, marked time is considered extraordinary while ordinary time is unmarked.[5] Yet, it is difficult to find political time that is entirely unmarked. People occupy specific times, however demarcated, just as much as they occupy territory.[6] Temporal boundaries carve borders around our nation-states and through populations via marked time and deadlines. Like any boundaries, temporal boundaries discriminate. They divide regimes, exclude outsiders, and distinguish between people who hold rights and those who do not. They also exercise considerable power by delimiting the exercise of rights and distributive justice. None of this is to say that temporal boundaries render territorial or other boundaries irrelevant. A state requires both a territorial and a temporal boundary to assert sovereignty, confer a work visa, or demarcate an electoral district. Nor is time the cause or creator of temporal boundaries. Time is a tool in the arsenal of a state and, while it is deployed frequently, it is not the argument of this chapter or this book that time somehow acts independently to create boundaries. Instead, the goal is to excavate the role that time plays in political boundary-marking in order to assess the normative potential of temporal justice at the margins.

Sovereign Political Borders

Time enters the political life of the state at its inception, as sovereignty is established. This embeds time as thoroughly as space in the act of asserting sovereignty. The first temporal boundary of any state is the one that identifies when the polity comes into existence. We identify the establishment of sovereignty with a precise date because a regime's dominion exists side by side with, and in contrast to, the dominion of other regimes. Just as geographic boundaries identify *where* one sovereign power begins and another ends, temporal boundaries show us *when* a sovereign regime begins or ends. While many have noted the degree to which clock and calendrical time are integral to the economy and society in modernity,[7] temporal laws are just as essential to, and pervasive within, modern

---

[4] Eviatar Zerubavel, *Time Maps: Collective Memory and the Social Shape of the Past* (University of Chicago Press, 2012), 12.

[5] Zerubavel, *Time Maps*, 26.

[6] Jed Rubenfeld, *Freedom and Time: A Theory of Constitutional Self-Government* (New Haven, CT: Yale University Press, 2008), 139.

[7] Anthony Giddens, *Consequences of Modernity* (Cambridge, UK: Polity, 1990); Michel Foucault, *Discipline and Punish: The Birth of the Prison* (New York: Vintage, 1979);

politics. We look to when, not just where, we are in order to ascertain the boundaries of our political units.

Scholars have noted that all political and social institutions are delimited chronologically as well as geographically.[8] To some, the temporal boundaries of politics may even precede the territorial. Margaret Somers illustrates that Locke's justification of a consent principle in his move from a pre-political to a contract-based polity is rooted in a "temporal narrative" that describes a causal sequence ending with the establishment of a citizenship that is spatially distinct from that which precedes it.[9] Chronological bounding is ubiquitous in modernity, but the practice is hardly confined to modernity. Consider these different examples of temporal boundaries that demarcate sovereign states. In 1793, the recently founded French Republic imposed an entirely new calendar and means of measuring time on the population as a way to demarcate the end of the monarchy and the creation of a sovereign citizenry. This act was intended to distinguish the new regime from the one that preceded it. It literally restarted the clock in step with the newly formed state. The new time line demarcated the end of one regime and the birth of a new one.[10] This calendar was the "original time of state formation."[11] But it was also intended to separate the French nation and people from all other nations and peoples. The "new time" of the FRC "offered a fixed point from which a new chronology commences, analogous to the originary or 'first' time of a new civilization."[12] Much the same role is attributed to the *Stünde Null*, which was invoked to signal the destruction of the Nazi regime, the installation of a new regime, and a complete cultural break with German traditions, many of which predated Nazism.[13] While the term "zero hour" is military in origin, referring to the moment a battle begins, shortly after 1945 it came to

Henri Bergson, *Time and Free Will: An Essay on the Immediate Data of Consciousness* (New York: Dover Publications, 2001).
[8] Jens Bartelson, *A Genealogy of Sovereignty* (Cambridge University Press, 1995), vol. XXXIX, 1221.
[9] *Genealogies of Citizenship: Markets, Statelessness, and the Right to Have Rights* (Cambridge University Press, 2008), 274–7.
[10] Sanja Perovic, *The Calendar in Revolutionary France: Perceptions of Time in Literature, Culture, Politics* (Cambridge University Press, 2012), 6.
[11] Perovic, *Calendar in Revolutionary France*, 30.   [12] Ibid., 26.
[13] Stephen Brockmann, "German Culture at the Zero Hour," *Dietrich College of Humanities and Social Sciences* (Research Showcase at Carnegie Mellon University, 1996), 7.

represent both the destruction and rebirth of Germany.[14] And "year zero" describes the defeat of General Lol Non and the ascent to total power of the Khmer Rouge.[15] In each case, the restarting of the calendar serves to mark a political break, a new regime, and a connection between members of the society living together in the newly created time. In each case a regime literally restarts time, marking the beginning of the new time as a political turning point at which a nation and a state have been formed.

Historiographical work hints at the political attributes of temporal boundaries. As Kathleen Davis writes, "[t]he history of periodization is juridical, and it advances through struggles over the definition and location of sovereignty."[16] From this fact flows a definition of who governs and is governed by a regime. "In this sense, periodization functions as sovereign decision."[17] Chronology allows events to be compared and contrasted, put in relation not just to one another but to a past and future more generally."[18] The mutual recognition of temporal boundaries by both people and institutions on all sides of those boundaries underscores the quiet consensus that exists regarding the political importance of time. It also strengthens the boundaries themselves. "Bede's periodization does, like Schmitt's decision and like medieval/modern periodization, establish forms of homogeneity, laying claim to a nomos of the earth, a territorialization of world and time."[19]

This is true not just for historiographical work and periodization, but for politics itself, and in particular the politics of the state. Even when no new calendar is imposed, this chapter will demonstrate that precise times and dates often form a sovereign boundary that divides a regime from its predecessor and its people from foreigners. Conceptions of historical time must therefore be understood as "political strategy" and periodization in the service of narrating a progressive history as nothing short of "aggression."[20] For Davis and other historiographers, "there is nothing legitimate about historical 'periods'; to the contrary, they are means of legitimizing political ends."[21]

---

[14] Brockmann, "German Culture," 12.
[15] Rosemary H.T. O'Kane, "Cambodia in the Zero Years: Rudimentary Totalitarianism," *Third World Quarterly* 14, no. 4 (1993): 735.
[16] *Periodization and Sovereignty* (Philadelphia, PA: Pennsylvania University Press, 2008), 6.
[17] Davis, *Periodization and Sovereignty*, 80.
[18] Perovic, *Calendar in Revolutionary France*, 13.
[19] Davis, *Periodization and Sovereignty*, 142.   [20] Ibid., 92.   [21] Ibid., 83.

Those ends can and do include the establishment of boundaries around states.

The assertion of temporal political boundaries around nations and states is imbricated in the process through which power was wrested from non-secular authorities.[22] Davis cites Antonio Negri's description of the religious secular break as illuminating how "constituent power has always had a singular relationship to time . . .Power becomes an immanent dimension of history, an actual temporal horizon."[23] The temporal side of sovereignty was regarded as an inevitability by natural law philosophers as they developed justifications for secular power. Pocock has described the slow extraction of authority from the church as a process in which the eternal authority of god is traded for an earthly, temporal, authority.[24] In contrast to eternal authority, temporal authority is non-sacred and hence non-eternal.[25] It takes effect at a precise point in time and it may also cease to exist at a precise point in time. This distinguishes political sovereignty from godly power. Religious dominion is eternal. Political dominion is not. A reign or a regime must be demarcated and distinguished from any other reign or regime. In place of referring to sacred texts to mark these boundaries we refer to secular and scientific texts and instruments. The calendar and chronology are among these texts and instruments. A calendar date is critical to this process. What can be numbered can be bounded and grasped by humans in a way that the non-numbered cannot.[26] The denumerable is controllable whereas that which cannot be numbered is indefinite, vague, and escapes human attempts to grasp and control it.[27] Political authority over a territory and its population exists with respect to a calendrical temporal boundary that is just as significant as the

---

[22] At this point, readers interested in the practical mechanics of temporal boundaries may wish to skip this brief history of political thought on temporality and move to the next section.

[23] Davis, *Periodization and Sovereignty*, 108 (citing Antonio Negri, *Insurgencies: Constituent Power and the Modern State* (University of Minnesota Press, 1999), vol. XV, 23).

[24] John Greville Agard Pocock, *The Machiavellian Moment: Florentine Political Thought and the Atlantic Republican Tradition* (Princeton University Press, 2009), 53–6. Scholars of time note that early theologians treated time as a "subsection of eternity." Carol J. Greenhouse, "Just in Time: Temporality and the Cultural Legitimation of Law," *Yale Law Journal* 98 (1989): 1634.

[25] Pocock, *Machiavellian Moment*, 8.

[26] Martha C. Nussbaum, *The Fragility of Goodness: Luck and Ethics in Greek Tragedy and Philosophy* (Cambridge University Press, 2001), vol. II, 107.

[27] Ibid.

geographic boundaries that are traditionally identified as integral to sovereignty.

Well before the revolutionary regime in France sought to announce its sovereignty by imposing a break with the old temporal order and an entirely new calendar, Hobbes presaged the need for attention to temporal politics, cautioning that people must live in the present because they are unable to imagine eternity. Hobbes sought to subvert the idea of the eternal in order to shore up political authority. Law could facilitate happiness by "transforming men's temporal consciousness."[28] The work of law is to carve a boundary into eternal time that permits people to live in the present. Once this is accomplished, humankind can circumvent living in a perpetual state of uncertainty.[29] The conquering of an uncertain future was necessary for the establishment of secular power.

Hobbes states one of the pivotal preconditions for secular politics: the future requires "taming" and certain actions and choices will accomplish this goal.[30] A future mastered by people living in the present motivates the development of future-oriented institutions underwritten by those secular political authorities. Davis points to the Treaty of Westphalia as a point at which, "[p]olitics thus begins to break the cyclic grip of prophecy, for which it substituted rational foresight and planning."[31] Bartelson makes a related point about modern sovereignty's distinctly rationalist foundations.[32] Similarly, Pocock observes that the eighteenth-century foundation of the National Debt in England marks a watershed because from that moment forward the entire society was able to extend credit for future actions based upon actuarial assessments of the past.[33] In a context in which an uncertain future was troubling enough to make people abandon any exercise of natural rights in favor of superstitious faith, the idea that an actuarial assessment of the past could facilitate the control of the future was tremendously alluring.

Once people subscribe to the idea that the future can be controlled, or at least influenced, actuarial assessment of the past quickly becomes pervasive. Modern sentencing practices, the assessment of a person's youth as training for enfranchisement, the transformation of foreigners into naturalized citizens, and many more temporal calculations made in

---

[28] Jose Brunner, "Modern Times: Law, Temporality and Happiness in Hobbes, Locke and Bentham," *Theoretical Inquiries in Law* 8, no. 1 (2007): 286.
[29] Ibid., 285–6.   [30] Ibid., 305.   [31] *Periodization and Sovereignty*, 105.
[32] *Genealogy of Sovereignty*, 194.
[33] John Greville Agard Pocock, *Virtue, Commerce, and History* (Cambridge University Press, 1985), 112ff.

modern bureaucratic states are all examples of this way of thinking. In each case, an assessment of the past is used to extend or retract "political credit" (by which I mean rights and status) in the future. Time serves such purposes well because it is so easily subjected to actuarial calculations, it can be treated as a rational variable, and it is embedded in secular practices, all while still attaching to normative evaluations of worth and legitimacy. This kind of thinking is critical to the development of capitalism, but its influence is hardly confined to commerce and finance. In according authority to the actuarial and the rational, it opened up a place for a variable such as time to become integral to politics. I will return to the ideas of political credit and actuarial assessment in the two chapters that follow.

Much as the temporal order can signify the establishment of a regime, the breakdown of a temporal order can serve as a benchmark for identifying the breakdown of political authority. A temporal order, "becomes a governing principle, which is dependent upon human practice for its visible meaningfulness and which, in turn, is capable of either legitimating rule or manifesting political instability."[34] When actions happen without respect to a temporal order this signals that there has been a breach of political authority and that no new authority is yet in place. This is most evident in cases where sovereignty is disrupted by war. As David Landes notes in his discussion of time and military action, "Combat began and ended without regard to hours and minutes."[35] Clocks eventually facilitate the coordination of battalions and allies, but battle itself, the signal of uncertain sovereignty, is not a scheduled affair as we might expect an election or even a coronation to be. The breakdown of sovereignty is signaled by the breakdown of a temporal order. This is the realization of Hobbes's fear of chaos as embodied by the temporal order he claimed was necessary for taming the future.

Bounding the Population of Political Subjects

Laws of time punctuate political *durées*, demarcate sovereign states, and coagulate nationhood. Once legitimized, temporal boundaries proliferate and diversify to accomplish a wide array of political boundary-marking purposes. As the discussion of sovereignty and time demonstrates,

---

[34] *Periodization and Sovereignty*, 124.
[35] *Revolution in Time: Clocks and the Making of the Modern World* (Cambridge, MA: Belknap Press of Harvard University Press, 1983), 96.

references to measured calendrical time permeate the foundation and maintenance of nation-state boundaries. Inevitably, then, temporal boundaries must also distinguish the subjects of different states from one another. Boundaries carved into time, as much as into territory, ground the formation of the population, and identify those parts of the population that will qualify for rights.

The preceding section dealt with temporal boundaries around states. The next two sections will look at the proliferation of temporal political boundaries *within* states. First, I will look at how temporal boundaries are drawn to indicate who may rightly be considered subjects of any given state. Then I will look at how temporal boundaries are drawn in ways that determine who will be entitled to exercise rights.

Temporal boundaries perform important functions required to create and enforce the political borders of populations. Whereas temporal boundaries around sovereign *nation-states* delineate institutional power arrangements, boundaries around *people* determine who may reside somewhere, who may move freely in which locations, and who is a recognized political subject of those sovereign nation-states. Historians of the border are quick to point out that the physical location of the territorial borders we often assume delineate the population is not always clear to the people who are policed by it. Even when the boundary is clear, it can be quite difficult to monitor it.[36] The physical geography of the border will often be difficult to identify in the absence of a human-made identifier. There are stretches of both the southern and northern US border that are not visibly marked. In the absence of a strongly policed boundary, people may not know precisely where (with respect to political geography) they are at any given moment and they may knowingly or unknowingly move freely over borders without the requisite permission and papers/ inspection. While it is theoretically possible to remain unaware of the date and time, reminders of these facts are pervasive. It is also far less costly to maintain a temporal border than a territorial one. No fences need be erected, no armed personnel occupy it, and it is not even clear whether or how it would be contested. A temporal boundary can impose a surgical precision on political power that geography cannot.

As the introduction to this chapter discussed, the boundary problem in democratic theory relates to questions of territoriality but it does not perfectly overlap with territoriality. Normative democratic theorists have

---

[36] Rachel St. John, *Line in the Sand: A History of the Western US–Mexico Border* (Princeton University Press, 2011).

generated a thriving debate about how a *demos* ought to be constituted. This debate has as its focal points the proper relationship of culture, nationality, territoriality, affected interests, and coercion. Liberal nationalists ground boundaries in a shared culture, history, and peoplehood. In this view, membership is unchosen, particularized, and heavily bounded.[37] Cosmopolitans have charged the liberal nationalist view with being parochial and unjust.[38] Relatedly, consequentialism has been invoked by Arash Abizadeh and Robert Goodin in the service of arguments that qualify people for membership in the *demos* by virtue of whether they are coercively affected by its decisions (Abizadeh) or affected more generally.[39] Territorialists have tried to carve out middle ground with reference to what they see as less ethnocentric arguments about connection to place.[40] And inclusive liberals have made strenuous arguments for placing very few boundaries on the *demos* at all.[41]

Each of these views espouses a set of normative principles about how *demoi* ought to be bounded, sometimes but not always with reference to actual boundary-marking practices. Each also takes for granted the background work that time does in the types of boundary-marking they are discussing. Yet, whether one takes a view of boundaries that is more nationalist, more territorial, or entirely cosmopolitan, the polity and its *demos* are both constructed temporally. Each type of boundary-marking has its own temporal tools and logic. Working backward, the next discussion in this section describes the process of establishing boundaries around political subjects without reference to norms. It focuses on the temporal boundary around all sets of political subjects, both democratic and non-democratic, and speaks to questions that would be relevant to liberal nationalists, territorialists, and consequentialist cosmopolitan theorists of boundaries.

---

[37] Anna Stilz, *Liberal Loyalty: Freedom, Obligation, and the State* (Princeton University Press, 2009).

[38] Thomas Pogge, *World Poverty and Human Rights: Cosmopolitan Responsibilities and Reforms* (Cambridge, UK: Polity, 2002); Goodin, "Enfranchising All Affected Interests," 40–68.

[39] Abizadeh, "On the Demos and Its Kin," 867–82; Goodin, "Enfranchising All Affected Interests," 40–68.

[40] Margaret Moore, *A Political Theory of Territory* (Oxford University Press, 2015); Song, "Significance of Territorial Presence."

[41] Joseph H. Carens, *Immigrants and the Right to Stay* (Cambridge, MA: MIT Press, 2010); Elizabeth F. Cohen, "Reconsidering US Immigration Reform: The Temporal Principle of Citizenship," *Perspectives on Politics* 9, no. 03 (2011), 575–83.

In the Anglo-American tradition, the practice of using a temporal boundary to define the population of a state is established most clearly in the foundational citizenship case know as *Calvin's Case* (1608). *Calvin's Case* involved the question of whether Robert Calvin, a Scottish person born after the Union of the Scottish and English crowns under James I, was a subject of the crown. The case asked whether Calvin, a Scottish person who had been born under the allegiance of King James, could legitimately inherit land. This right of inheritance was a signature right of subjects. At stake was the political status of Scots, people in other parts of the kingdom, aliens who had been admitted for residence or temporary travel to England, and, finally, people residing in territories that had non-standard political relationships to the crown. In short, it was a case that took up where Magna Carta's constitutive vagueness left off. It asked how to differentiate between subjects and foreigners, and also how to differentiate among the different kinds of aliens who were present within the kingdom.[42] Procedures for addressing non-subjects (deciding who could be present and enjoy which protections of the king, as well as whether anyone not in the allegiance of the king could somehow be made a subject anyway) would follow therein.

Coke invoked a temporal principle in order to determine who was in the allegiance of the king. He argued that jurists must scrutinize birthright in order to ascertain a person's allegiance. Subjects were people born fully and solely in the allegiance of the king's natural body, which ruled both England and Scotland.[43] In other words, a person's spatial location at the precise moment of their birth determined their allegiance. While Magna Carta made vague references to birth in the realm, Coke is explicit that the time of birth is at least as important for determining allegiance as the place of birth. He wrote, "the time of his birth is of the essence of a subject born; for he cannot be a subject to the king of England, unlesse at the time of his birth he was under the ligeance and obedience of the king."[44] Merely swearing

---

[42] As I have written elsewhere, these kinds of "semi-citizenships" are integral to the instantiation of the modern state. Elizabeth F. Cohen, *Semi-Citizenship in Democratic Politics* (Cambridge University Press, 2009).

[43] Bernadette Meyler, "The Gestation of Birthright Citizenship, 1868–1898: States' Rights, the Law of Nations, and Mutual Consent," *Georgetown Immigration Law Journal* 15 (2001): 519; Polly Price, "Natural Law and Birthright Citizenship in *Calvin's Case* (1608)," *Yale Journal of Law and Humanities* 9, no. 1 (1997): 83–4, 113, 115.

[44] *Calvin v. Smith*, 77 Eng. Rep. 377, 399 (KB 1608).

an oath could not constitute subjecthood because "ligeance doth not begin by the oath in the leet ... swearing in a leetmaketh no denization."[45] Obedience itself was a birthright, not a decision, choice, or act, and determined whether one would enjoy the protection of the freedoms spelled out in Magna Carta as well as the rest of the common law tradition.[46] By stating that allegiance was set at the time of birth, Coke made the time of a potential subject's birth as important as their place of birth.[47] This principle serves as important a role as place of birth or parentage in determining who would enjoy the freedoms spelled out in Magna Carta and other parts of the common law tradition.

In order to specify who actually was born into the allegiance of the natural body of King James, Coke gives a detailed political history of each of the territories potentially containing subjects of James.[48] This included primarily Scotland, Ireland, Normandy, Aquitaine, Calais, Gascony, and Guyana. He traces the history of each territory's political relationship to the crown. Through these political histories, Coke very carefully detailed what Magna Carta had left undefined: namely who could be considered a subject based not only on political principle, but also on historical circumstance. Foremost among the territories whose peoples were of special interest when Coke wrote were the Scottish and the Irish. Coke sifts through the arguments presented to the court and a lengthy history of the subjects in question and comes to the conclusion that the Irish were not full subjects of James. Of the Scottish, *postnati* (born after the union of the crowns), of which Calvin was one, were indeed subjects. The *antenati* (persons born prior to the union of the crowns) were not.

In drawing a line between the *antenati* and *postnati*, Coke draws a temporal boundary around the subjects of James I. Calvin was born after James had assumed the throne, joining England and Scotland in political union. In elaborating this principle, Coke does not simply show how to draw political boundaries around sovereign territorial boundaries. He demarcates sovereign temporal boundaries that are every bit as powerful as those drawn in the soil.

---

[45] Ibid., 382.

[46] The case does discuss the fact that noble titles to which people had been born in Scotland would not entitle them to the equivalent in England, though this fact is not central to the argument of this article (ibid., 394).

[47] A few others have noted this parenthetically. See Price, "Natural Law and Birthright Citizenship," 117; Mary Sarah Bilder, *The Transatlantic Constitution: Colonial Legal Culture and the Empire* (Cambridge, MA: Harvard University Press, 2004), 36.

[48] *Calvin v. Smith*.

Coke was no doubt able to achieve the drawing of a temporal boundary around the British population because time already held significance within the constitutional tradition in England. Magna Carta's age itself was cited as a decisive element of its supremacy. As Pocock states, "If the constitutionalists could show that the laws were as, or older than, kings, they might go on to assert a contractual or elective basis for kingship."[49] It is the long-standing Englishness of Magna Carta, as well as its sources, that lend each the authority to establish sovereign dominion. In fact, one of Coke's arguments against considering the Irish full subjects hinged on the fact that the Irish were governed by their own law that was itself ancient and historically distinct from that governing the English and, post Union, Scottish. Coke wrote, "they retain unto this day divers of their ancient customs, separate and diverse from the laws of England."[50] What *Calvin's Case* shows us is how dates become just as integral to sovereignty as physical borders of nation-states. In other words, the classic definition of sovereignty – supreme authority within a geographic territory – contains an unarticulated temporal assumption.

The establishment of temporal line that differentiates members from non-members is not unique to the early modern era or the British context. "Zero option rules," as they are now known, are common.[51] These rules specify a date or dates at which anyone physically present may be considered a subject or citizen. Zero-option rules are not exclusively a function of *jus soli* regimes that accord citizenship to people born within a territory. Despite its association with blood-based citizenship (*jus sanguinis*), Germany's Basic Law allows citizenship for persons present or related to those present as of December 31, 1937, as well as anyone expelled between January 30, 1933 and May 8, 1945, as long as those persons were also present after May 8, 1945.[52] Soviet citizenship was revoked in 1921 for those who had resided abroad for more than five years and for those who had left Russia after November 7, 1917 without

[49] John Greville Agard Pocock, *The Ancient Constitution and the Feudal Law: A Study of English Historical Thought in the Seventeenth Century* (Cambridge University Press, 1987), 56.

[50] *Calvin v. Smith*, 398.

[51] *Diasporas and Ethnic Migrants: Germany, Israel and Russia in Comparative Perspective*, eds. Rainer Munz and Rainer Ohliger (London: Routledge, 2004), 109.

[52] Basic Law for the Federal Republic of Germany in the revised version published in the Federal Law Gazette Part III, classification number 100–1, as last amended by the Act of 11 July 2012 (Federal Law Gazette I p. 1478), at Article 116.

permission of the Soviet government. This was a decree of the All Russian Central Executive Committee.[53]

In many cases states use these fixed date temporal boundaries around populations to accomplish via time what cannot be done physically – a return of the boundaries of the population to a past iteration of itself.[54] Temporal boundaries are thus manipulated in ways that return a people to a previous self. This process of resetting the clock involves reestablishing boundaries around the nation and the population that existed at one time but were reshaped over time. Culture requires forms of boundaries that do not lend themselves to territorial definition. Because ideas about time and its measurement are, at least in part, artifacts of shared social life, temporal boundaries can serve purposes that territorial boundaries do not. Starting the political clock of a society over to mark the commencement of a new regime, as the French did after their revolution, has the effect of creating an important cultural boundary around a nation whose territorial boundaries have not shifted at all.

The ability of temporal boundaries around a people to return that people to a prior state is illustrated well by the fact that the reconfiguration of empires is often accompanied by zero-option rules. In such cases, nationalism – both ethnic and liberal – is realized through temporal laws. Ayad Akhtar's play *Disgraced* features a lead character born in the US but straddling the sociopolitical consequences of the 1947 temporal divide between Pakistan and India, after the birth of his father but before his mother's birth. Hong Kong's handover from the British to Chinese control occurred on the schedule of a 99-year lease that expired in 1997. In 1952, the US granted citizenship to anyone living or born in Guam on or after 1899.[55] The post-Soviet era saw many such rules, empowering ethnic nationalism in the face of colonialization projects that had resettled Russians in the ethnic homelands of various other peoples. After the breakup of the Soviet Union, Latvia and Estonia excluded from citizenship large numbers of people who had been born in their territories during the Soviet era and who were present during separation but whose parents and grandparents had not been present prior to the moment when the Soviet occupation began.[56] More recently it

---

[53] Isabel Kaprielian-Churchill, "Rejecting 'Misfits': Canada and the Nansen Passport," *International Migration Review* 28 (1994): 283.

[54] This is closely related to the phenomenon of "irredentism." See Thomas Ambrosio, *Irredentism: Ethnic Conflict and International Politics* (Westport, CT: Praeger, 2001).

[55] 8 USCA § 1407 (West 2015).

[56] Jeff Chinn and Lise A. Truex, "The Question of Citizenship in the Baltics," *Journal of Democracy* 7, no. 1 (1996): 133–47.

has been reported that the reappropriation of Crimea by Russia caused ethnic minorities in contested and threatened areas of Ukraine to scramble to birth and register their children as Ukrainian before the deadline set for the Russian takeover.[57]

Kuwait's 1959 Nationality Law defines nationals as persons who were settled in Kuwait prior to 1920 and who maintained their normal residence there until the publication of the law (one-third to one-half of the population is recognized as full-fledged citizens).[58] The law has been amended fourteen times, always becoming more restrictive.[59] In Cyprus, persons can be citizens if they were born before August 16, 1960, are citizens of the United Kingdom and its former colonies, and originate from Cyprus from the male side. People born after August 16, 1960 to a female Cypriot citizen and a foreign father may also apply for citizenship, as may adults who were born after August 16, 1960 and were born to a parent who became a British citizen based on the Annexation of Cyprus Orders in Council 1914 to 1943 or a person born in Cyprus after November 5, 1914 and prior to August 16, 1960.[60]

Zero-option rules and related constitutional stipulations that make political status dependent on presence or birth on a specific date can be used to do more than partition states. They can also shape the ethnic composition of the nation. The former Soviet republics accomplished its de-Russification without having to move geographic boundaries or forcefully expel populations. Such rules structured the decomposition of the British Empire and its reconstitution into separate sovereign nations. Along the way, temporal borders were also erected to differentiate among the persons who would be permitted to return to the UK, either temporarily or permanently, and those who would be considered fully foreign.

These kinds of nostalgic returns to past borders have also been deployed in the US. The 1924 National Origins Quota Act looked for a rationale for the specific quotas the congressmen sought to enact. The goal was to shape a polity that would include very few people from countries

[57] Davide Greene, "Crimean Tatars Pressured to Become Russian Citizens," National Public Radio (Oct. 28, 2014, 4:39 AM ET), www.npr.org/2014/10/28/359512062/crimean-tatars-pressured-to-become-russian-citizens

[58] Kuwait: Ministerial Decree No. 15 of 1959 promulgating the Nationality Law, http://gulfmigration.eu/kuwait-ministerial-decree-no-15-of-1959-promulgating-the-nationality-law; Justin Schuster and Eric Stern, *Diplomatic Discourse* (The Politic, 2015), 454.

[59] Katherine Southwick and Maureen Lynch, "Nationality Rights for All: A Progress Report and Global Survey on Statelessness," *Refugees International* (March 2009): 51.

[60] Rainier Baubock, *Migration and Citizenship: Legal Status Rights, and Political Participation* (Amsterdam University Press, 2006), ch. 2.

whose genetic stock was deemed inferior to that of white northwestern European Protestants.[61] This could have been accomplished in any number of ways. Congress could have used percentages of the total population to set quotas that would admit few or even no undesirable immigrants. They could have completely banned immigration from some countries. At the time there was no legal immigration from a number of countries including but not limited to all countries on the continent of Africa, India, and the Philippines. What the congressmen did instead was decide that they were going to key the restrictions to earlier censuses. Instead of dickering directly about how many Polish people, for example, would be allowed into the US, they dickered over how to construct a temporal formula using an outdated census. The congressmen negotiating the bill reverse-engineered the population, and in a sense, the nation. The question they had to decide was which moment in US history they sought to recreate using their temporal formula. It is no accident or decision of pure convenience that they ended up using the 1790 and 1890 censuses. What they were doing was instantiating a highly rationalized version of a practice that is common to nation-states – an attempted nostalgic return to origins.

Interior Temporal Boundaries

Temporal borders do not just bound the exterior of states and control the makeup and movement of states' populations. They also traverse the interior of states, dividing the population and controlling movement. These interior temporal boundaries perform functions similar to those of external territorial boundaries, regulating people's rights to legally reside in any given place and their rights of free movement. Polities are crisscrossed with various kinds of invisible temporal boundaries. Curfew laws carve temporary boundaries around public spaces, limiting the free movement of specific groups and people in particular communities. While many academics reading this text may think of curfews as exceptional to "business as usual," and not worth attention, if one is a minor, a person of color, or both, curfews are a familiar obstacle to exercising one's right to free movement.[62] Like curfews, temporal restrictions related to citizenship can be summarily imposed, causing free movement and other rights to vanish. In 2013 the

---

[61] Daniel J. Tichenor, *Dividing Lines: The Politics of Immigration Control in America* (Princeton University Press, 2002), ch. 5.

[62] Terry Shropshire, "Mayor Kasim Reed Considers Curfew in Atlanta," *Atlanta Daily World* (July 15, 2016), http://atlantadailyworld.com/2016/07/15/mayor-kasim-reed-con siders-curfew-in-atlanta

Dominican Republic imposed a deadline for people of Haitian descent born in Dominican territory to claim citizenship in Haiti or be subject to deportation. This effectively stripped thousands of people of citizenship, leaving a sizeable number stateless.[63] Similarly, parole status restricts the movement of individuals who have been released following a period of incarceration. Quarantines follow a similar logic, as do temporary restraining orders. These and other temporal boundaries have some but not all of the characteristics of territorial boundaries. They regulate, govern, and restrict movement, separating insiders from outsiders in a context where inside and outside denote not just physical presence, but permission to reside somewhere, and the rights associated with this status.

In the US, an elaborate system of interstate boundaries enabled both southern and northern states to restrict the movement of sick, disabled, immigrant, non-white, and otherwise unwelcome people in the US.[64] Such interior temporal boundaries were particularly important to restricting the movement of the slave and free black population. Slaves who were permitted to travel had to acquire "passes" that came with time limits for travel.[65] Free blacks were prevented from entering from many states and some states precluded the reentry of free blacks who left for extended periods of time.[66] Like their enslaved counterparts, free blacks had to produce documentation of their permission to leave one state and enter another. This was not only true in southern states but also northern states.[67]

---

[63] Roque Planas, "Thousands of Dominicans Woke Up This Week without Citizenship in Any Country," *Huffington Post* (Feb. 3, 2015), www.huffingtonpost.com/2015/02/03/dominicans-citizenship_n_6606336.html

[64] Anna O. Law, "Lunatics, Idiots, Paupers, and Negro Seamen – Immigration Federalism and the Early American State," *Studies in American Political Development* 28, no. 2 (2014): 107–28.

[65] Homer Hawkins and Richard Thomas, "White Policing of Black Populations: A History of Race and Social Control in America," in *Out of Order? Policing Black People*, eds. Ellis Cashmore and Eugene McLaughlin (New York: Routledge, 1991): 68; Allan Colbern, "Regulating Movement in a Federalist System: Slavery's Connection to Immigration Law in the United States," 10–12 (unpublished manuscript) (on file with the author).

[66] Rogers M. Smith, *Civic Ideals: Conflicting Visions of Citizenship in US History* (New Haven, CT: Yale University Press, 1997), 253–4.

[67] Colbern, "Regulating Movement in a Federalist System," 17–18. Some might argue that the creation of a "new Jim Crow" through racialized aggressive policing and sentencing policies effectively recreates temporal restrictions on the free movement of black Americans through the requirement that people on probation request permission to move between states. See Michelle Alexander, *The New Jim Crow: Mass Incarceration in the Age of Colorblindness* (New York: The New Press, 2010).

Interior temporal boundaries were also erected around the Chinese population by the rules that institutionalized Chinese Exclusion. The 1882 Chinese Exclusion Act specified that the entry and subsequent residence of any Chinese laborers in the US would be prohibited from ninety days after the passage of the Act until ten years later. It exempted from removal any Chinese person who was in the US on or before that ninety-day mark and created a documentation system (itself deeply flawed) that would enforce these rules.

The temporally delineated documentation systems that prevailed in the past paved the way for the far more elaborate documentation system that now polices the boundaries between temporary immigrants, permanent residents, and full citizens in many countries. In the US and abroad, visas and one's eligibility for different visa statuses determines how long one can legally reside in a foreign country. Visas specifying a length of legal residence create a temporal boundary for non-citizens living abroad. A person who overstays a visa essentially crosses a border in time rather than a geographic boundary, becoming "illegal" by virtue of when it is, not just where they are. The temporal limit that a visa imposes carves a border in time that corresponds to a political boundary. In many countries, including the US, a large proportion of the undocumented population does not cross a geographic border illegally but instead crosses a temporal border, becoming "illegally" resident by overstaying their visas. This process can also work in reverse. "Registry dates" and one-time amnesties will regularize immigrants based on their presence in the country by specific cutoff dates. The best-known example of this kind of rule is the 1986 Immigration Reform and Control Act (IRCA) that offered "amnesty" to undocumented immigrants and guestworkers who had been present and working in the US since 1982.[68] But other democratic states have also held amnesties. Italy had five between 1987 and 2002; Portugal held three major amnesties, in 1992–3, 1996, and 2001–3; and Greece held two major amnesties, in 1998 and 2000–1.[69]

Such interior temporal boundaries crop up regularly outside of the US as well. Before the fall of the Iron Curtain, Soviet citizens needed a temporary "propiska" (an interior passport) in order to leave their domicile and relocate on a temporary but extended basis. There were rules

---

[68] Immigration Reform and Control Act, 8 USC § 1254a (1986).
[69] Willem Maas, "Freedom of Movement Inside 'Fortress Europe,'" in *Global Surveillance and Policing: Borders, Security, Identity*, eds. Elia Zureik and Mark B. Salter (Cullompton, UK: Willan, 2005), ch. 14.

governing not just the location and purpose of interior movement, but the length one could stay somewhere. Similarly, the South African interior passport system, designed to enforce apartheid, stipulated how long and where black African people could live and travel within the country.

Temporal boundaries carve up populations into hierarchically ordered groups with different rights. It is not just residency and free movement rights that are affected when one's visa expires, but eligibility for a host of other rights that legal non-citizen residents enjoy. Similarly, when temporal barriers are imposed on an existing population, they form borders between groups of persons who enjoy differentiated sets of rights. California water rights laws distinguish between those that were acquired before 1914 and those that were established after 1914, making it almost impossible to impose environmentally responsible restrictions on the rights established earlier.[70] The Bundy family's conflict with the federal government is rooted in their claim that their family had rights to contested land long before the Bureau of Land Management was formed.[71]

Respect for a temporal standard is established while the preconditions for sovereign states are put into place and is subsequently baked into the boundaries of sovereign nation-states. For most individuals, encountering a sovereign state boundary involves either receiving permission to move freely or having their movement restricted. This also holds true for the interior temporal boundaries described above. As should be evident from the instances of temporal boundaries that I have mentioned, race and nationality will often be salient to a person's experience of a sovereign nation-state boundary. Some people move freely with ease while others run into boundaries. Often one's race or country of origin will affect the ease with which one can enter a nation-state. This also holds true in the case of interior temporal boundaries. Many of the US, Soviet, and South African rules about free movement refer directly to race/origins and other facially neutral temporal rules (such as curfew and parole) are applied in ways that restrict movement in racialized ways.[72] I take from this a cue that

---

[70] State Water Resources Control Board, "The Water Rights Process," California Environmental Protection Agency, www.waterboards.ca.gov/waterrights/board_info/water_rights_process.shtml (last visited Aug. 8, 2016).

[71] Driadonna Roland, "Sovereign Law Made Cliven Bundy a 'Patriot' But Korryn Gaines 'Crazy': An Explainer on the Controversial Beliefs Gaines May Have Held," *Revolt* (Aug. 8, 2016), https://revolt.tv/stories/2016/08/10/sovereign-law-made-cliven-bundy-patriot-korryn-gaines-crazy-3517d33d30

[72] P.J. Brendese, "Black Noise in White Time: Segregated Temporality and Mass Incarceration," in *Radical Future Pasts: Untimely Political Theory*, eds. Romand Coles, Mark Reinhardt, and George Shulman (University Press of Kentucky, 2014).

attention to race and political time is important. From my analysis, it seems evident that temporal boundaries are frequently being used to restrict the inclusion and free movement rights of racial minorities. Political time, like many features of political systems, reinscribes social and structural inequalities.

I have presented interior temporal boundaries that restrict the free movement of a state's population as extensions of the kind of temporal boundaries that restrict free movement across sovereign borders. Indeed, they bear many similarities to those kinds of boundaries. At the same time, they are also examples of rules that dissect populations into differently entitled groups. Free movement is but one instance of a host of rights that states offer their citizens. There are other temporal boundaries on the interior of a state that determine who will be eligible for all kinds of rights. An age of majority, retirement, unemployment benefits, residency qualifications for public education, and innumerable other laws impose temporal boundaries between those who can claim important rights and who cannot. This considerably complicates the normative picture of temporal boundaries. The next section explores how temporal boundaries are invoked to include and exclude people from the *demos*, conferring and denying the signature rights of democratic citizenship: political participation and representation.

Temporal Boundaries Around Demoi

Simple date-based rules, such as the one expounded by *Calvin's Case* or zero-option laws, are precise in their ability to carve borders that include or exclude *people* from membership. However, these rules are fairly crude tools with which to disaggregate *rights*. They tend to restrict/permit single rights, for example free movement, or confer/deny an entire bundle of rights. But other types of temporal rules exist to shape more complex power and rights relationships. As the concept of sovereignty develops to denote not just a sovereign ruler, but also a sovereign rights-bearing people, calendrical temporal boundaries are built around the rights-bearing population. This includes the membership in the *demos* as well as the portion of the population that will enjoy various other types of rights. Because enfranchisement is the hallmark of a democracy I will focus on temporal boundaries around the *demos* rather than surveying temporal restrictions on all fundamental rights.

Temporal boundaries around the *demos* impose restrictions on who may vote and who receives representation. Perhaps the most ubiquitous temporal boundary around the *demos* is the age cutoff that determines eligibility to vote. This essentially creates a countdown from the moment of birth to the moment when one enters the *demos*. It falls into a category of age boundaries that demarcate various aspects of legal adulthood.[73] While distinct from ages of consent, majority, etc., it shares with those other temporal boundaries an assertion that one's fitness to exercise rights can be identified with a moment in time. Other very stark temporal boundaries delimiting the *demos* include residency requirements for voting eligibility, rules disenfranchising people such as felons/ex-felons or the mentally ill, and electoral timing.[74]

The question of who is represented presents a more complex picture of temporal boundaries. Temporal boundaries circumscribe the population of persons who are represented via districting and apportionment processes, among other means. Electoral districts impose boundaries that divide *demoi* into politically relevant subunits for the purpose of achieving representation formulae. Districts are the product of varying combinations of geography and political structures such as electoral systems in which "winners take all" or in which parties receive proportional representation. But districts are also bounded in temporal terms. In any representative system, a formula determines how representation will be apportioned. There are myriad ways of producing a formula for representation – it would be a voluminous digression to survey all of them. However, an overwhelming number of the formulae for apportioning representation in established democracies rely on measures of the population that are themselves produced by periodic censuses. In effect this means that the precise meaning of membership in the *demos* – how much representation one can expect from one's political party or in one's home district – is determined on the temporal schedule that determines apportionment. Once a threshold is surpassed and a formula dictates that more or less representation is in order due to shifts in the population, the *demos*'s political weight is altered to reflect how its population has changed in comparison with the populations of other districts. Reapportionment is performed periodically. In the US, it occurs

---

[73] Age restrictions on legal consent to sex are not the same as those for consent to marriage and other contractual arrangements. The age restrictions on consent to sex originate with concerns to protect the virginity of young and unmarried girls. Thus, ages of sexual consent have not always been gender neutral. Ages of consent to sodomy have also been imposed to reflect inegalitarian social norms. For a brief discussion of the importance of these distinctions, see Chapter 5.

[74] Parts of the temporal boundary question in democratic politics have been well explored in the political science of electoral timing. I touch on this literature in the next chapter.

on the temporal schedule of the census. In addition to predictable events such as births, deaths, and movement of voters between districts, apportionment will be affected by the opening and closing of prisons (whose population is counted as resident in the district of the prison despite the fact that inmates are not permitted to vote) and the influx of undocumented persons.[75]

Consider the fact of periodic reapportionment in light of the earlier interpretation of *Calvin's Case*. Coke's rendering of the decision created a date that served as a temporal boundary that divided subjects and non-subjects. Membership turned on a date. This is too simple a formula for representative democracy based on consent. Among the demands of democracy is the need for renewals of consent. Effectively this means that the boundary problem that Coke solved with a single date must be solved with a repeating set of dates. If consent must be renewed, we must know whose consent is sought and how that consent will be translated into representation. For many political theorists, this has set up the challenge of determining how often elections should occur and how to best calculate a ratio of representatives to the electorate. However, it also requires regularly recalculating the actual content of the *demos*. The membership of a district changes nearly constantly. People move geographically, others reach the age of majority, some members will die, and some will gain or lose eligibility for the franchise, to name only a few of the circumstances that affect the *demos*. In this sense, democratic citizens are no different than King James's potential pool of subjects in the seventeenth century. These changes to a district and to the *demos* obtain political influence at the moments that the reapportionment schedule dictates that a recalculation must occur. An influx of citizens arriving from another district, or out migration from the district, will only change the representative weight of a district once a census is performed and analyzed for the purposes of apportionment. Adam Cox points out that compliance with the one-person one-vote rule would actually require revisions after each election cycle.[76] But this would be highly inefficient. While the transplanted citizens can vote prior to the moment of reapportionment, their presence does not count toward the weight of their district in the legislature.

This picture is further complicated by attempts to tinker with representation formulae that themselves reflect ambivalence about how to

[75] Sanford Levinson, "'WHO COUNTS?' 'SEZ WHO?,'" *St. Louis Law Journal* 58 (2014): 937–1189.
[76] "The Temporal Dimension of Voting Rights," *Virginia Law Review* 93, no. 2 (2007): 409–10.

achieve representation. In the US, this is exemplified by provisions contained within the Voting Rights Act (VRA). The VRA traditionally carved its own temporal boundary by keying the applicability of Section 4 to voter registration rates in 1964 and authorizing the provision for a period of five years. Over time, Congress repeatedly reauthorized the provision for specific periods of years and changed the temporal boundary to 1968, then 1972, and so on, until the court struck down the provision in 2013 in the *Shelby County, Alabama* v. *Holder* ruling.[77] It is noteworthy that the *Shelby* decision repeatedly refers to the fact that over forty years have passed since the racially motivated laws that justified the Act were made illegal.[78] No explanation is offered for why forty-plus years (or any number of years) is the precise amount of time required to obviate the need for the Section. But the Supreme Court has traditionally used time in partisan gerrymandering cases as a way of determining when a gerrymander is responsible for voter losses.[79] Using White's logic in *Bandemer*, Cox shows that losses over a period of time represent the kind of "continued frustration" that rises to the level of a harm requiring remediation.[80] However, Cox is adamant that there is no consensus or discussion about what constitutes the precise temporal frame in which we identify "continued frustration" or the permanent conclusion of such frustration.[81] Such discussion would no doubt be illuminating and it is warranted. If the VRA was put into place to right a historic wrong, then some discussion of how we know that wrong has been righted – in a fashion we believe will be enduring – is in order.

Political philosophers have long theorized a relationship between temporal authority and stability. Pocock's ancient constitution derived its authority from its age.[82] In *Shelby*, the court could have in mind a corollary to Pocock's idea of the "ancient constitution" in which the effects of a malevolent law dissipate over a period of time after a remedy is put into place. The idea of dissipation is suggested by the language of the *Shelby* but neither the precise parameters of the time required for dissipation nor the justification of the calculation are explored in this or any related decision. The decision cites no precedent citing any formula for the dissipation of past electoral exclusions. The logic of the forty-year rule functions like a statute of limitations on the offense of racist voting laws. The decision implies that, once a certain amount of time has passed, the

---

[77] *Shelby County, Alabama* v. *Holder*, 133 S. Ct. 2612 (2013).   [78] Ibid.
[79] Cox, "Temporal Dimension of Voting Rights," 379.   [80] Ibid., 377–8.
[81] Ibid., 381–2.   [82] Pocock, *Ancient Constitution*.

damage will have been reversed. In *Shelby*, the court implies that the dissipation of racism's effects can be quantified and expressed in a unit of time, or at least that a threshold can be observed at which point dissipation can be said to have taken place. But the decision leaves unanswered the two critical questions that follow logically from this implication. How do we decide that this is the case? And what is the formula for determining when the consequences of specific provisions (for example a poll tax) have dissipated? By suggesting the idea of a statute of limitations on something as significant as remedies for racial discrimination, and leaving unanswered the question of why this might exist or how it can be calculated, the court invites serious reflection on the normative justifications and implications of temporal boundaries. This lacuna is all the more salient in light of the fact that earlier sections of this chapter noted that temporal boundaries have frequently been used to separate and distinguish racial minorities from full-fledged members of polities. In the final section of this chapter I will survey some of the normative justifications for different kinds of temporal boundaries in order to test their potential for fulfilling the normative promises of democratic nation-states.

ANALYSIS

The preceding three sections of this chapter described temporal boundaries around three types of political units: the nation-state, the population, and the *demos*. Through these descriptions there emerges a second way of analyzing temporal boundaries that organizes them according to *how* they form boundaries rather than *what* they bound. Among the most significant kinds of temporal boundaries, I observe three main types: single moment fixed deadlines; countdown deadlines; and repeating deadlines. The first are fixed single dates, such as those associated with zero-option countries, *Calvin's Case*, and the FRC. The second involve countdown timelines of the sort one might experience with a visa or a statute of limitations. The third involves recurring deadlines such as a reapportionment. Each has a different logic and relationship to democratic norms and political justice more generally. I turn now to interrogating the normative potential and limitations of the way in which each type of temporal boundary functions.

Fixed single-moment boundaries are simple and relatively efficient. In comparison to, for example, declaring that sovereignty is in place when certain conditions for democratic decision-making have been met, identifying the establishment of a state with a specific date is efficient. But can fixed single-moment boundaries be just? At first glance this seems possible because these boundaries can be associated with normative justifications. For example, *Calvin's Case* refers to a norm of duties that exist between a single sovereign and his subjects. The moment that distinguishes subjects from non-subjects is the moment at which the sovereign is empowered to fulfill and demand the fulfillment of those duties. Hence, that moment is normatively significant. Single moment fixed boundaries are highly effective complements to other means of establishing sovereign political boundaries.

This establishment and maintenance of sovereignty is a necessary precondition for any more demanding norms of justice. But it fulfills only the most minimal demands of justice. Thus the reference in the preceding chapter to the fact that the imposition of sovereignty is necessary before popular sovereignty can legitimize a democratic state. Sovereignty itself can never be democratic. The more complex dispersion of power in a democracy requires boundaries that can accommodate complex normative justifications. Single-moment fixed boundaries cannot reflect these complexities. From the perspective of democratic theory, there is no salient difference between someone who arrived in the US on December 31, 1972, and the person who arrives January 1, 1973. But the former is eligible to naturalize based on the registry provision of US immigration law and the latter is not. Single-moment fixed boundaries also cannot accommodate gradation or nuance. People who fled Nazi Germany before 1937 fall outside of the boundary even if they fled out of justified fear for their lives. Much like a territorial boundary, a fixed single-moment boundary does not have any means for incorporating subtlety or for adjudicating claims. Even when they are put into place with reference to substantively meaningful dates, the outcome of fixed single-moment boundaries will have an arbitrary quality. One might say that identifying a fixed single-moment boundary is a precondition for creating democratic justice, insofar as it is difficult to imagine democracy developing outside of the context of a nation-state with a clearly defined temporal perimeter. But it would be a stretch to say that the *Stünde Null* or *Calvin's Case* make promises of justice. Zero-option logic can be put into place with the intent to achieve a justice-oriented outcome – for example in the case of German Basic law that used dates to offer citizenship to anyone displaced by the Third Reich. But even in cases such as those, which rely on multiple iterations of single dates, the fixed nature of the deadlines makes them relatively blunt instruments. On its own, a single fixed temporal deadline cannot accommodate the nuance of differently situated parties.

Fixed single-moment temporal boundaries also have limited normative potential because they make no allowances for the fact that time, unlike land, is not static. This is brought to light in a headline published by the satirical newspaper, *The Onion*; "Nation's Historians Warn the Past Is Expanding at An Alarming Rate."[83] The location of a fixed geographic boundary will stay in the same place relative to other relevant markers. The US border is not growing steadily further away from Washington DC or Mexico or any other geographic location. But a deadline is always approaching in the future or receding into the past at the exact speed of the clock. Take the example of the registry date. The registry date of 1972 is continually moving further away from the present moment in time. If we were to imagine the registry date as if it were our own geographic boundary, it is as if we were slowly moving the US border by keeping the date fixed in relation to ever-advancing time. As each year goes by, registry date grows further away. Thought of in geographic terms, fixed temporal boundaries are akin to superimposing a geographic boundary on sand that will be blown steadily away by the wind.

From the perspective of the population rather than the geography, a single unchanging deadline rather than repeating deadline leads to democratic attrition. The farther out we get from the registry date the fewer people are eligible to register and the larger the population of disenfranchised people grows. If we take the figure of 55,000 who adjusted their status in the three years that followed the last update to the registry date and invert it (meaning that now there are 55,000 people each year who cannot adjust their status) the fixed temporal deadline is equivalent to ceding the entire population of, to take one borderland example, Maverick County, Texas, every three years. A similar effect occurred after the implementation of Chinese exclusion and the 1925 National Origins Quota Act. The idea of ceding that much land sounds absurd. But for purposes of democratic legitimacy, the failure to allow adjustment of status to an ever-larger portion of the population is just as problematic. As time marches on, the proportion of the population that is excluded and/or disenfranchised grows ever larger.

[83] "Nation's Historians Warn the Past Is Expanding at an Alarming Rate," *The Onion* 51, no. 3 (Jan. 22, 2015), www.theonion.com/articles/nations-historians-warn-the-past-is-expanding-at-a,37827

A second type of temporal boundary is a countdown deadline in which a boundary is linked to two dates by a precise quantity of time. A clock is started when an event occurs and runs down at the moment when the temporal limit is reached. An example of this kind of boundary would be a non-immigrant visa or a statute of limitations. These laws impose a boundary on claims that can be made based on the passage of an amount of time following an event. Debts cannot be collected after certain amounts of time have elapsed and charges for various crimes cannot be filed once the temporal delimitation has been surpassed. Immigration amnesties also often rely on a countdown boundary logic in which people who arrive somewhere without documentation during a specific period of time may apply for regularization during another delimited period of time.

Countdown boundaries accommodate some of the complexity that I argued single-moment boundaries lack. In effect, they take a single-moment boundary and append to it a precise quantity of time to create a second boundary. The second boundary is not fixed insofar as it is contingent upon when the first boundary is pinned. But it is fixed insofar as it will occur within a precise interval of the first boundary. Together, the two boundaries mark out a period of time in which claims may be justified. The quantity of time is thought to have meaning. For example, the statute of limitations is based on beliefs about how long evidence can be reliable and the seriousness of types of crimes. By virtue of their structure, countdown boundaries leave room for more normative complexity than fixed single-moment boundaries. If nothing else, they allow decisions to be made over longer periods of time than do fixed single-moment boundaries. Compared to having one's fate determined at birth, having a period of time in which claims may be staked leaves open the possibility for judgment, reasoning, and changes of circumstance. This is a significant departure from the logic of *Calvin's Case* or a zero-option rule. The creation of a period of time disperses the process of judgment and claim staking over many more points than the single moment of judgment affixed to one moment. As will be elaborated in the next chapter, this has important implications for democratic norms. Just as power is distributed over a wider swath of the population in a democracy than in an autocracy, so too is power distributed over a wider stretch of time in democratic boundary formation than in undemocratic boundary formation. However, many of the traits of single-moment fixed boundaries are ultimately also inherent in countdown boundaries. Once the time window has elapsed, the door slams shut. Exceptions may be made by pausing the countdown. For example, the practice of "tolling" pauses statutes of

limitations in specific instances. However, in the absence of democratically minded alterations to the basic form of a countdown boundary, its
limitations are similar to those of single-moment fixed boundaries.

These limitations are indirectly expressed by complaints that political
boundaries having to do with age, maturity, and consent are arbitrary. In
US law, a standard exists so that people below a precise age (children) are
tried differently from those who are above that age (adults). The Willie
Bosket Case (1978) created the precedent for trying juvenile offenders as
an adult.[84] The Willie Bosket law prescribes that all 13-year-olds charged
with murder be tried as adults and all 14–15-year-olds charged with an
array of seventeen felonies be tried as adults. Many states also provide that
once a child has been tried as an adult in criminal court that person
remains an adult for the purposes of any future accusations even if those
later crimes are not serious enough to have triggered a transfer from
juvenile to criminal court on their own. Only about half of the offenses
that trigger the trial of a child as an adult are violent crimes.[85]

Childhood can also be recalibrated for the purposes of sexual consent
and marriage laws. In the US, each state sets its own age of sexual consent
and a separate age at which marriage is legal. It is illegal for an adult to
have sex with a minor. Within that category of acts, the size of the age
difference also determines the legality or criminality of the act. However,
in some states, marriage overrides the age of sexual consent, decriminaliz-
ing what would be criminal sexual behavior on the part of older adults
(usually men) toward young children (usually girls).

The formula for adulthood is thus complicated by the insertion of
caveat transforming a person from a child to an adult, or the
reverse, even as that person remains a child or adult in all other
ways and for all other purposes. Reasoning from the position that
children are protected and governed paternally until they reach the
age of legal adulthood, because it is seen as critically important for
them to be allowed to mature before they are saddled with the
responsibilities of adulthood, we are led to the following conclusion:
children accused of serious crimes or desired by older adults for the
purpose of marriage and sexual relationships receive less time in

---

[84] Eli Hager, "The Willie Bosket Case: How Children Became Adults in the Eyes of the
Law," Marshall Project (Dec. 29, 2014), www.themarshallproject.org/2014/12/29/the-
willie-bosket-case

[85] Patrick Griffin et al., "Trying Juveniles as Adults," 13, www.ncjrs.gov/App/abstractdb/
AbstractDBDetails.aspx?id=172836

which to mature than all other children. The reverse, however, is never true. Children are never awarded the right to vote and participate politically before they reach the age of 18 even when they demonstrate ample rational capacities.

Selectively treating children as adults for the purposes of marriage and punishment highlights the degree to which countdown temporal boundaries of all sorts can be arbitrary. It is difficult to justify an age of consent that can be adjusted down when charges of extraordinary brutality are lodged, or to erase the possibility of marital rape, but is never adjusted down in cases of extraordinary accomplishment. The idea that we measure maturity using a temporal threshold rather than evaluating someone's rational capacities may be efficient, but it hardly seems maximally effective or accurate. Many children can and should be able to give consent, but even those who we believe are not qualified to consent are quite evidently dominated by the fact that they have not lived long enough to acquire rights to determine their own fate.[86] Furthermore, rampant inconsistency about ages of consent makes apparent the fact that adulthood is a threshold manipulated by adults to achieve adult ends, not all of which prioritize the good of the persons who are not yet adults. While children are never exempted from the age threshold for voting, they can be exempted from some of the other privileges of childhood.

The third kind of temporal boundaries, repeating boundaries, are those that perpetually and periodically repeat themselves. They are not fixed to single events or moments but rather occur on a repeating basis. The census and reapportionment exemplify the idea of a repeating temporal boundary. They create a schedule for the periodic reevaluation and alteration of the boundary they demarcate. Whereas the justification for a single-moment boundary derives from the significance of the single moment (an ascent to power, the establishment of a state, etc.), the justification for repeatedly reset boundaries is similar to that of the countdown boundary. Both countdown and repeating boundaries are justified based on the meaning of the interval of time carved out by the multiple points in time at which the boundaries are imposed. Like election cycles, repeating boundaries hold out the possibility for incorporating new information and change in the distribution of power that is associated with democratic norms.

---

[86] www.nbcnews.com/health/health-news/judge-cassandra-c-cant-go-home-amid-cancer-treatments-n334086

More so even than countdown boundaries, which are still linked to single events, repeating temporal boundaries comport with the expectations of a political system in which power is distributed among the many. In the same way that decision making is considered democratized when it is dispersed over a larger rather than smaller portion of the population, so too might we think of boundaries and rights as more democratically structured when they are built using multiple points in time rather than single dates. Of the three types of temporal boundaries, repeating boundaries disperse power over the largest number of points in time. In so doing, they also impose a kind of accountability that is present only in a limited form in countdown deadlines and not at all in single-moment fixed deadlines. There is no finality to any repeating temporal boundary because it may be adjusted after the next increment of time has elapsed.

Repeating temporal boundaries circumvent the objection to the single-moment fixed boundaries that fixed boundaries do not account for the non-fixed nature of time. The boundary is continually moving further away as time passes. The one-time nature of the establishment of sovereignty or an immigration amnesty therefore cannot accommodate change that transpires over time after these single events. By contrast, repeating temporal boundaries can keep up with time. The schedule on which they are set may or may not be adequate to the task of keeping up with the changes that come over time, but they hold the potential to do so in a way that fixed single-moment boundaries do not.[87]

As the chapters that follow will explain, this instills in repeating deadlines the potential to accomplish important goals within democratic politics. It is already clear from the discussions of establishment, sovereignty, and time, that states can and do command the time of their subjects. Liberal democratic states must do so in ways that conform to the basic tenets of liberalism and democratic theory. There are multiple versions of both of these sets of norms, and hence there are multiple temporal arrangements that can satisfy them. But there are also ways of structuring both the time of institutions and individuals that contravene fundamental principles of liberal democracy. When a temporal arrangement violates such a principle it undermines the legitimacy of the state. Repeating temporal boundaries are highly significant to the architecture of democracy because they instantiate procedures like regularly scheduled elections, without which no political system can meet even the most

---

[87] In so doing, they fulfill Thomas Jefferson's exhortation to ensure that the dead ought not to have power over the living by ensuring that boundaries are negotiable over time.

minimal bar for democraticness. When a repeating boundary such as that which ensures opportunities for political participation is suspended, the legitimacy of the democratic state is called into question.

We can therefore expect that the transition to political regimes that emphasize participation and representation over absolute and divine right will be accompanied by a transformation of *institutional* temporality that reflects the difference between these different types of authority. To move beyond the territorial sovereignty of a state and create a sovereign citizenry – popular sovereignty – requires a complex set of institutional refinements. Chief among them is the shift from locating legitimate authority in a single body to vesting it in a citizenry of enfranchised equals. The division of sovereignty is the division of a single locus of authority into many loci of authority. If a moment in time identifies a single sovereign such as a king, it stands to reason that a sovereign citizenry will require more than a single moment in time in which to exercise its political authority.

CONCLUSION

If time is invoked in the establishment of any regime, then all political orders will exist in reference to some kind of temporal order. Calendrical time does not replace but rather complements other forms of boundary marking. In some cases, temporal boundaries make the job of physical boundary keeping easier, and in other cases temporal boundaries perform wholly unique functions. This chapter has focused on the types of temporal boundaries that circumscribe states, nations, populations, and *demoi*.

Temporal boundaries enter early modern politics as a means of wresting power from religious authorities and justifying its location in the offices of earthly sovereigns. As sovereignty matures, temporal boundaries are carried into the practices that distinguish states from one another and demarcate the population of each state and, eventually, into the interior of states as means of making distinctions regarding who among the population is entitled to which rights. As is the case with any other type of boundary, temporal boundaries necessarily discriminate. They divide rights-bearing people from non-rights-bearing people. Whenever individuals or groups are excluded from political systems or enfranchisement, the justifications for doing so and the outcomes of such rules warrant scrutiny.

Temporal boundaries can be imposed to shape the ethnic makeup of a citizenry, control who votes, return a nation to a previous version of itself, and an array of other ends. Because time is integral to nations as well as states, temporal boundaries transmit nationalist biases regarding race and ethnicities. Many instances of temporal boundaries that traverse the interior of states intentionally or effectively constrain and exclude structural minorities.

The normative effect of temporal boundaries may be shaped most directly by the intentions of the people and institutions that impose them, but their potential to be inclusive also depends on how they are configured. Single-moment fixed boundaries may be justified based on normatively meaningful events, however on their own they lack any mechanism for making fine-grained distinctions. They also fail to account for the fact that time is not static. Temporal boundaries that create a countdown between an event and a deadline offer more opportunities than single moments for the practice of democratic norms like judgment, however ultimately they also bluntly circumscribe the exercise of rights. Finally, repeating boundaries that recur in perpetuity offer the greatest potential for keeping up with progress in time. The normative argument for boundaries that repeatedly adjust over time is an important one. At its core, it suggests that there is an important relationship between multiple intervals of time and the realization of democratic principles. In the chapter that follows I will explore this idea in depth, examining what happens between temporal borders, and detailing the history of political thought that assigns normative value to specific durations of time. In moving from moments on a calendar, to schedules and measured quantities of time, we can identify more precisely what kinds of temporal rules confer rights and we can test the limits of temporal rules' potential for egalitarianism.

3

Democracy, Duration, and Lived Consent

INTRODUCTION

Chapter 2 began with a simple point about the inextricable relationship between precise moments in time and sovereign boundaries. But, as the chapter's analysis pointed out, the temporal arrangements associated with sovereignty have no normative valence. Sovereignty itself is not particularly normative and there is very little, if any, normativity to the single moment that identifies the boundary of a sovereign regime. Yet, the political systems that structure sovereign states inevitably justify themselves with reference to norms. Democracies, for example, are pursued for normative ends that derive from shared values and goals and prioritize consent and representation. Over the course of the chapter, increasingly complex forms of temporal boundaries were identified and discussed. Among the conclusions of the chapter was that there is normative potential in temporal arrangements that invoke multiple points in time.

Multiple and recurring deadlines insert a new element into the discussion of temporality and politics. Instead of indicating only single moments, they carve out quantities – durations – of scientifically measured time, and mark those durations as politically significant. Recurring deadlines are more conducive to realizing the normative aspirations of democratic theory than are single-moment fixed deadlines. The most obvious instance of temporal arrangements that invoke repeating deadlines are political schedules and calendars, but recurring deadlines appear in all manner of political procedures. Often, they demarcate value-laden durations of time.

The normativity of durational time is terrain that contemporary democratic theorists have skirted, for example in the case of epistemic democrats who see the accumulation of political knowledge as a process that occurs not just among a specific number and type of people in any given territory, but also over time.[1] Likewise, APD scholars have long focused on how temporal

---

[1] Hélène Landemore, *Democratic Reason: Politics, Collective Intelligence, and the Rule of the Many* (Princeton University Press, 2013), 20.

structures both constitute some political processes and reveal political patterns.[2] And theorists of equality recognize that time is one of the means with which the terms of equality are laid out.[3] Like this chapter, each of these areas of inquiry draws a connection between processes that have political implications and the practical political procedures that structure a democratic state.

However, the normative and practical implications of durational time for democracy are multifaceted and have not yet been fully explored. Aphorisms like Benjamin Franklin's "time is money," as well as the experience of everyday life, prime most people to accept the idea that time has value. And, as the introduction to the book described, there are innumerable instances in which it is clear that durational time has political value. Waiting periods, schedules for elections, and various other political procedures offer clues about the value of time by making clear that durational time is a common prerequisite for the acquisition and exercise of rights. But, outside of the work world, time's value and the way in which it is derived are largely unspecified.

This chapter describes how durational time is transformed into a good with a distinct political value arising from time's connection to a set of processes that have special importance to liberal democratic politics. It does so by pointing to traditions in the history of political thought that implicitly and explicitly assign a political value to durational time. The chapter also looks at how the establishment of citizenship in the US put elements of these traditions into practice. In Chapter 1, process was identified as a pivotal conduit through which durational time is accorded importance in politics. Without ignoring the many ways in which this premise can be qualified, it is both intuitive and widely accepted that social and political processes occur in durations of time. The relating of process to duration has ancient origins. Whatever is not innate, and also that which is innate but requires cultivation, occurs in durations of time. Plato and Aristotle addressed readers to the connection in multiple contexts including the development of knowledge, expertise, and judgment.

---

[2] Daniel Kryder and Sarah Staszak, "Constitution as Clockwork: The Temporal Foundations of American Politics" (prepared for annual meeting, American Political Science Association, working paper, 2006); Karen Orren and Stephen Skowronek, *The Search for American Political Development* (Cambridge University Press, 2004).

[3] For example, Douglas Rae writes, "Answers to the question, 'Equal what?' refer to *domains of equality* – that is the *classes of things to be divided equally*. Usually the natural language terms of kind ... of quantity ... of special reference ... and of time, are used to sketch out the boundaries of equality." *Equalities* (Cambridge, MA: Harvard University Press, 1981), 45.

These connections remain relevant as modern democratic theory is applied to the task of designing political institutions.

The goal of the chapter is to show how its relationship to process transforms durational time into a political good that can then be used in much the same way that Marx postulated time is used to measure work in discussions of socially necessary labor time. The Marxian comparison paves the way for Chapter 5's discussion of commensuration. Time acquires forms of value that allow it to be used in political transactions over the acquisition and exercise of power and citizenship rights. Ultimately, what we see is that the normative potential of durational time is closely associated with important political processes through which outcomes like reason, consent, and truth are produced. Politics that follows a political schedule is premised on the idea that durational time is integral to understanding the good, reasoning, informedness, stability, deliberation, consent, character development, and relationships that are an important part of citizenship. Durational time is a political good with political value insofar as it is crucial to these processes, without which politics could not be democratic and people could not be citizens. It is necessary, although not sufficient, for these processes to occur. Time's value is drawn into political practice by procedures that make important forms of rights and status contingent upon deadlines and the passage of precise durations of time. A deadline, waiting period, or other durational element inserts either direct or indirect references to process into political procedures.

A few brief notes on definitions: for something to be considered a good, it must be widely regarded as having value to members of the society in which the good exists. Elizabeth Anderson describes goods as acquiring their value in the "pluralistic, contestable, historically contingent and socially informed practices in which people participate."[4] This stipulates two things about goods. First, the value of any good can be inferred from the practices of a society or subunit of any society. This chapter relies on such inferences to come to initial conclusions about the political value of time. Second, the value of any good is rarely if ever a matter that is entirely settled. Value is often contested. It may be evident that a society values life, for example, and yet the value of life – or even what is included in the definition of life – will remain in question. For this reason, the chapter does not include any claim to be able to systematically translate amounts of time into precise quantities of something such as consent. There are no

[4] *Value in Ethics and Economics* (Cambridge, MA: Harvard University Press, 1993), 15.

tables with temporal exchange rates, as one might find in a book on international monetary currencies, nor are such tables possible to construct.

In addition to treating goods as acquiring their value from within the social and political contexts in which they exist, the chapter requires attending to the distinction between processes and procedures.[5] Processes involve actions and transformations.[6] Here one need not subscribe to all of the views of a thinker like Henri Bergson or Alfred North Whitehead, both of whom were process philosophers, to accept this book's argument. One only needs to accept some version of a phenomenology of change. People and societies are not static and the changes that they experience occur in time. Procedures are the institutional mechanisms through which a practice, in this case the practice of democratic politics, is conducted. Political procedures are superimposed on institutions, and therefore political subjects, in order to make politics as predictable, orderly, and efficient as possible. The insertion of either direct or indirect references to process into political procedures makes the political value of time manifest, threading the normative fiber of process through the governmental needle of procedure.

Finally, in keeping with the spirit of the book, the discussion of durational time and procedural politics is limited to prescribed durations of time that are intentionally and explicitly a part of political procedures. Delays, even those that seem inevitable when a procedure is imposed, are qualitatively different forms of waiting which I develop in an independent manuscript.[7]

THE POLITICAL VALUE OF TIME IN THE HISTORY OF POLITICAL THOUGHT

The idea that time is accorded value in the history of political thought hinges on connecting two key points drawn from distinct traditions in the history of political thought. The first point is one that Pocock fleshes out in *The Machiavellian Moment*, but also appears throughout ancient and early modern philosophy: science, including but not limited to scientifically measured time, is valuable because of its ability to tame chance and offer a predictable,

---

[5] Paulina Ochoa Espejo notes that procedures are specific methods while processes are less directed, if not completely random. *The Time of Popular Sovereignty* (University Park, PA: Pennsylvania State University Press, 2011), 143, 148.

[6] Stephen Linstead and John Malarkey, "Time, Creativity, and Culture: Introducing Bergson," *Culture and Organization* 9, no. 1 (2010), 6. Bergson believed that culture, society, and history were all processual.

[7] See unpublished manuscript on file with author.

safer future. The authority of science and scientific measurements comes from their relationship to security and the betterment of the human condition.[8]

The second point on which time's value hinges is the idea that it is possible to determine which processes are of particular importance to democratic politics and how much time those processes require to transpire. States pursue all sorts of security, but for democratic states, the processes that produce character development, deliberation, reflection, and consent are particularly critical to securing legitimacy and stability. Democratic politics unfolds over time, occurring on a particular schedule that can be controlled by particular processes that are assigned precise durations of time.

Plato and Aristotle, in their capacity as moral and political philosophers who predate the development of the modern state, both single out scientific measurement for attention. In the Protagoras, Plato calls for a science that makes it possible to measure practical deliberation.[9] This science, *technē*, is akin to practical judgment of the sort needed for planning, prediction, and progress.[10] To secure human life requires a "science of deliberative measurement."[11] This isn't solely a statement about the conduct of politics, however it expresses well the connection between a polity that will be able to secure its citizens lives and the need to count and scientifically assess political processes.

Aristotle focuses on process as well. For Aristotle, the particulars of sound political judgment are "not in the province of *episteme*, but are grasped with insight through experience."[12] Good decision-making, to his mind, requires experience. We know someone has this kind of accumulated experience in part by observing the duration of time in which they have lived. By elevating the process of achieving insight through experience, he introduces the idea of durational time's importance to politics. Aristotle's foil for Plato's potentially reductive approach to practical wisdom is one in which time actually figures prominently, if not explicitly. Nussbaum makes this point by referring to Aristotle's conviction that children and young adults do not yet possess practical wisdom (*phronêsis*): "Young people can become mathematicians and geometers

---

[8] The classic formulation of the connection between science and security can be found in Foucault's lectures on biopower. Michel Foucault, *Security, Territory, and Population: Lectures at the Collège de France, 1977–78*, ed. Arnold I. Davidson (Basingstoke, UK: Palgrave Macmillan, 2009).

[9] Martha Craven Nussbaum, *The Fragility of Goodness: Luck and Ethics in Greek Tragedy and Philosophy* (Cambridge University Press, 2001), vol. II, 90 (quoting David Ross, trans., *Aristotle: The Nicomachean Ethics* (Oxford University Press, 1925), Book VI. 8).

[10] Nussbaum, *Fragility of Goodness*, 95.   [11] Ibid., 107.   [12] Ibid., 299.

and wise in things of that sort; but they do not appear to become people of practical wisdom. The reason is that practical wisdom is of the particular, which becomes graspable through experience, but a young person is not experienced. For a quantity of time is required for experience."[13] Aristotle draws a direct normative relationship between quantities of time – duration – and the process of judgment. To him, time is intimately linked with experience. Even in the Aristotelian view, durational time is important for rendering political judgments. By according time special meaning, processes that require the passage of precise quantities of durational time can be critical to either of these opposing arguments about practical wisdom. Durational time has been identified as a political good without which important processes cannot take place.[14]

Durational Time in Modern Political Theory

As the modern state comes into existence, political theorists adjust their conception of time and process to accommodate the changing form of politics. The idea of constituting consent through time is apparent in Locke's formulation of consensual citizenship, which invokes durational time. Less than a century after *Calvin's Case* had advocated for nonconsensual birthright citizenship, Locke advocates shifting the conferral of political status from the moment of birth to the *duration of time in which a child born into a polity matures and acquires the capacity to give consent*.[15] Margaret Somers identifies Locke's consent as "embedded in a narrative in which an anterior, pre-political state is replaced with institutions constituted by a social contract. These narratives are sequential and hence temporal and culminate in a moment – the moment of time in which consent is given."[16] Here Locke implicitly relies on reasoning described in the preceding chapter of this book. For Locke, two temporal boundaries (birth and the age of maturity) are necessary to confer citizenship. The transition from drawing boundaries using only a moment in time to bounding the population using durations of time marks the shift from non-democratic to democratic forms of rule. In fact, upon achieving maturity, children can opt out of citizenship rather than accepting it as a

---

[13] Ibid., 305.   [14] This view is consistent with Bergson's invocation of time in process.

[15] John Locke, *1690. Two Treatises of Government*, ed. Peter Laslett (Cambridge University Press, 1988).

[16] Margaret R. Somers, *Genealogies of Citizenship: Markets, Statelessness, and the Right to Have Rights* (Cambridge University Press, 2008), 32.

fait accompli. This position on the importance of maturation represents Locke's broader turn away from seeing political relationships as the realm of the innate rather than the experiential. This is consistent with his preference for empiricism rather than scholasticism.[17]

What Locke did not accomplish was a detailed model for constitutional design. For this I turn to the French mathematician Condorcet. The work of Condorcet accomplished what others only gestured at: a detailed institutional prescription for democratic decision-making articulated with scientific precision. Condorcet's writings bring together normative argumentation about what makes for good democratic decisions with a mathematician's inclination to look for numeric ways of measuring and plotting the good. His "social mathematics"[18] was a companion to a political arithmetic that is integral to the political economy of time be described in Chapter 5.[19]

Condorcet's work is important not because it *should* serve as a model for institutional design but because so many of his prescriptions *are* reflected in the most successful institutional designs that the Enlightenment produced.[20] Condorcet was avidly interested in the procedures that would achieve the outcomes to which he and his more abstractly inclined philosopher peers were committed. His constitutional plan was written after a study of the writing of the US Constitution and although he rejected some elements of what the founders produced (notably bicameralism) many other elements are admiringly reproduced in his own writings.

Reading Condorcet is therefore like reading a social scientific explanation of the pace at which democratic political procedures should occur in order to meet the standards of democratic theory. Political procedures are generally scheduled affairs. When a schedule for a procedure is omitted, significant problems can and do arise. Condorcet's focus on a temporal political schedule is notable for his detailed attention to the reasons that

---

[17] Steven Forde, *Locke, Science and Politics* (Cambridge University Press, 2013),ch. 2.

[18] Steven Lukes and Nadia Urbinati, *Condorcet: Political Writings* (Cambridge University Press, 2012), 573.

[19] Iain McLean and Fiona Hewitt, trans. and eds., *Condorcet: Foundations of Social Choice and Political Theory* (Aldershot, UK: Edward Elgar, 1994), 11.

[20] Here I note that Condorcet studied the American founders, in particular Franklin, Jefferson and Paine, but do not intend to comment on the precise degree of influence Condorcet had on them. See Iain McLean and Arnold B. Urken, "Did Jefferson or Madison Understand Condorcet's Theory of Social Choice?" *Public Choice* 73, no. 4 (1992): 445–57; Guillaume Ansart, *Condorcet: Writings on the United States* (University Park, PA: Pennsylvania State University Press, 2012).

democratic decision-making ought to happen at a particular pace. Reason, that crucial ingredient of liberalism, has been called "timeless."[21] But reason is not in fact timeless, although it may seem so. Reason, along with other processes that are integral to decision-making and consent, requires durational time that has been structured in ways conducive to those processes.

We see versions of Condorcet's ideas about time incorporated into an array of democratic constitutions.[22] Constitutions schedule elections and censuses and create all kinds of temporal triggers for many fundamental political processes. In turn, scholars study the outcomes of such procedures with the intention of explaining and predicting various political outcomes. So significant is the subject of duration to empirical social science that there is a branch of methodological scholarship instructing researchers on how to measure and interpret durational time as a variable in their studies.[23] Moreover, it is well understood that a constitution can schedule (or fail to schedule) political procedures such as elections or legislative calendars in ways that delegitimize any claims a state might wish to make to being democratic. Staggered elections in which various executives and legislators are elected at different times tend to lower turnout and decrease chances for radical and direct democracy.[24] Infrequent elections can entirely delegitimize a democracy.[25] In 2016 the Supreme Court of the United States was placed in indefinite limbo following the death of Antonin Scalia. The Senate refused to consider the president's nominee, Merrick Garland, prompting one analyst to point out, "the Constitution actually does not have a timeframe for when a

---

[21] Melissa Lane, "Political Theory and Time," in *Time in Contemporary Political Thought*, ed. P.J.N. Baert (1st edn, Amsterdam: Elsevier, 2000), 235.

[22] Kryder and Staszak, "Constitution as Clockwork"; Paul Pierson, *Politics in Time: History, Institutions, and Social Analysis* (Princeton University Press, 2004); Orren and Skowronek, *Search for American Political Development*.

[23] For example, Gryzmala Busse cautions against misinterpreting the role of durational time as causal in cases for which duration is not the mechanism. She also claims that duration can proxy for specific processes. For example, "Longer duration makes it possible for diffusion, accumulation, saturation, and tipping effects to unfold. If a tipping process is cut short, it cannot not reach its threshold." Anna Grzymala-Busse, "Time Will Tell? Temporality and the Analysis of Causal Mechanisms and Processes," *Comparative Political Studies* 44, no. 9 (2011): 1279.

[24] Simon Nix, "Elections, Parties, and Institutional Design: A Comparative Perspective on European Union Democracy," *West European Politics* 21, no. 3 (1998): 19–52.

[25] One of Dahl's basic prerequisites for a democracy is the regular schedule of frequent elections. Robert A. Dahl, *A Preface to Democratic Theory* (University of Chicago Press 2013), 12–14.

President's nomination for the Supreme Court must be voted on. That's not in the Constitution. So, we're sort of in a constitutional limbo land."[26] Not only did this lead to uncertainty regarding the functioning of the Court during the interregnum, but the discovery that there is no temporal mechanism for ensuring that someone will ever be appointed to the Court remains disconcerting.[27] As I asserted in the introduction, states can legitimately order and claim the time of their members. But not all temporal claims that states make are legitimate. Furthermore, the absence of state claims on time can delegitimize the exercises of power that follow. What happens in a Supreme Court interregnum, much like what happens in states of emergency that suspend broader sovereign powers, lacks the legitimacy of procedurally standard politics.[28]

Where philosophers have often been less precise with regard to political calendars and schedules, Condorcet is painstakingly detail oriented. Condorcet saw voting as comparable to decision-making, about which he wrote extensively.[29] Because Condorcet's theories about voting require multiple stages of decision-making, it was inevitable that he would have to build into his theory a temporal structure.[30] He creates an elaborate democratic calendar based in part on his own original mathematical formulae and in part on formulae that were implicit in democratically minded documents like the US Constitution. Indeed, Condorcet was frustrated with scholars like Voltaire, who shared his commitment to legal reform and innovation, but lacked the mathematical prowess to

---

[26] Interview by Diane Rehm with Lisa Desjardins, Political Director, PBS Newshour, in the *Diane Rehm Show*, National Public Radio (Apr. 1, 2016, 10 AM), http://thedianerehm show.org/shows/2016–04-01/friday-news-roundup-domestic

[27] This discomfort with the lack of a schedule led some experts to suggest deriving a temporal boundary beyond which the president would be permitted to appoint his nominee. The boundary was determined using a calculation of how long confirmations had taken in the past. See Gregory L. Diskant, "Obama Can Appoint Merrick Garland to the Supreme Court if the Senate Does Nothing," *Washington Post* (Apr. 8, 2016), accessed Apr. 27, 2016, www.washingtonpost.com/opinions/obama-can-appoint-mer rick-garland-to-the-supreme-court-if-the-senate-does-nothing/2016/04/08/4a696700-fc f1-11e5-886f-a037dba38301_story.html

[28] Split decisions made prior to the appointment of a ninth justice either defer to a lower court (bypassing the Supreme Court) or will be held over until the appointment of a ninth justice, whenever that may occur. Either way, the Court remains only semi-functional until Congress approves a ninth justice.

[29] "On the Constitution and Function of Provisional Assemblies," in *Condorcet: Foundations of Social Choice and Political Theory*, trans. and eds. Iain McLean and Fiona Hewitt (Aldershot, UK: Edward Elgar, 1994), 157.

[30] On the importance of two-stage elections, see Condorcet, "On the Forms of Elections," ibid., 169–71.

effectively express abstract norms in their correct mathematical form.[31] Kreider and Staszak, building on Orren and Skowronek, describe a layered pacing of democratic procedures in the US Constitution that embodies Condorcet's focus on political tempo and duration.[32] In both Condorcet's writings and APD analysis, durational time and scheduling are recognized as crucial to ensuring that democratic politics proceeds based on informed, if tacit, consent, and in a way that is fair, thoughtful, and sound. As will be discussed in the second half of this chapter, a Condorcetian focus on durational time and political scheduling permeated the political procedures that the authors and early interpreters of the US Constitution created.

THE ROAD TO CONSTITUTIONAL VALUATION OF TIME

In Condorcet's prescriptive writings, the value of time for politics is explained in detail, showing time to be a good without which democratic practices would be impossible. Condorcet's inclination to seek mathematical measures for good decision-making conjures images of Plato's *technē*, and led him directly to scientifically measured durational time. Condorcet's Enlightenment peers circled the connection between scientifically measured durational time and politics. Condorcet homes in on this relationship and produces a theory of politics in which durational time is pivotal to ensuring democratic processes. He premises his conclusions about politics on the observation that producing consent in a single instant yields political systems that discourage reasoning.[33] Just as the previous chapter argued that the sovereign political boundary instilled at one single moment in time is arbitrary and undemocratic, Condorcet believed that popular sovereignty could not be enacted simply in the single moment of a vote. In Condorcet's view, Rousseau had failed to theorize a viable model of popular sovereignty because he "collapsed the time of politics into the instant of voting."[34] Condorcet, who strove to give

---

[31] McLean and Hewitt, *Condorcet*, 33.

[32] Kryder and Staszak, "Constitution as Clockwork."

[33] Nadia Urbinati, *Representative Democracy: Principles and Genealogy* (University of Chicago Press, 2006), 2577. The question of whether legitimate consent is created or given in a single fixed moment has vexed many political theorists, most recently Jürgen Habermas in his work on dynamic constitutionalism. *Between Facts and Norms: Contributions to a Discourse Theory of Law and Democracy* (Cambridge, MA: MIT Press, 1996).

[34] Urbinati, *Representative Democracy*, 2582.

mathematical form to procedures for seeking the general will,[35] thought Rousseau failed to focus adequate attention on the relationship between durational time and democracy, and in so doing had neglected to treat duration as a distinct political good.

Condorcet expresses a sentiment that is widely held by democratic theorists (including Rousseau): voting alone cannot ensure democracy.[36] Voting only produces a democratic outcome when the proper ingredients in proper proportions precede the moment in which people register their decision. Voting itself is not democratic when it is not preceded by decisions made through deliberation and truth-seeking. Without reflection, deliberation, and inquiry, votes, and the decisions they express are neither consensual nor democratic. He argues that the thoughtful decision-making required by consent entails complex consideration, deliberation, and knowledge that can only be acquired in due time. He was aware that some decisions had to be made quickly (a sort of proto-emergency powers doctrine), others required time in order for people to become informed and invested, and that taking too much of people's time for politics would defeat the purpose of democratic procedures. Excessive temporizing and haste are equally the enemies of democracy.[37] Condorcet is clearly channeling but not replicating thoughts expressed in *The Federalist Papers*, which includes multiple references to judicious means of pacing politics to encourage desirable behaviors and outcomes and discourage problematic ones. People who rush to vote before they have truly reflected, deliberated, investigated, and then decided, are prone to express extremism, impulsiveness, and conformity rather than deliberation and knowledge. However, the opposite of haste – unduly long periods

---

[35] McLean and Hewitt, *Condorcet*, 38.

[36] A consensus that democracy cannot be reduced to the act of voting exists in other wise divergent literatures ranging from political behavioralists (Christopher H. Achen and Larry M. Bartels, *Democracy for Realists: Why Elections Do Not Produce Responsive Government* (Princeton University Press, 2016)) to deliberative democrats like Joshua Cohen and James Fishkin (Joshua Cohen, "Deliberation and Democratic Legitimacy," in *Debates in Contemporary Political Philosophy: An Anthology*, eds. Derek Matravers and Jon Pike (New York: Routledge, 2003); James Fishkin, *Democracy and Deliberation: New Directions for Democratic Reform* (New Haven, CT: Yale University Press, 1991)) to epistemic skeptics like Jason Brennan (*Against Democracy* (Princeton University Press, 2016)).

[37] Condorcet writes, "We therefore needed to find procedures which could prevent the dangers of excessive haste, without at the same time rendering speedy decisions completely impossible; for, although the law cannot determine in advance the cases in which a quick decision is needed, these cases sometimes arise." "A Survey of the Principles Underlying the Draft Constitution (1793)," in McLean and Hewitt, *Condorcet*, 202.

between elections – is equally problematic. Infrequent opportunities to change political course allow past decision-makers to tyrannize citizens in the present. Put another way, democratic decision-making requires properly proportioned durations of time just as surely as it requires a properly proportioned ratio of electors to representatives. Condorcet describes five pathologies that arise from failing to understand the place of durational time in politics: corruption, misunderstanding the good, instability, conformity, and presentism.

First, a government that imposes inadequate limits on the amount of time that decisions take, or decision-makers stand in office, risks the very likely outcome that "partisan influence and intrigue" will take over.[38] Condorcet worries that assemblies lasting too long will encourage members to become "lazy and consequently dangerous."[39] He therefore distinguishes different types of assemblies and specifies a distinct temporality for constitutional decision-making and other types of demands and decisions required by the population.[40] Minimizing the time that people hold office and the amount of time that can transpire prior to the conclusion of a decision-making procedure will bolster the trust of the population and the trustworthiness of its representatives. Relatedly, Condorcet also believed in a minimum age (25) for anyone seeking office as a means to ensure "sufficient time, between obtaining political rights and becoming eligible for public functions, for the new citizens to be judged, their behaviour observed and their principles recognized."[41]

Second, Condorcet is committed to pacing decision-making in order to rein in "excessive enthusiasm."[42] Without a proper amount time to acquire the requisite situated knowledge for conferring consent, the people often misunderstand the good. Acquiring both the knowledge and experience that consent demand takes time, as does thoughtful deliberation with one's peers. An impulsive politics is a poorly informed and likely wrongheaded one. An assembly that decides too quickly will become oppressive.[43] Here again he agrees with Hamilton. In Federalist 70, Hamilton writes, "The ingredients which constitute energy in the Executive are, first, unity; secondly, duration; thirdly, an adequate

---

[38] "Survey of the Principles Underlying the Draft Constitution," 196.   [39] Ibid.
[40] Ibid.   [41] Ibid., 215.   [42] Ibid., 201.
[43] "If the short duration of public office, frequent elections and various legal protests are effective ways of assuring freedom, they must also be sufficient to protect public prosperity or individual rights from the errors which could occur in a large assembly through haste, prejudice or even excessive enthusiasm. Condorcet, "Survey of the Principles Underlying the Draft Constitution," 201.

provision for its support; fourthly, competent powers." Hamilton was concerned that "In the legislature, promptitude of decision is oftener an evil than a benefit."[44] In Federalist 71, he goes on to advocate longer terms for officeholders as a means of reducing obvious ills, such as instability and haste, and less obvious ones, such as pandering by politicians.[45] Kant expresses Condorcet's connection of haste with ignorance in *Toward Perpetual Peace* when he says that "a public can only slowly arrive at enlightenment. A revolution is perhaps capable of breaking away from personal despotism and from avaricious or power-hungry oppression, but it can never bring about a genuine reform in thinking: instead new pre-judices will serve as a guiding reign for the thoughtless masses."[46] Without taking proper time, political movements will not liberate their participants, and could not be called democratic, but instead subjugate people to their own bigotries and lapses in judgment.

Time compression is a phenomenon that contemporaries have worried over as much as did Condorcet. Bob Jessop and Hartmut Rosa have each decried the compression of decision-making time in democracies.[47] Giddens and Connolly have pointed out related features of politics that take place in temporally accelerated contexts.[48] One wonders whether innovations, such as early voting, which have the effect of not only desynchronizing the electoral process, but also of altering the amount of time that candidates have to campaign for some constituents' votes, would pass muster with someone such as Condorcet or one of his contemporary counterparts.[49]

---

[44] "Federalist no. 70," *The Federalist Papers*, ed. Clinton Rossiter (New York: Penguin Putnam, 1961).

[45] "Federalist no. 71" (ibid.).

[46] Immanuel Kant et al., *Toward Perpetual Peace and Other Writings on Politics, Peace, and History* (New Haven, CT: Yale University Press, 2006), 18.

[47] Bob Jessop, *State Power* (Cambridge, UK: Polity, 2007), 191 (citing William E. Scheuerman, *Liberal Democracy and the Social Acceleration of Time* (Baltimore, MD and London: Johns Hopkins University Press, 2004)); *High Speed Society: Social Acceleration, Power, and Modernity*, eds. Hartmut Rosa and William E. Scheuerman (University Park, PA: Pennsylvania State University Press, 2009).

[48] Anthony Giddens, *A Contemporary Critique of Historical Materialism* (Berkeley and Los Angeles: University of California Press, 1981); William E. Connolly, *Neuropolitics: Thinking, Culture, and Speed* (Minneapolis, MN: University of Minnesota Press, 2002); William E. Scheuerman, *Liberal Democracy and the Social Acceleration of Time* (Baltimore, MD and London: Johns Hopkins University Press, 2004).

[49] While early voting has been touted as a means to expand the population of eligible voters who actually do vote, it also has the effect of recalibrating campaigns. Paul Gronke, Eva Galanes-Rosenbaum, and Peter A. Miller, "Symposium: Early Voting and Turnout," *PS: Political Science and Politics* 40, no. 4 (2007); Patrick Healy, "Early Voting Limits

Condorcet argues that decisions of the moment are also unstable. Whims do not lay a solid foundation for politics but instead reflect momentary views that pass in the same way that fashions or other trends pass. Condorcet teases out a relationship between durational time and commitment. Impulsiveness is unstable and lacks the qualities of reasoned sustained contemplation and discussion that are required by commitments. So, it should not surprise us that those seeking loyalty or other qualities associated with serious commitments, whether they be commitments of country or commitments of penitence, would connect those acts and decisions with quantities of time. Dennis Thompson echoes the conviction that government by whim is undemocratic, writing, "[Popular control]... is valuable only insofar as it expressed a genuine will, not transient impulses or uninformed preferences."[50] Condorcet, in making an argument about instability, turns Pocock's observation about the ancient connection of time and instability on its head. In Pocock's words, "A world in which justice rode the wheel of fortune was a frightening prospect, but a certain intelligibility was paradoxically imported by the notion of cyclical recurrence."[51] In opposition to *fortuna, virtu* is universal and the product of human intentionality. Whereas Polybius was "concerned with time as the dimension of instability,"[52] Condorcet solves the pre-modern problem of how to tame the infinite and establish stability by subjecting decisions to a science of political time in which progress is linear rather than cyclical. Properly structured, politics need not ever descend into disorder. This should cue us to the idea that there will be democratic potential in durational time, but also the possibility for the exercise of very powerful state authority in ways that are not democratic. A political system can treat the time of its subjects in ways that are democratizing or authoritarian.

Third, and relatedly, haste enables a weakness for passing fads and encourages a herd mentality. Faddishness and groupthink are precarious bases for politics. Mobs stampede whereas citizenries advance slowly and deliberately. To be deliberate, one must deliberate, and deliberation

Donald Trump's Time to Turn Campaign Around," *New York Times: Election 2016* (Aug. 16, 2016), www.nytimes.com/2016/08/17/us/politics/early-voting-limits-donald-t rumps-time-to-turn-campaign-around.html

[50] "Democracy in Time: Popular Sovereignty and Temporal Representation," *Constellations* 12, no. 2 (2005): 247.

[51] John Greville Agard Pocock, *The Machiavellian Moment: Florentine Political Thought and the Atlantic Republican Tradition* (Princeton University Press, 2009), 78.

[52] Ibid., 77.

requires time. But deliberateness requires more than discussion with peers. It also requires time spent in solitude, reflecting and gathering knowledge. Condorcet very carefully marks out a democratic process that allows for both the social and the solitary actions required to deliberate.[53] The solitary acts as a check on the pull of the herd, and the social acts as a check on the solipsistic.

Fourth, giving people adequate time reduces that the chances that they will become uninformed and disinterested. Condorcet was sensitive to the fact that decisions and decision-making procedures should not take up so much time that democracy itself becomes a burden or blunts its own authority. However, he did not believe that people would cotton to the task of voting if they did not have enough time to become invested in any given decision.[54]

Fifth, Condorcet believed that hasty decisions also risk the problem of presentism. Given adequate time, people can come to understand and incorporate views other than the views they possess at the exact moment when they are asked to choose. They can consider not only the past – the wisdom of experience referenced in Condorcet's first concern – but also the question of the future. Condorcet's second and fourth objections to haste – the problems of passing trends and of presentism – are two sides of one issue: that of obsolescence. Only over time can we extricate ourselves from our immediate setting enough to gain the perspective of past experience and knowledge, and adequately consider the interests of future generations.

Here we see Condorcet arguing for a more radical and less tempered form of democracy in which the representation of some (future citizens) by others (past citizens) is illegitimate. He demands a temporal limit on the legitimacy of even documents as fundamental as constitutions.[55] Generalizing from our experience and imposing our conclusions on future generations precludes the very likely possibility that in another time there will emerge information that contradicts our beliefs. This view of presentism in democratic theory is one that Condorcet shared with Locke. As Brunner shows us in his reading of Locke:

> [Locke] suggests that the legislative body, which is to hold supreme authority, will convene only for limited periods, while the executive power, although located below the legislative branch in the governmental hierarchy, will be in continuous

---

[53] Condorcet thought electoral agendas needed to be "examined quietly" and be discussed "with friends, relations, and neighbours." "The Theory of Voting," in McLean and Hewitt, *Condorcet*, 245. On the importance of solitary action, see Ira J. Cohen, *Solitary Action: Acting on Our Own in Everyday Life* (Oxford University Press, 2015).
[54] "Theory of Voting," 245.   [55] Ibid.

activity. Locke explains the temporal distinction between the two powers as follows: '[B]ecause those Laws which are constantly to be Executed, and whose force is always to continue, may be made in a little time; therefore there is no need, that the Legislative should always in being, not having always business to do.' By contrast, 'because the Laws, that are at once, and in a short time made, have a constant and lasting force, and need a perpetual Execution, or an attendance thereunto: Therefore 'tis necessary there should be a Power always in being, which should see to the Execution of the Laws that are made, and remain in force.'[56]

Whereas Hobbes's absolutism sought to prevent instability and political precariousness by removing temporal limits on political rule, Locke's liberal democratic commitments required time limits to accommodate what cannot be predicted and ensure a mechanism for political revision.[57]

Presentism also troubled Condorcet's friends and peers, including Jefferson, who made an even more dramatic argument that, "the earth belongs in usufruct to the living."[58] Jefferson was concerned that the US Constitution must free future generations from the beliefs of predecessors who were dead and gone. Jed Rubenfeld argues that many enlightenment thinkers, notably Mill, ignore their own presentism in ways that hobble the normative potential of their political aspirations.[59] By contrast, Thompson would have us act as trustees for the future. But he also says that we are only competent to be sovereign for specific durations of time. We cannot be permitted to impose restrictions that would prevent future sovereigns from enacting rules that present sovereigns would not enact or approve.[60] This can be restated in a way that resonates with contemporary democratic theorists; the "all affected principle" (all those affected by a decision must be permitted to participate in the making of the decision) automatically creates temporal threshold issues.[61] Future citizens are among the group of persons affected by decisions. Decision-makers must therefore consider future generations and future generations must be able to reconsider the decisions they are bequeathed. It also seems

---

[56] Jose Brunner, "Modern Times: Law, Temporality and Happiness in Hobbes, Locke and Bentham," *Theoretical Inquiries in Law* 8, no. 1 (2007).

[57] Ibid., 298.

[58] Thomas Jefferson, Letter to James Madison (Paris, Sept. 6, 1789), www.let.rug.nl/usa/presidents/thomas-jefferson/letters-of-thomas-jefferson/jefl81.php

[59] Jed Rubenfeld, *Freedom and Time: A Theory of Constitutional Self-Government* (New Haven, CT: Yale University Press, 2008), 48.

[60] Thompson, "Democracy in Time," 248–9.

[61] An extended argument for realizing this in a utilitarian framework is Jon Elster's case for "ethical individualism." "Ethical Individualism and Presentism," *The Monist* 76, no. 3 (1993): 333–48.

consonant with epistemic democrats. Such reasoning informs decisions like those that have awarded children victories in lawsuits challenging current environmental practices.[62] Landemore seems to see the temporal questions of epistemic democracy as occurring over durations long enough to categorize the problem as one of intergenerational change.[63]

The move to avoid presentism marks Condorcet and other like-minded thinkers as doing more than just echoing a simplistic interpretation of Burkean commitments to slow change and to Burke's description of citizenship as a compact between generations. It imposes an expiration date on consent. Rubenfeld compares time to space, arguing:

Just as the citizens living on a certain block in New York City lack the right to determine the meaning of the nation's commitments, so too do the citizens living on a certain day in 2001. If the people as a temporally extended whole could somehow declare at one moment, in one voice, its interpretation of its own commitments, this impossible declaration could be taken as supreme. But a temporally extended people cannot speak in such a voice. It can only inscribe itself, over time, into the world. Constitutional interpretation in written self-government must itself be a written project; an enterprise in which one text is intermeshed with another and another over a long period of time. It cannot be reduced to a single clarifying pronouncement by the people, even a pronouncement made in unison by every living citizen at a sublime constitutional moment.[64]

These concerns about presentism argue in favor of incorporating limits to the temporal reach of any decision, as well as temporal considerations during the process of decision-making. Once the consenting parties have expired, so too does the legitimacy of their agreements. Indeed, Condorcet believed that actuarial tables should be used to limit the validity of any contract by calculating the probability that one of the parties to the contract had died.[65] Jefferson took this so seriously that he proposed that any constitution ought to become invalid and be rewritten every nineteen years.[66] There is a window in which consent can be given and received. Offer a decision too quickly and the verdict is not legitimately consent. Let the decision stand in place for too long without reconsidering

---

[62] James Conca, "Children Win Another Climate Change Legal Case in Mass Supreme Court," *Forbes: Opinion* (May 19, 2016), www.forbes.com/sites/jamesconca/2016/05/19/children-win-another-climate-change-legal-case-in-mass-supreme-court/#5dc9412c556b

[63] Landemore, *Democratic Reason*, 20.   [64] *Freedom and Time*, 173.

[65] This view was shared by Jefferson who likely adapted it from Condorcet. McLean and Hewitt, *Condorcet*, 58.

[66] Julian P. Boyd, ed., *The Papers of Thomas Jefferson* (Princeton University Press, 1958), vol. xv, 394.

it and it also cannot be considered consensual. Unlike sovereign boundaries, which required only one date, democratic decision-making deploys multiple dates that carve out durations of time. This confirms the normative conclusions of the preceding chapter, which pointed to the connection between democratic norms and durational time. Condorcet treats durational time as a good with multifaceted political value.

To avoid the preceding five pitfalls of a hasty democracy: the imposition of an ignorant, unstable, herd-like, and despotic will, Condorcet's constitution proposes a complex democracy that enforces temporal layers in which there are multiple times and locations for reasoning, learning, and deliberation. He removes authority away from a single moment of decision (the vote) and disperses it over multiple points in time, thus extending but limiting the time in which decisions are made and consent is given. He sought to avoid spontaneous and intemperate acts of self-legislation by ensuring that citizens had adequate time (neither too little nor too much) in which to form considered judgment.

Condorcet seems hyperaware that deadlines make people susceptible to the pathologies of bounded rationality that are linked to time (e.g. a person's tendency to harden their views once a deadline is in place and to experience framing effects under time pressure).[67] In some ways his prescriptions also resemble those adopted in labor and other types of law to create "cooling off periods" that protect people from making decisions in "transient emotionally or biologically 'hot' states.'"[68] Such cooling-off periods often govern negotiations but they also are invoked to prevent corruption, for example in laws that restrict how quickly one can become a lobbyist after leaving one's congressional seat or how quickly one can enter a civilian position such as secretary of defense after having been in the US military. Congressional procedures are filled with examples of such rules. For example, the Senate requires that thirty hours elapse after the Senate has voted to cut off a filibuster before a vote on final passage can be held. These are in turn similar in spirit to waiting periods for marriage or abortion, but the latter two cases use only single deadlines rather than multiple stages of decision-making. At stake are several factors, notably

---

[67] For a discussion of bounded rationality that bridges political decision-making, see Marco Pinfari, *Peace Negotiations and Time: Deadline Diplomacy in Territorial Disputes* (Abingdon, UK: Routledge, 2012).

[68] Brishen Rogers, "Passion and Reason in Labor Law," *Harvard Civil Rights–Civil Liberties Law Review* 47 (Summer 2012): 334 (citing Camerer et al., "Regulation for Conservatives: Behavioral Economics and the Case for 'Asymmetric Paternalism'," *University of Pennsylvania law review* 151 (2003): 1238).

deliberation, considered judgment, and the tempering of impulses. His is a rigorously structured "slow democracy" that encourages careful consideration and truth seeking. At moments he even seems attuned to problems related to "decision fatigue" in which people are asked to make too many decisions in circumstances, often in less than ideal decision-making environments.[69] Urbinati calls Condorcet's theory of democracy "a third way between representative democracy and radical democracy."[70] Distinctive to Condorcet's theory is "a complex system of time delays."[71] Various temporal intervals for intermediate deliberations were built into his constitution.[72] In contrast to Rousseau, who collapsed the moment of proposing legislation with the vote,[73] for Condorcet, "[e]lection is one moment in the continuum of political action that involves citizens and representatives."[74] Condorcet believed that citizens would more likely arrive at truthful conclusions if they were given precise durations of time to both deliberate with each other and consider their acquired knowledge independently. Reasoning takes time. Only with time can people master their impulses, and only when they have mastered their impulses is the mere act of voting elevated to the level of consent.

By drawing a causal connection between haste, instability, conformity, and presentism, Condorcet elevates durational time in his diagnoses and prescriptions for democratic politics. Time becomes not just a means to an end, but a political good in its own right. While the mastery of momentary impulses is an Aristotelian preoccupation, Condorcet's recommendation channels Plato's quest to systematize democratic processes. Time is harnessed in the service of creating and implementing democratic dispositions. For both Condorcet and Plato, reasoning must be *measured* in the multiple senses of the word. It must be measured in the sense of being slow, rhythmic, and thoughtful. It must also be measured scientifically using variables that can be quantified. But, in building into his theory a concern for future generations, Condorcet was also implicitly acknowledging Aristotle's skepticism about an eternal science of politics.

Condorcet gives us a political schedule made up of carefully proportioned blocks of time for different elements and phases of self-government. While there is no shortage of like-minded prescriptive work on democratic

---

[69] On decision fatigue, see Kathleen D. Vohs, et. al., "Making Choices Impairs Subsequent Self-Control: A Limited-Resource Account of Decision Making," *Motivation Science* 1 (2014).

[70] Urbinati, *Representative Democracy*, 2770.   [71] Ibid., 2772.   [72] Ibid., 2772.

[73] Ibid., 2897.   [74] Ibid., 2846.

theory, Condorcet's mathematical bent imparts his prescriptions with an unusual degree of specificity and precision. Toward the goal of producing a science of democracy, Condorcet essentially offers formulae with which citizens can produce informedness, deliberation, stability, and insight. These are, in short, formulae for democracy. His formulae are not the strongly worded abstract assurances about deliberation, knowledge, truth, or consensus that are characteristic of political philosophy. Instead, they specify the many variables that go into decision-making and place them into relation with one another using mathematical principles. The quantifiable elements of Condorcet's study distinguish his work from so many of his peers because they enable him to give us a formula for doing the work of democracy.

For Condorcet, time is crucial to the process of making of something that some treat as intangible and/or qualitative into something concrete and tangible. He believes that a science of politics is not only possible but necessary. Durational time ensures stability for Condorcet but not because it was cyclical, as was true of Polybian cycles. To Condorcet, durational time allowed for measured progress. In short, democracy is simultaneously cyclical, insofar as political calendars prescribe regular and repeated series of events like elections, and linear insofar as no cycle of rise and decline is expected as long as the citizenry is judiciously engaged in truth-seeking and prevented from imposing their will on future citizenries.

Condorcet explains why different phases of the decision-making process ought to take certain amounts of time. But his recommendations did not take root in France, which instead descended into terror and eventually chaos after its revolution. His prescriptions for measured deliberate decision-making went unheeded. To carve out a place for consent in a sovereign state would require something more than the imposition of a shared temporal context through the invention of a calendar. The French experiment failed, not because it misunderstood the symbolic importance of trying to replace birthright hierarchy with a shared temporal context, but because it lacked the institutional framework necessary for consensual decision-making. In this sense the French Republic was no improvement on Coke's British monarch. Each lacked, among other things, effective and stable government by consent and rights.

Given this failure, Condorcet's discussions of temporal formulae for democratic decision-making could be dismissed as the abstracted musings of a philosopher rather than insights into the practice of politics. But Condorcet's work doesn't just describe a normative aspiration. It also describes practices that are characteristic of both ancient and modern democratic design. To see a liberal democracy instantiated, one can turn to the establishment of citizenship in the US. It is in part the US accomplishment that Condorcet translated into normatively prescriptive language. In the US, one can see a transition from thinking about durational time as a political good necessary primarily for judicious decision-making to implementing a political system in which durational time actually serves to structure a host of the procedures for determining who would exercise which rights. While work like Orren and Skowronek's focuses heavily on how duration is incorporated into institutional prescriptions for processes such as elections and other forms of collective decision-making, the underlying message of Condorcet is that duration is important to processes that transcend institutions and permeate the conferral and exercise of the rights of citizenship.

   In both cases – decision-making and rights distribution – durational time is treated as a good that has a kind of political value. I will examine in greater detail the nature of the value of durational time in Chapter 4. The section that follows scrutinizes how durational time is inserted into the procedures for determining rights in a liberal democracy.

DURATIONAL TIME AS A GOOD IN LIBERAL DEMOCRATIC PRACTICE

For Condorcet, durational time is a good whose judicious application to decision-making truth, stability, and free thought, will yield liberating practices of democratic politics. His notion that political decision-making should adhere to some kind of predictable and staggered schedule has become widely accepted even as it engenders the critique that it tempers direct democracy, populism, and truly radical democracy. As we saw in Chapter 2, uncertainty plays an outsized role in the establishment of secular states. In order to supersede the promise of eternal salvation offered by religious authorities, sovereigns had to assure would-be subjects of the security offered by earthly authority. They did this in part by establishing political systems with reference to secular time. The management and reduction of contingency plays an important part in the establishment of the laws that will govern people. Here we see the role of time in creating laws intended to produce normatively desirable outcomes. Condorcet's schedules and calendars ensure that periodic reconsideration of decisions and political arrangements occurs. While they were designed to thwart radicalism and immediacy, it is also the case that even radical democrats would almost certainly have to work within some temporal framework to maintain legitimacy. As long as states are constituted as the primary guardians of sovereignty, democratic legitimacy will require some kind of temporal order.

However, it is not just constitutions or institutional design and rights of participation and representation that embody the idea that time is a good with political value. In fact, an almost endless array of rights is distributed on the basis of formulae that treat durational time as a good with a precise political value. These formulae and the value that they accord time were implemented as the world's first liberal democratic state set about creating procedures for determining how one became eligible to bear and exercise the fundamental rights of citizenship. This was a process that followed the writing and ratification of the US Constitution and unfolded in the legislature and court.

Most citizens acquire rights via a formula that includes birthplace and age. Persons born to citizens or born in a given territory receive some rights at birth, and many other rights following the passage of the duration of time it takes to reach the age of majority. This is a common temporal formula. Equally common is a formula for assigning rights to people who are not on a birthright trajectory for the acquisition of rights. This formula usually involves residency within the boundaries of the state for a duration of time as well as other requirements. The formula is often one that culminates in naturalization, but it need not apply only to immigrants. In fact, it was fundamental to the establishment of boundaries around the population of the United States.

The initial determination of who qualified for the rights of US citizenship was complicated by a diverse analog to the group Coke had termed *"antenati"* (people born before the ascent of James to the throne). Among the US *antenati* whose rights were in question after the founding were: persons born before the Revolution; before the treaty concluding the Revolution; and before the adoption of both the national and state constitutions. Intersecting with these divisions were differences among people who had sided with Americans, loyalists who had sided with the British but whose circumstances of birth, residence, or behavior led US authorities to consider them American, and finally "Real British Subjects," whose affiliation with the Crown was never in question.[75] In addition, there were questions about people from America who had fled to Britain

---

[75] James Kettner, *The Development of American Citizenship, 1608–1870* (Chapel Hill, NC: University of North Carolina Press, 1978), 183.

but who at one time had shared allegiance to the same sovereign as their compatriots who stayed behind.

The political status of the would-be Americans required clarification in order for the US to affirm its sovereignty and political legitimacy. A country predicated on citizenship had to be able to say with certainty who qualified for citizenship. The Constitution had enumerated the rights of citizens, but it had not adequately specified who would enjoy those rights. In fact, it hardly even gestured toward the idea of citizenship. This job fell to the courts and legislature. At issue, first and foremost, were cases in which people sought the right to inherit and bequeath property. Prior to the establishment of participatory democracy, property owner-ship and the right to inherit and bequeath property were considered the signature rights of a political subject. Perhaps marking a hangover from the pre-democratic membership defined in *Calvin's Case*, these three related rights were proxies for citizenship rights far more than was the franchise.[76] Unsurprisingly, property rights remained highly salient mar-kers of citizenship as democratic politics were established. In fact, prop-erty is still an important part of fundamental rights disputes. Both the landmark cases that sought to overturn anti-miscegenation laws and anti-gay marriage cases have been brought in part on behalf of people who wished to pass property to heirs that the state did not recognize as legal spouses.[77] At the time of the founding, just as was the case for subjects of the British crown, only citizens of the US could inherit and bequeath property.

US jurists did not replicate the *Calvin's Case* rule of *jus soli* by simply ordering that anyone not born on US soil was not eligible for full rights of citizenship. Instead they tempered the rule by prioritizing consent.[78]

---

[76] Kettner, *Development of American Citizenship*, 117–18. On the relative openness of the franchise, see Ronald Hayduk, *Democracy For All: Restoring Immigrant Voting Rights in the United States* (New York: Routledge, 2006), 250; "Noncitizen Voting Rights: Extending the Franchise in the United States," *National Civic Review* 92, no. 4 (2003): 57–62; Jamin B. Raskin, "Legal Aliens, Local Citizens: The Historical, Constitutional and Theoretical Meanings of Alien Suffrage," *University of Pennsylvania Law Review* 141, no. 4 (1993): 1391; Sarah Song, "Democracy and Noncitizen Voting Rights," *Citizenship Studies* 13, no. 6 (2009): 607.

[77] *United States v. Windsor*, 133 S. Ct. 2675 (2013); Lynn D. Wardle, "*Loving* v. *Virginia* and the Constitutional Right to Marry, 1790–1990," *Howard Law Journal* 41 (1998).

[78] Peter H. Schuck and Rogers M. Smith, *Citizenship Without Consent* (New Haven, CT: Yale University Press, 1985); Daniel Scott Smith, "Population and Political Ethics: Thomas Jefferson's Demography of Generations," *William and Mary Quarterly*, no. 3 (1999): 591–612. Schuck and Smith illustrate in careful detail how consent came to dominate US conceptions of citizenship. However, even the nation's most purely

Allegiance in Coke's terms began at birth and could not be foresworn. By contrast, Lockean consent was neither ascribed at birth nor perpetual; it could only begin at the age of consent, and the kind of political status it produced could be abjured.[79] The US marriage of consent and *jus soli* was predicated on the idea that durational time is a political good that can be included in procedures for transacting over citizenship rights. Having written a constitution in which durational time was linked to consent, it was now possible to apply the idea that durational time is a political good to a procedure in which people not born into citizenship could consent to becoming citizens.

US CITIZENSHIP: DURATIONAL TIME AND THE IDEA OF LIVED CONSENT

Coke had established allegiance as perpetual; it began at birth and could not be abjured. By contrast, Lockean consent was not ascribed; it was only conceivable once a child reached maturity (the age of consent) and it could be foresworn.[80] This marriage of consent and *jus soli* was made possible because US citizenship revised the temporal reasoning found in *Calvin's Case* to confer authority on periods of time bounded by specific dates rather than just single sovereign moments.

Beginning in 1804, a series of court decisions established a set of understandings about who was a US citizen. The Supreme Court's earliest words on the subject of the US *antenati* came in the case *McIlvaine v. Coxe's Lessee*. Leading up to this confrontation had been a series of squabbles between the British and Americans about the exact date on which US sovereignty, and hence citizenship, was established (1783, upon the conclusion of the Treaty of Paris, as the British contended, or 1776, as the Americans contended).[81] As was true of many of the early citizenship cases, *McIlvaine* involved a question of whether an *antenatus* could

---

consensual rules of citizenship attribution required physical presence and therefore some element of *jus soli* is omnipresent.

[79] Kettner, *Development of American Citizenship*, 55; Schuck and Smith, *Citizenship without Consent*; Scott Smith, "Population and Political Ethics," 591–612. On expatriation, see Gerhard Casper, "Forswearing Allegiance" (University of Chicago, Maurice and Muriel Fulton Lecture Series, 2008).

[80] On Locke and expatriation, see Aristide Zolberg, *A Nation by Design* (New York: Russell Sage Foundation, 2006), 48.

[81] The difference of opinion between the British and the Americans is directly noted in *Inglis v. Trustees of Sailor's Snug Harbor*, 28 US 99, 161–4. It may be useful at this point to recall that the period under examination roughly corresponds to the period in which

inherit land. In this case, Daniel Coxe's allegiance and eligibility for citizenship were brought into question by virtue of the fact that he had been a loyalist during the Revolutionary War. The arguments on each side were complex, pointing to where Coxe resided at specific intervals marked by the declaration of war (1776), the signing of Jay's Treaty in 1794, and interim legislative acts in New Jersey that explicitly enumerated the actions that would henceforth be considered treasonous.[82] Ultimately, the decision declared Coxe to be a citizen by virtue of the fact that he had tacitly given consent through residence in New Jersey from the time of its founding (the adoption of the state constitution) all the way to the point at which the state passed laws defining its citizenship.[83] In the language of *McIlvaine*, Coxe's citizenship existed because he elected not to reject it, or to not "adhere to his allegiance to the king," by virtue of his continued residence in New Jersey during this period of time.[84] The ratification period was a critical duration of time that Daniel Coxe quite literally chose to spend in New Jersey. His consent was consent not to reject allegiance to the US. And it was signaled by durational time and place.

French authorities were playing all manner of games with time, including, notably the imposition of an entirely alien calendar for which time began with the Revolution.

[82] The Judge wrote, "The inquiry which the jury is directed to make, by the act of the 18th of April, 1778, in order to lay a foundation for the confiscation of the personal estates of these fugitives is, whether the person had, between the 4th of October, 1776, and the 5th of June, 1777, joined the armies of the king of Great Britain, or otherwise offended against the form of his allegiance to the state. The 7th section of this law is peculiarly important, because it provides not only for past cases, which had occurred since the 5th of June, 1777, but for all future cases, and in all of them, the inquiry is to be whether the offender has joined the armies of the king, or otherwise offended against the form of his allegiance to the state. During all this time, the real estates of these persons remained vested in them; and when by the law of the 11th of December, 1778, the legislature thought proper to act upon this part of their property, it was declared to be forfeited for their offences, not escheatable on the ground of alienage. This last act is particularly entitled to attention, as it contains a legislative declaration of the point of time, when the right of election to adhere to the old allegiance ceased, and the duties of allegiance to the new government commenced." Mary Sarah Bilder, "The Struggle Over Immigration: Indentured Servants, Slaves, and Articles of Commerce," *Missouri Law Review* 61 (Fall 1996): 8–9.

[83] The decision reads, "Daniel Coxe lost his right of election to abandon the American cause, and to adhere to his allegiance to the King of Great Britain; because he remained in the state of New-Jersey; not only after she had declared herself a sovereign state, but after she had passed laws by which she pronounced him to be a member of, and in allegiance to the new government." Bilder, "Struggle Over Immigration," 6.

[84] Kettner makes the corollary point that, prior to states passing treason laws, individuals were not prosecuted for treason even though Congress had defined the crime, implying "that individuals were generally allowed to choose sides before that time." *Development of American Citizenship*, 194

The mutually constitutive relationship between time, place, and consent is fleshed out in even more useful detail in the decision written by Justice Thompson, as well as Justice Story's frequently cited concurrence in *Inglis* v. *Trustees of Sailor's Snug Harbor*.[85] This case involved an even lengthier hashing out of both the moment at which US sovereignty commenced and the appropriate duration in which consent, or election, could take place.[86] In the decision, Justice Thompson states, "The rule as to the point of time at which the US *antenati* ceased to be British subjects, differs in this country and in England, as established by the courts of justice in the respective countries. The English rule is to take the date of the treaty of peace in 1783. Our rule is to take the date of the Declaration of Independence."[87] On the subject of durational time and consent he states, "To say that the election must have been made before, or immediately at the declaration of independence, would render the right nugatory."[88] In this way he gave voice to a belief repeated throughout *antenati* cases, asserting that a government that imposed itself at a specific date was arbitrary and non-consensual, while one to which citizens could subscribe within the space of a reasonable period of time was consensual. Condorcet himself could not have written a more perfect application of his own conclusions about consent. Consent requires reason and reason requires time.

Justice Story's concurrence affirmed this relationship between time and consent, although he acknowledged that the precedent of *McIlvaine* contradicted his precise conclusion with respect to when allegiance could commence. Story thought the British occupation of New York that began on September 15 of 1776 effectively muddled any allegiances claimed to begin on July 4, 1776. He therefore strenuously argued that 1783 be regarded as the cutoff date for the period of election. Still, he emphasized that the nature of the Revolution made it crucial that individuals be allowed an appropriate duration of time in which to choose their allegiance. He wrote, "This choice was necessarily to be made within a reasonable time. In some cases that time was pointed out by express acts of the legislature; and the fact of abiding within the state after it assumed independence, or after some other specific period, was declared to be an election to become a citizen."[89] And he also specified the origins of this principle, saying: "[t]he general doctrine asserted in the American courts, has been, that natives who were not here at the declaration of independence, but were then, and for a long while afterwards remained, under British protection, if they returned before the

---

[85] *Inglis* v. *Trustees of Sailor's Snug Harbor.*   [86] Ibid., 99.   [87] Ibid., 121.   [88] Ibid.
[89] Ibid., 160.

treaty of peace, and were here at that period, were to be deemed citizens. If they adhered to the British crown up to the time of the treaty, they were deemed aliens."[90] Again, consent requires reason, and reason is measured in durations of time.

These Supreme Court decisions were not anomalies. Even during the war years, most states were also already moving toward a conception of "volitional allegiance" that embraced the idea of a temporal duration in which people could elect their own citizenship.[91] By instituting such a policy, many states effectively created a temporal formula, or equation, that both expressed and "solved" the problem of Americanization by taking into account a person's age, length of absence, and period of reimmersion in America society, economy, and politics.

The treatment of time in the early citizenship cases highlights a critical difference between the British model of birthright citizenship and the US model of consensual citizenship. In the course of making decisions about the US *antenati*, the Court became increasingly strident about the fact that electing citizenship required a period of time in which reason could occur and culminate in consent. The time was demarcated by two dates rather than identified with a single moment as in *Calvin's Case*. Judges writing decisions about the *antenati* explicitly called for "reasonable" periods of time in which persons could elect to become citizens. These durations were times of crucial political reasoning during which people had information (newly adopted constitutions and social and political context) to help them to make "enlightened" decisions about their consent.[92] In *Calvin's Case*, an unchosen lifelong obligation (allegiance) to the sovereign commenced at the moment of birth.[93] Citizenship was now predicated not just on birthright allegiance, but also consent. Coke's conception of *jus soli* seemed arbitrary to the colonists, who replaced the model of conquest with a "right of election" in determining the citizenship of the *antenati*.[94] They solved this problem by creating times of political reason to legitimize consent. The consensus that emerged from the citizenship decisions was that, in living in the time of election and the sovereign territory of the new country, *antenati* created "lived consent" that was not entirely tacit in exchange for their citizenship.

---

[90] Ibid., 161.   [91] Kettner, *Development of American Citizenship*, 40.

[92] "Enlightened understanding" one of Robert Dahl's prerequisites for democratic decision-making. *Democracy and Its Critics* (New Haven, CT: Yale University Press,1989), 21.

[93] Elizabeth F. Cohen, "Jus Tempus in the Magna Carta: The Sovereignty of Time in Modern Politics and Citizenship," *PS: Political Science & Politics* 43, no. 3 (2010): 464.

[94] Kettner, *Development of American Citizenship*, 193.

Durational time infused the US version of *jus soli* with reason, thus avoiding the arbitrary quality of Coke's perpetual allegiance. The decision to assign durational time a political value stood in opposition to Blackstone's related writing on the subject, which expressly stated that natural allegiance was due from the moment of birth, because infants were incapable of protecting themselves, and "cannot be forfeited, cancelled, or altered by any change of time, place, or circumstance."[95] This contrast was noted in the *McIlvaine* case, among others.[96]

Indeed, time is critical to conferring legitimacy on the kind of "tacit consent" that Locke discusses and that is integral to social contract democracy.[97] But lived consent measured by durational time isn't entirely tacit, as Kettner's term "volitional allegiance" suggests. Justice Story says as much in his *Inglis* concurrence, arguing that durational time and residence together formed an "*overt* act or consent. . . to their [citizens'] right of election."[98] Time has value and the choice to spend it in one place and one political system over another place and political system is overt. Time does not just happen to us. We make choices to spend it in particular ways.

The US Supreme Court, like Condorcet, thought most of time's value had to do with acts of reasoning that precede consent. But others saw a larger family of acts, processes, characteristics, and relationships that develop in durational time. The section that follows examines the more extensive meanings accorded to temporal durations by legislators concerned with citizenship and naturalization rules. It also highlights the establishment of a process through which durations of time that had been valued in connection with important norms could be exchanged, in this case for political rights and status. The precedent of exchange sets the stage for the creation of a political economy of time.

---

[95] Schuck and Smith, *Citizenship without Consent*, 43.
[96] *McIlvaine* v. *Coxe's Lessee*, 6 US 280, 330 (1804).
[97] A. John Simmons, "Tacit Consent and Political Obligation," *Philosophy & Public Affairs* (1976), 279.
[98] *Inglis* v. *Trustees of Sailor's Snug Harbor*, at 159 (my emphasis). Regarding the question of whether *jus soli* is consensual, see Matthew J. Lister, "Citizenship, in the Immigration Context," *Maryland Law Review* 70 (2011), 10–16. On Locke's discussion of the political status of children, see Ian Shapiro, *Democracy's Place* (Ithaca, NY: Cornell University Press, 1996), 70.

BEYOND CONSENT: TIME'S VALUE FOR DEMOCRATIC PROCESS

If we look beyond the *antenati* court cases to legislative debates about acquiring citizenship, we can see that other relationships, actions, values, and characteristics besides consent are associated with durational time. The establishment of citizenship requires not just a statement about the existing population, but also rules for transforming newcomers, who were essential to the settlement and survival of the young nation, into citizens. The bulk of early debates over political incorporation occurred at one of two points: during the Constitutional Convention when the matter of prerequisites for national office holding were discussed, and a few years later when naturalization legislation was debated. The myriad worries and aspirations of the representatives – their concern about foreign influence and purchase of offices, about creating inequalities among the population, about what people with foreign attachments might accomplish, and about becoming an illiberal society – were expressed using the language of durational time. The sheer volume and range of discussion about the meaning of time, the fairness of temporal rules, and the effect time has on the division of citizenship into lesser statuses, is impressive. Parsing these debates makes evident the degree to which linking intangible values such as loyalty and civic incorporation to durational time, measurable in precise increments by clocks and calendars, created a formula for the extension of citizenship status and rights to foreign-born persons.

At the Constitutional Convention, discussion was devoted to deciding how many years of residence *after* naturalization should new citizens be required to wait before becoming eligible to hold congressional office. Some advocated no waiting period while others went so far as to advocate a seven-year bar for the House and a fourteen-year bar for the Senate. Madison's record of the deliberations shows intense disagreement over whether the waiting periods were so long as to "give a tincture of illiberality to the Constitution."[99] George Mason demanded a seven-year period for the House in order to prevent "[f]oreigners and adventurers" from making American law and to ensure adequate civic knowledge for all lawmakers.[100] Gouverneur Morris, who sought a fourteen-year waiting period, claimed the loyalty of foreigners would always be to their first

---

[99] James Madison, *Notes of Debates in the Federal Convention of 1787* (Ohio University Press, 1966), 419.

[100] Kate Mason Rowland, ed., *The Life of George Mason, 1725–1792* (New York: Putnam's, 1892), vol. II, 149#.

governments.[101] The final result of this temporal haggling was a nine-year waiting period for the Senate and a seven-year waiting period for the House.

The congressmen referred to a diverse yet limited set of values that they believed could be achieved with time. Like Coke and the US judges who drew on his thought, some legislators identified probationary time periods prior to naturalization as a means of measuring "fidelity and allegiance."[102] Others nudged the debate beyond allegiance into the valuation of the government and citizenship. Hartley said, "an actual residence of such a length of time would give a man an opportunity of esteeming the Government from knowing its intrinsic value, was essentially necessary to assure us of a man's becoming a good citizen."[103] Madison connected the amount of time an immigrant is in residence with understanding the value of citizenship itself, rather than just the government and laws.[104] Sedgwick also connected it with shedding "prejudices of education, acquired under monarchical and aristocratical governments [that] may deprive them of that zest for pure republicanism which is necessary in order to taste its beneficence"[105] and, taking this one step further, with forms of civic knowledge that will make them good citizens.[106] Besides the length of the probationary period, other subsidiary temporal issues were raised. For example, a debate ensued over how important continuity in time is in the context of questioning the citizenliness of people who frequently traveled outside of the US.[107] A few even wanted to expatriate citizens who left and stayed abroad for a specified length of time.[108] Continuous residence has remained integral to the naturalization of permanent residents in the US.[109]

As the Court would affirm with respect to the lived consent of the *antenati*, the probationary period of the 1790 Act allowed people not born with US citizenship the opportunity to exchange two years of their time for the status of citizen. The architects of the legislation were explicit that this was a market-style exchange in which time was the measure of

[101] Madison, *Notes of Debates*, 421.   [102] Annals of Congress 1 (1790), 1147.
[103] Ibid., 1147–8.   [104] Ibid., 1156.   [105] Ibid.   [106] Ibid.
[107] Frank George Franklin, *Legislative History of Naturalization in the United States* (New York: Arno Press, 1906), 42.
[108] Annals of Congress, 1149.
[109] US Citizenship and Immigration Services, "Continuous Residence and Physical Presence Requirements for Naturalization," United States Department Homeland Security, www.uscis.gov/us-citizenship/citizenship-through-naturalization/continuous-residence-and-physical-presence-requirements-naturalization (accessed Aug. 20, 2016).

fitness for citizenship. Direct reference was made to the fact that time has a political exchange value, excoriating states in which people could become citizens immediately upon arrival at all for making citizenship too "cheap."[110] By the time of the Alien and Sedition Acts, the threshold had been raised to fourteen years, though further dickering revised it to five by 1802.[111]

The concept of a probationary duration was not a US or even a modern innovation. It can be traced back to Roman laws pertaining to the status of newly conquered people.[112] However, the English common law precedents to which Americans turned for guidance in creating their own citizenship rules did not allow for the full naturalization of newcomers. US legislators advocating probationary periods prior to naturalization looked to the Roman practice of requiring probationary periods. But the US legislators' valuation of the probationary period of time identifies distinctively US citizenly qualities and values. Indeed, among the virtues of temporal metrics is their ability to represent different values, both in different contexts and for different actors who share a context.

The creation of a formula in which time-in-residence was valued was also not unique to immigration and naturalization. The predication of rights on a commitment to settling in the territory of the state granting the rights, and the use of continuous residence for set durations of time to represent this commitment, are pervasive practices, extending well beyond questions of naturalization. One potent example was the repeated use of probationary residence periods upon which property ownership rights were contingent in laws like the Homestead Act, the Armed Occupation Act, and the Donation Land Claim Act, to name just a few.[113] In these cases the political economy of time predicated the right to own a piece of land on continuous residence upon that land.[114] This period of occupation transformed the land into property that could be privately owned by the occupant as long as the occupant was a free, white male. It also purposefully displaced long-time residents who were not white.

---

[110] Annals of Congress, 1148.
[111] Daniel J. Tichenor, *Dividing Lines: The Politics of Immigration Control in America* (Princeton University Press, 2002), 54.
[112] A.N. Sherwin-White, *The Roman Citizenship* (Oxford University Press, 1973), 61; Randall S. Howarth, *The Origins of Roman Citizenship* (Lewiston, NY: Edwin Mellen Press, 2006), 4–5.
[113] Paul Frymer, "'A Rush and a Push and the Land Is Ours,'": Territorial Land Expansion, Land Policy, and U.S. State Formation," *Perspectives on Politics* 12, no. 1 (2014).
[114] There were also laws that contained provisions about cultivating the land and building one's primary residence there.

The US founders, legislators, and jurists charged with deciding how rights would be accorded to potential citizens expressed Condorcetian beliefs about the connection between durational time, normative ideals of democratic citizenliness, and procedural democracy. The processes of becoming informed, developing attachments, reasoning, and consent all require durations of time upon which rights became and remain contingent. Waiting periods are not just intended to exact a cost on those who wait. They are intended to allow processes to unfold in the time they mark out. The temporal formula for acquiring citizenship is not unique. Temporal formulae confer rights on people as they become adults, they determine who may get an abortion, what the consequences of a criminal conviction will be, and innumerable other procedures for conferring or denying rights. Temporal formulae are also not unique to any type of political system. They can and do appear in all kinds of contexts. The preceding excavation of the meaning of temporal formulae for core rights of citizenship uncovers some of the meaning accorded to time in a liberal democracy. We see time invoked in all kinds of circumstances that require reasoning, consent, learning, deliberation, character development and any number of other abstract processes that are important to being democratic. Time is a singularly valuable ingredient in the realization of democratic politics.

The durations of time in which people experience the processes of reason, deliberation, consent, etc. reveal time's value to politics. Once valued in this way, time becomes, for practical purposes, a political good. As broached earlier, goods are that which is valued from within spheres of a society. Abstract goods that are of great importance to non-abstract things like the functioning of a political system must somehow be translated into less abstract terms. Consent must somehow be represented, whether through a spoken oath, a tick on a ballot, or waiting for a period of time. Scientifically measured durational time is hardly the only means with which abstract goods could be translated into terms that are friendly to political procedures. But it is uniquely ubiquitous and hence fundamental to the structure of democratic politics. The attributes of durational time that lead to this ubiquity are discussed in the chapter that follows. Much like Marx showed that wage labor remunerated work based on the quantity of time spent performing work, many political formulae measure fitness for rights based on a quantity of time. Just as time acquires an entirely new form of value once it becomes the medium of exchange in a labor-based economy, so too does time acquire a new form of value once it becomes the medium of exchange in a rights-based politics. The idea of time as a medium of exchange in transactions over rights and political power will be scrutinized more closely in Chapter 5.

One of the primary purposes of this book is to infer from political practices the value that time acquires in politics, particularly liberal democratic politics. From that can follow an understanding of the effect of contestation over the value that time is assigned. By relying on democratic theory, we can see a clear relationship between specific norms about how politics should be conducted and processes that take place within precise durations of time. Although the primary normative conclusions of this book are contained in the second half of Chapter 5, there is one normative conclusion that can be drawn based on the content of Chapters 2 and 3. In Chapter 2 an argument was made that single moment deadlines are somewhat arbitrary and not conducive to democratic justice. Chapter 3 builds on this idea by showing that time acquires value in politics because it is instrumental to processes that themselves have political value. This leads to a consideration of political procedures that not only have deadlines, but whose deadlines have unusual finality. Examples of such procedures include court proceedings that end in a death penalty or a sentence of life in prison with no change of parole, exile,[115] and less common procedures such as reproductive sterilization. If a political system has adopted practices that predict character development and other phenomena that time purports to facilitate and measure, permanently disabilities, exclusions, or even deaths, become very difficult to justify. They are predicated upon the idea that some people are impervious to process, that no new evidence will be discovered or produced to show that someone's character or deservingness is other than what we think of it at the precise moment when their rights or even their life is terminated. The idea of such permanence does not square readily with a political system that has embraced an understanding that human character and deservingness changes over time.

What is not yet clear is why time, rather than some other good, comes to hold this place in politics. In Chapter 4 time's value is scrutinized more closely as a means of answering the question of, "why time?"

---

[115] Elizabeth F. Cohen, "When Democracies Denationalize: The Epistemological Case Against Revoking Citizenship," *Ethics & International Affairs* 30, no. 2 (2016).

CONCLUSION

Chapter 2 began by pointing out the role of single moments in carving out political boundaries. The second half of the chapter described additional temporal boundaries within sovereign state boundaries and how they carve out durations of time that have normative potential. Chapter 3 has elaborated on the importance of durational time in democratic theory and practice. In the context of democratic theory, durational time is transformed into a good with a distinct form of political value. Initially it seems like durational time is a good that has a niche political role: it is a necessary ingredient in decisions that are well informed, stable, lasting, and consensual. But as democratic politics is joined by liberal aspirations to be inclusive, durational time's meaning expands. It is a political good that is linked to all kinds of processes, relationships, and characteristics that are prerequisites for holding rights.

The political role of durational time in modern political practice shares a great deal in common with the arguments about time that Plato makes in the *Protagoras*. He urged the development of a science of measurement for resolving ethical disagreement and identified time as one means of distilling and translating human experience into a scientific language that could be understood by all. Condorcet's prescriptive theory of slow democracy elaborates on Plato's *technē* by precisely stating a relationship between duration and stable, carefully considered, consensual decision-making. By identifying the necessity and specific functions of time for democracy, durational time comes to be treated as a good with a set of valuations in Condorcet's formulaic version of the democratic process. Condorcet's formulae bring us to a better-developed understanding of the relationship between time and democracy than many of his peers. By making political formulae possible, time allows us to put different elements of democracy into relation with one another. US legislators and jurists put into practice a political system in which not only were elections scheduled in ways that deliberately linked durational time to decision-making, but also based procedures for granting and denying rights to people on durational time.

The practices of the US and the many other liberal democracies that carefully schedule elections and create temporal formulae for carving out *demoi* and conferring and denying rights assign a normative meaning and form of value to durational time. The next chapter more systematically studies the instrumental and representational relationship between time and process in order to add depth to the understanding of time developed in Chapter 3. Process and time are inextricably connected. However, many of the most important temporal procedures use time as a proxy for process. Rather than asking people to endure waiting periods, schedule elections, or meet temporal thresholds because it is evident that an important process has taken place in those periods of time, many political procedures insert a temporal element as a placeholder for various processes that people think should take place. These temporal referents are proxies for process rather than the actual processes themselves. The use of time to proxy for processes opens up an array of political possibilities that would not be possible if procedures were not able to use time to represent process. Chapter 4 will also focus attention on the reasons that temporal procedures for conferring and denying rights are so ubiquitous and important in liberal democratic states. This sets the stage for exploring how the political economy of time works and for critiquing the normative implications of using time to transact over rights.

4

Time's Political Value

The preceding chapter highlighted how critical durational time is to the establishment of procedures for conferring and exercising fundamental rights in a liberal democracy. In each procedure, precise durations of time have value that is associated with foundational political norms. We schedule elections or establish probationary periods for citizenship because there is a belief that the duration of time involved has meaning that is relevant to the election or conferral of rights. These durations of time are inserted into formulae along with other requirements for conferring or denying rights.

The value of time appears in a plethora of important procedures that confer or deny liberal rights as well as in the basic structures of democratic decision-making. These procedures are expressed in formulae. Naturalization is often *time+residence and good moral character=citizenship*. Punishment is calculated using the factors of *crime+criminal history + age–good behavior=years in prison*. *Maturity=age 18*. Abortion has often been available to people in the first two trimesters of a pregnancy, if they wait for a specific period of time after requesting the procedure. Military service of different kinds requires different lengths of commitment to various tours and inactive assignments. The list goes on and on. These are procedures that can and sometimes do use measures other than time in order to determine who qualifies for which rights. For example, prison sentences restrict a person's rights using units of time rather than units of money or pain. Political maturity is measured by one's age rather than a test of reasoning, skills, or education level. The range of procedures that could be deployed for distributing rights underscores the fact that the use of temporal procedures is intentional, meaningful, and merits our attention. This brings to the fore questions about what kind of value time has. It also provokes us to ask why durational time is so often a measure of choice.

This chapter responds to these two questions, beginning with an analysis of the kinds of value time has. First, it describes how time acquires both instrumental and representational value for politics. Because time is integral to processes that are themselves essential for politics, time comes to have an instrumental political value. And because time has an instrumental value to politics it also comes to be treated as having symbolic value. Durations of time are often used to represent processes and characteristics that are otherwise too abstract to insert into political formulae.

Next, the chapter argues that temporal formulae become ubiquitous in political decisions and procedures that administer rights because durational time has a unique relationship to otherwise conflicting imperatives of liberal democratic states. Durational time can be scientifically measured and quantified in ways that appear objective and impartial, and ultimately even egalitarian. And yet, durational time is also embedded in any given society, allowing it to reflect subjective qualities of a democratic people. Although liberalism and democracy are rarely practiced in the absence of each other, the impartiality of liberalism and the embeddedness of democracy are actually in conflict with one another. Durational time can appear to be an objective scientific measure of the characteristics, processes, and relationships that a society decides are prerequisites for holding rights while also being a familiar, societally specific referent to embedded norms and ways. Temporal formulae are among the few procedures for transacting over rights that can meet the requirements of these conflicting values.

WHAT KINDS OF VALUE DOES TIME HAVE?

Durational time is explicitly accorded political value in ancient and modern democratic theory. Much as was the case in the discussion of temporal boundaries, the ubiquity of temporal referents could be dismissively chalked up to necessity: nothing, political or otherwise, happens outside of time. But throughout the history of democratic theory, an array of thinkers refers to durational time deliberately and thoughtfully; not in a way that suggests they are assuming its importance to politics or taking it for granted. Durational time is not just an uninteresting necessity in politics: something omnipresent but only because the laws of nature and physics make it thus. Nor is it an afterthought or an inescapable circumstance of human existence that has an inevitable but unintentional and insignificant political place. Durational time is intentionally described as having explicit value throughout the history of democratic political thought. In each case, time is intentionally accorded a very specific and precise political value that is justified with extensive argumentation.

This claim that time has political value is bolstered by observing that time has two distinct forms of value in politics: instrumental and representational. The instrumental value of time is derived from its role in the unfolding of specific political processes. The representational value of time is linked to the need to represent in a concrete, preferably quantifiable form, that which is politically important but intangible. Time's instrumental and representational value are not necessarily mutually exclusive. But the distinction is important because it is tempting to some to write off an argument about the political value of time as a mix-up in which time is not an important unit of analysis, but rather is just a proxy for the underlying value or process that really matters. So, for example, one might be tempted to shrug off the omnipresence of temporal measurements of residence in naturalization formulae as just a convenient proxy for the real values that actually matter to citizenship. This is not an absurd thing to think. But, in fact, time has instrumental value based on its connection to the processes through which one becomes citizenly. Time would be a far less persuasive proxy for underlying values if people did not also believe that there is an instrumental relationship between the processes that realize these values and the passage of time. Because it is easy to agree to the idea that developing one's character or making a thoughtful decision requires the passage of time, time is well suited to proxy for these and other processes, relationships, and characteristics that are meaningful for citizenship and difficult to represent. Both the instrumental and the representational value of time are important to democratic politics.

Durational Time's Instrumental Value

Time's instrumental value originates in its relationship to process. Processes can only occur in durational time, and not in single moments of time. Time has instrumental political value because it is inextricable from specific processes, for example character development and the acquisition of wisdom, that are fundamental to the institutions and actions on which democratic politics depends.

Although they disagree on how to regard this fact, for both Plato and Aristotle durational time is integral to the process of acquiring the qualitative experience that is essential to politics. It is a necessary (though insufficient) condition for experience. For Plato, experience could be measured by durational time and subjected to quantitative analysis.

The insights garnered can be applied scientifically. Aristotle seeks to supersede *tuche* – fortune and the intemperate passions – with practical judgment that is acquired over time. He does this with reference to the process of gaining experience over time. As an integral part of political, social, and human processes, time has its own distinct value in Aristotelian *arête* (moral virtue). In these cases, time does not symbolize the acquisition of practical knowledge or maturity. It is one element of the process through which those qualities come into existence, a prerequisite for their existence, and therefore one observable sign that the processes through which they form have occurred. This is a predecessor to the views about the human experience of time that Bergson and Deleuze would later develop and complicate.[1]

In the modern context, the lines between time as instrumentally valuable and time as a proxy look like they begin to blur. A cursory pass at Condorcet's thought might suggest that the only goods he thinks are instrumentally valuable to politics are truth and good judgment. If this were true, durational time is just a proxy for the value of these goods in his thought. His temporal schedule for decision-making is a means for achieving the end of producing truth and good judgment, and if he were presented with an instant fix for misinformed decisions he might agree to eliminate the temporal restrictions in his prescriptions. This would lead us to conclude that Condorcet believed durational time is not a good with inherent political value.

But, as we saw in Aristotle's thought, for Condorcet, time is not only a proxy for elements of decision-making. It is an actual element of a consensual decision. Condorcet critiqued Rousseau for collapsing consent into a single instant and argued for structuring periods of time to maximize a variety of elements of judicious decision-making including solitary reflection, deliberation, fact gathering, and negotiation. Measured durational time is also essential to democratic processes culminating in consent. This was borne out in the legislation and jurisprudence that established how consent could be produced and identified in the US citizenship cases and naturalization debates. Time is necessary, though not sufficient, for these processes to occur. It is an irreplaceable part of the processes that develop good judgment and an ability to see truth. Just as there is no other substance besides blood for carrying oxygen to human

[1] J.C. Muller, *The Temporality of Political Obligation* (New York: Routledge, 2015); Henri Bergson, *Time and Free Will: An Essay on the Immediate Data of Consciousness* (New York: Dover Publications, 2001).

cells, a politics cannot be a measured one without taking proper amounts of time for decisions. We can infer this from the fact that something like an instant referendum is seldom called for by political theorists. Time is not just a proxy for being measured and deliberate. It is integral to being measured and deliberate.

In this critique, Condorcet is essentially making a version of the point expressed in Chapter 2: single moment deadlines are undemocratic and arbitrary. Condorcet seeks to enable decisions that reflect collective as well as individual judgment, that achieve stability, and that are revisited as the population is renewed. These ends cannot even be imagined outside of the context of durational time. We cannot be simultaneously alone and together, we cannot anchor stability in a single moment, and new generations cannot revisit decisions made by previous generations at the same time the original decisions were made. Deliberation, civic education, loyalty, etc. all develop over time. They are not innate, and they must be cultivated.

Durational Time's Representational Value

The fact that durational time is commonly recognized as having instrumental value to politics makes it easy for durational time to also become a widely accepted proxy in political formulae. The development of politically salient relationships, traits, habits, etc. are all contingent upon processes. But these qualities and the processes that produce them are often intangible and difficult to precisely define, identify and measure. There are not abundant tangible objects associated with character development or affection for one's countrymen. Since durational time is integral to process, and processes are difficult to represent, time becomes a convenient way to represent process in political procedures. Legislation or rules that refer to time as a proxy make an abstraction in which time becomes a, perhaps even, *the* defining characteristic of the process. This aligns with the standards of the state.

Examples in which time represents processes abound. The age of maturity is a representation of a consensus about fitness for citizenship more than it is an exact measure of maturity. Similarly, a statute of limitations takes a qualitative process – the deterioration of evidence – and uses a quantity of time to represent that process.[2] A similar assessment

---

[2] In reality, it is widely known that many factors contribute to whether a piece of evidence or eyewitness account is reliable. However, time is treated as an ultimate limiting factor.

could be made about any number of temporally rooted laws, for example common law marriage and adverse possession, both of which use durations of time to represent the processes that can legally transform relationships to other people or to property. Rarely does someone draw a direct relationship between a precise prison sentence or immigrant probationary period and a specific outcome. Instead, those durations of time become more loosely associated with processes we associate with law-breaking or foreigners naturalizing. Time's instrumental value to political processes such as rehabilitation, punishment, political acculturation, etc. suggests the use of durations of time in transacting over rights in cases of law-breaking or naturalization, even when no argument or evidence proves that specific processes are unfolding in the exact time period that is at issue.

The establishment of a US citizenry vividly illustrates how durational time came to be used, not only to carve sovereign boundaries around a population of equally situated *subjects*, but also as a means of translating the intangible qualities that are integral to democratic *citizens* in the process of distributing powers and rights among the state and citizens on a consensual basis. The deliberations of legislators who debated naturalization practices in the US indicate that time represents certain processes, traits, and relationships, in addition to being integral to them. For example, not wanting to make citizenship "too cheap" points at a symbolic value to time that goes along with the more direct references to the acquisition of civic knowledge and commitment that can only occur over time. If no one ever checks to see whether people become loyal to an adoptive country and its government in a given amount of time, or if such a test is not even possible to design, then the practice of making people wait for a certain duration of time becomes symbolic. In these cases, time serves as a proxy for the traits, processes, and relationships that are thought to be important to democratic politics.

Someone could still go ahead with a prosecution based on the eyewitness testimony of an unreliable witness. But prosecution is impossible after the statute of limitations has expired. For example, evidence of "flight" – where a defendant leaves a jurisdiction immediately after the commission of a crime or after he is accused of a crime – may be offered to show "consciousness of guilt." However, one factor of whether admission of such evidence is proper is the length of time between the alleged commission of the crime and the defendant's flight. Compare, *United States* v. *Rowan*, 518 F.2d 685, 691 (6th Cir. 1975) (flight instruction not improper where defendant left community within thirty-six hours of the time at which the charge crime was committed) with *United States* v. *White*, 488 F.2d 660, 662 (8th Cir. 1973) (instruction improper where five months had elapsed between the date of the charged offense and the attempted arrest).

The representational, or metaphoric, role of time is widely recognized, although more often by social theorists and anthropologists than by political theorists. Societies across the world exhibit a common reliance on the value of time for the purpose of creating the building block metaphors that are essential to any system of communication.[3] In democratic politics, this metaphoric function allows amounts of time to approximate sufficient learning, attachment, reasoning, etc. for citizenship. We often purport to measure the presence of these traits and relationships using precise durations of time. This departs from the idea of instrumental value insofar as time is necessary for maturation but does not actually guarantee that it will occur. An 18-year-old person may not be mature enough to exercise the judgment required for citizenship. However, for political purposes, that amount of time becomes a proxy for maturity. In more complicated temporal formulae such as naturalization procedures or prison sentences, durational time sits beside other variables. In each of these two examples there is a formula that combines a temporal variable with non-quantitative modifiers such as good behavior and good moral character. A lot of work is done by the temporal variable but there is room for modification both within the calculation of the temporal variable (non-citizens who marry US citizens and non-citizen members of the military get two years knocked off of their probationary period) and alongside the temporal variable (solitary confinement can heighten the severity of a prison sentence). In each case there is a formula that combines a temporal variable with non-quantitative modifiers such as good behavior and good moral character.

Durational time also often proxies for multiple things simultaneously. We can see this very clearly in the case of prison sentencing. There is widespread disagreement about the purposes of imprisonment, which include incapacitation, deterrence, retribution or expiation, and reformation.[4] Durational time can represent each of these goals simultaneously, allowing people to agree to complicated sentencing formulae even when they are seeking very different ends. The vagueness about what is happening in a given duration of time works to evade potentially divisive disagreements. I will return to how durational time is used to produce consensus and smooth over normative disagreement in Chapter 5.

---

[3] Mark Johnson and George Lakoff, "Conceptual Metaphor in Everyday Language," *Journal of Philosophy* 77, no. 8 (1980): 453–86.

[4] Norval Morris and David J. Rothman, *The Oxford History of the Prison: The Practice of Punishment in Western Society* (Oxford University Press, 1998).

Political time is deliberately accorded value by a diverse array of political theorists. The question of *why* durational time is singled out to play the parts that both ancient and modern thinkers assigned to it remains open. And the fact that time is pervasively treated as having value in political practice, and not just political theory, demands explanation. After all, many goods have instrumental and symbolic value and could be used to transact over rights, structure political decision-making, and serve related core political purposes. Property ownership can and has been used as a means to qualify people for rights. So too has birth into a politically privileged class.

There are five attributes of time that make it an ideal means for valuation and transacting over rights in liberal democratic states. These are: (1) ideas about time are embedded in contingent social circumstances and histories that are of particular relevance to the formation of national communities; (2) time can be scientifically measured and quantified; (3) time's quantification lends it an air of scientific objectivity and impartiality; (4) the connection of time's supposed impartiality with the appearance of fair, or even egalitarian political rules; (5) time is able to be both embedded and appear objective, while most other means of valuation are either one or the other.

The section that follows elaborates these four explanations of the importance of time and, in so doing, shows why procedures that feature durational time can serve as a hinge, flexibly connecting the embedded *demos* with its aspirations to fair treatment. This helps explain why durational time is such a common element of procedures for administering rights. It also raises questions about whether temporal valuations and measurements can fulfill any, let alone all, of these normative expectations.

Situated Political Time

The first attribute of scientifically measured time that makes it a likely candidate for valuation in politics is its situatedness. The other attributes of scientifically measured time: its quantifiability, its valence of impartiality and objectivity, and its purported egalitarianism, are all prerequisites for a liberal state. In order to erect liberal procedures in any realistically sized modern state, quantitative measures that can claim impartiality and egalitarianism are crucial. This leads Thomas M. Allen to conclude that, "time is highly differentiated, the medium for heterogeneous forms of economic and social organization."[5] The first attribute of time is not an outgrowth of the liberal state but rather of the embedded *demos* and its nation.

Time is the medium in which we experience democratic politics, develop as citizens, and forge ties to nations. Historian Lynn Hunt describes modern time schema as a dimension that is *"universal, homogenous,* and *deep."*[6] It is in expanses of measured time that the situated experiences, attachments, and characteristics of democratic citizens develop. Time is therefore a singular means via which particularistic *attributes, actions, and relationships* can be translated into rights-bearing statuses because it manages to simultaneously connote impartiality and context-specific meaning.

In Chapter 2, one way in which time becomes embedded in politically situated context was broached. Specific moments in time of special import come to form boundaries around polities while other temporal boundaries delineate rights-bearing parts of the population. But periods of durational time have even more potential to exhibit embeddedness. Benedict Anderson points out that shared temporal context, facilitated by the regularization of clock and calendrical time, was crucial to the development of the modern nation-state.[7] Anderson also writes, "The idea of a sociological organism moving calendrically through homogeneous, empty time is a precise analogue of the idea of the nation."[8] Time can seem tangible and yet does not hold out all of the constraints of a territorial border. Rainer Baübock asserts, "Cultural communities are more strongly anchored in historical time than space. Societies are territorial units more than historical ones. For polities, historical continuity and territorial boundaries are equally essential features."[9] The fact that

---

[5] *A Republic in Time: Temporality and Social Imagination in Nineteenth-Century America* (University of North Carolina Press, 2008), 41. Allen convincingly argues against scholars who have claimed that the temporal boundaries of the nation-state that developed in the eighteenth century enclosed timeless states in which no aristocratic legacy determined one's fate and no threat of corruption ensured one's demise. See Myra Jehlen, *American Incarnation: The Individual, the Nation, and the Continent* (Cambridge, MA: Harvard University Press, 1986), 253; and David W. Noble, *Death of a Nation: American Culture and the End of Exceptionalism* (University of Minnesota Press, 2002), 352, for discussions of the thesis of liberalism's claims to timelessness.

[6] *Measuring Time, Making History* (Budapest: Central European University Press, 2008), 25.

[7] *Imagined Communities: Reflections on the Origin and Spread of Nationalism* (London: Verso, 2006), 22.

[8] *Imagined Communities*, 26. Justin Muller points out that Anderson's use of time in this context is "Bergson's conception of the social role of time and space ... filtered through Benjamin." *Temporality of Political Obligation*, 27.

[9] "Sharing History and Future?" *Constellations* 4, no. 3 (1998), 320–45.

time has a special relationship to nationhood enhances the strength of national boundaries. Writing about the effect of the French Revolution on European identity, Peter Fritzsche proposed a dualist thesis about European identity in which shared context and differentiation were produced by the "specific temporal identity not unlike the feeling of generation, and separated or decoupled ... from their forebears two or three generations earlier."[10] Thomas M. Allen illustrates this process at work in eighteenth century America, writing that America made "time the medium for an effusive nationalism."[11] Indeed, in the US, the creation of four standardized time zones in 1883 was accomplished by railroad officials so that everyone would know what time it was, but served to bring people more fully together as a nation.

Even prior to European nation-states establishing hard boundaries, temporal orders were unavoidable markers of distinct political systems and their individual embeddedness. Each burgeoning nation-state had its own temporal order. David Landes notes that in the sixteenth and seventeenth centuries:

> Different countries and places began their day at different hours – some at sunrise, some at sunset, some at noon, some at midnight. Basel began at noon, but designated that as one o'clock, so that its clocks always ran an hour ahead of those of its neighbors. Some places divided the day into twenty-four consecutive hours (so-called Italian time); this was very hard on bell-ringing clocks. Others marked it into two rounds of twelve hours each ('German hours in Bohemia; 'French hours in France) ... [T]he experienced traveler never went abroad without his conversion tables. In the long run, of course, the needs of commerce and communication were such as to encourage standardization, and usage shifted gradually toward the diurnal pattern we know today.[12]

Davis interprets the work of Benedict Anderson as "undo[ing] periodization based upon feudalism and reinscrib[ing] it on the basis of 'absolutism.' These intertwined paradigms of periodization, however, both emerge from the doubling back of feudal historiography upon itself in an act of mapping sovereign boundaries onto a universalized chronology."[13] Eventually, in the late nineteenth century, states across

[10] *Stranded in the Present: Modern Time and the Melancholy of History* (Cambridge, MA: Harvard University Press, 2004), 53.
[11] *A Republic in Time: Temporality and Social Imagination in Nineteenth-Century America* (University of North Carolina Press, 2008), 23.
[12] *Revolution in Time: Clocks and the Making of the Modern World* (Cambridge, MA: Belknap Press of Harvard University Press, 1983), 94.
[13] Kathleen Davis, *Periodization and Sovereignty* (Philadelphia, PA: Pennsylvania University Press, 2008), 41.

the world would move toward the standardization of time, describing such decisions in the language of national security.[14] However this "global transformation of time" was a transformation of the measurement of time in the service of comparisons that only further highlighted contestation over national identities.[15]

It would require a vast digression to rehearse a survey of the literature in sociology and anthropology on the many forms of cultural time that correspond to as many societies, and in some cases even subcultures within societies. The subject of this chapter is politics and durational time, and in this section I seek only to make two points: that durations of time will have distinct meanings to the people who deploy those durations in the procedures that administer rights; and that those meanings allow time to represent political values in democratic procedures. If a *demos* seeks to impose a procedure for deciding who has demonstrated adequate loyalty, and time is serving as a proxy for loyalty, then a probationary period of time spent among a people or within a nation is associated with a panoply of cultural and social meaning. The same holds true for a period of punishment or a duration of time required to prove maturity.

Time as a Quantifiable Good

Not all forms of time are scientific or measurable, but the procedures referred to in this book have in common a reliance on a kind of time that can be measured and quantified. According to Ian Hacking, the English initiated the practices of political arithmetic in 1662, although in his telling the statistical state does not fully flower until the nineteenth century.[16] This development was presaged by Greek thinkers who had sought to systematize knowledge in the quest for human security well before the development of the modern state. As Nussbaum and Hursthouse noted of Plato's *Protagoras*, "And it would be natural that, confronted with a subject matter as confusing in its variety and indeterminacy as human valuation and choice, a thinker with an interest in order and progress should ask himself whether this area of our lives could be, or become, a science of measurement."[17] Hacking's is an account of how

---

[14] Vanessa Ogle, *The Global Transformation of Time: 1870–1950* (Cambridge, MA: Harvard University Press, 2015), 5.

[15] Ogle, *Global Transformation of Time*, 45.

[16] *The Taming of Chance* (Cambridge University Press, 1990), 16.

[17] Martha C. Nussbaum and Rosalind Hursthouse, "Plato on Commensurability and Desire," *Proceedings of the Aristotelian Society, Supplementary Volumes* 58 (1984): 57.

states seek to master chance through actuarial study and assessment of the population. Once inaugurated, political arithmetic became pervasive. We measure anything and everything, including things that may not initially appear to lend themselves to quantification. As the instruments that measure time scientifically become reliable, they are adopted pervasively by public authorities, including religious and state or state-like institutions.[18] Clocks and calendars appear in all manner of public places, and rules are made that refer to the measurements these instruments facilitate. Even before those instruments were very sophisticated, scientifically measured durations of time took on a singular importance in political thought. Plato emphasized two attributes of time: its measurability (it can be quantified and calculated) and its universality (it is common to all political subjects and processes). Both attributes remain significant to modern political theories that invoke time.

Quantifying the measure of something serves at least three functions that are politically salient. First, quantification creates a measurement that can be understood and applied universally. Math is a lingua franca. A loyalty oath will vary from country to country and perhaps even engender dispute in different regions of the same country. But a five-year waiting period for citizenship lacks the qualitative features of the oath about which there might be bitter dispute. Some may still disagree about whether five is the correct number of years to make someone prove their loyalty. But the disagreement between the person advocating three years and the person advocating five years is conducted using the same numeric terms. This contrasts with a debate in which someone thinks a loyalty oath should require swearing allegiance to god and another person thinks the loyalty oath should require swearing allegiance to the Constitution. Arguing over the quantity of time in a probationary period at least has the advantage of a common currency, so that the parties trying to create a procedure embodying the norms, processes, and relationships they prioritize are speaking the same language.

In Plato's telling, the possibility of measuring the variables that are central elements of goodness is irresistible. "Socrates evidently believes that . . . the urgency of our ethical difficulties requires the life-saving power of a *technē* of measurement. The relevance of a science of measurement to the resolutions of ethical disagreement and uncertainties is evident."[19]

---

[18] David S. Landes, *Revolution in Time: Clocks and the Making of the Modern World* (Cambridge, MA: Belknap Press of Harvard University Press, 1983).
[19] Nussbaum and Hursthouse, "Plato on Commensurability and Desire," 57.

Without it, our practical wisdom will be difficult to understand or apply in a systematic fashion. In particular, deliberations become difficult when we grow mired in particularities. In the absence of a science to organize our experiences, we cannot learn or gain insight. We will not be able to pick out important facts or patterns and turn our experience into wisdom. This limits people's ability to plan and live a good life.[20] Plato therefore argues for a science of ethics "that weighs and measures using a single standard ... Such a science needs a measure of value that will be single, ubiquitous, and relevant to the choices in question."[21] Because time can be subjected to the kind of scientific and mathematical treatment that Plato embraced, we find in the idea of experience, measured by time, a point of overlap between the position that embraces a science of decision and the position that rejects it. In fact, the idea of using one's experience over time to render judgments is akin to a science of probability and that science is only improved if generalizations are made from the experienced judgment of many people rather than just one.[22]

Second, a quantifiable measurement of vague or hard-to-identify qualities and relationships makes the intangible more tangible. Loyalty, reasonable maturity, or even the rehabilitation that we seek for convicted criminals are intangible states of mind, characteristics, and relationships that sometimes refer to a plethora of related characteristics, circumstances, and relationships. By representing them using quantities of scientifically measured time, they become more tangible than they would otherwise be. A number of years can be specified in a way that a state of mind cannot. In the example of an age of majority, a temporal threshold is used to embody the somewhat ineffable condition of maturity. Time is not the only embodiment of maturity that one could imagine, but it is widely deployed for this purpose because the processes of maturing occur in time, and temporal measures put the terms of maturation in the concrete and universally recognizable form of calendar years.

Third, quantification is important to the sciences of control and governmentality that develop along with the modern state. In this sense the state's reliance on quantitative measures of whether a criminal has paid their debt to society through a prison sentence, or whether someone has

[20] Martha Craven Nussbaum, *The Fragility of Goodness: Luck and Ethics in Greek Tragedy and Philosophy* (Cambridge University Press, 2001), vol. II, 298–9.
[21] Nussbaum and Hursthouse, "Plato on Commensurability and Desire," 58–9.
[22] John Greville Agard Pocock, *The Machiavellian Moment: Florentine Political Thought and the Atlantic Republican Tradition* (Princeton University Press, 2009), 23–4.

lived in a country long enough to qualify for social welfare rights, are part of a much larger turn toward the quantification of the science of politics. Temporal laws fit right in with the gathering of quantitative data about populations exemplified by the census or any number of other actuarial statistics for life expectancy, birth rates, disease manifestation, and so on. As many, myself included, have discussed and demonstrated, the development of the liberal state is a march toward the scrutinized and scientifically calculated life in which the state uses quantitative data about its population in order to govern efficiently. In this context, it would be a surprising aberration to find that rights and decision-making were not structured by any quantitative measure.

Time takes highly subjective, abstract, and qualitative processes and expresses them in highly precise, tangible, and quantifiable terms. These features make temporal measurements very useful proxies for character traits, processes, or relationships that are deemed important to politics. Units of time can effectively serve as political metrics. Using durations of time as proxies for value appears to enact liberal standards for fair treatment in procedural justice more faithfully than almost any other means of representing value in politics.

Quantifiable measures of qualitative experiences, relationships, and characteristics are therefore also important to the political process of commensuration. Commensuration is the "transformation of different qualities into a common metric."[23] All political systems require some kinds of commensuration, but liberalism takes on a special burden of reconciling differences within the population. Liberal politics aspires to offer a way in which people's differences can be reconciled to allow them to coexist and self-govern collectively.

To Plato, time is a resource whose instrumental universality facilitates commensuration among conflicting values. Plato notes, "a subject matter as confusing in its variety and indeterminacy as human valuation and choice" should whenever possible be subject to "a science of measurement."[24] He embraces the idea that conflicting values can be reconciled through a science of commensuration that relies on measurement. The fact that it is common to all political subjects allows it to translate otherwise abstract truths into precise, scientifically calculable terms. Marx's assertion that time becomes the universal measure of exchange value is rooted in a similar argument.

---

[23] Wendy Nelson Espeland and Mitchell L. Stevens, "Commensuration as a Social Process," *Annual Review of Sociology* 24 (1998): 314.

[24] Nussbaum and Hursthouse, "Plato on Commensurability and Desire," 57.

Capitalists cannot and prefer not to deal with differences in production. They need a quantifiable measure for exchange value. And they certainly cannot easily quantify effort, skill, or any of the other ways in which one might measure the work that goes into production. They converge on time – hours in which work is conducted – as a means of measuring the work that goes into the production of a commodity. Out of this way of thinking comes the idea of socially necessary labor time. Socially necessary labor time is the amount of time an average worker will require under average conditions to produce any given commodity. The cost of the labor for the production of the commodity is measured in time, which is in turn compensated in money. Time serves to measure and translate something abstract – labor – into concrete and regularized terms.

Barbara Adam describes the process thusly, "[T]ime is the decontextualized asituational abstract exchange value that allows work to be translated into money."[25] Work itself could be measured in various ways: effort, output, profit, etc. However, measuring work in units of time, often demarcated by uniform start-and-stop times as well as regularized quantities (e.g. the eight-hour day), mediates between the uniformity required by efficient capitalist production and the less regularized, lived experience of people doing and being paid for work.

Analogizing this insight about work and standardized temporality to observations about how time functions in politics is useful for understanding the value of political time, and ultimately for understanding how a political economy of time functions. The political value of time facilitates transactions over rights such as the according of rights to people upon reaching political maturity, or the denial of rights to people being punished for law-breaking. Using scientifically measured time to quantify and represent processes and traits, such as reason and citizenliness, citizenly relationships, loyalty, maturity, etc., mediates between the uniformity required by a government bureaucracy and the less regularized, lived experience of people actually engaged in political reason and other acts of citizenship. This makes the valuation of time and its use in procedures for granting rights, a process of commensuration. Commensuration allows us "to reduce and simplify disparate information into numbers that can be easily compared. This transformation allows people to quickly grasp, represent, and compare differences."[26] A politics that facilitates commensuration is the very kind of political system Plato envisioned

---

[25] *Time* (Cambridge, UK: Polity, 2004), 38.
[26] Espeland and Stevens, "Commensuration as a Social Process," 316.

when he stated that "a science of deliberative measurement would be an enormous advantage in human social life."[27]

I will return to the importance of temporal measurement in political commensuration in the chapter that follows. For now, it is enough to note that the turn toward reason, rational decision-making, and the pursuit of the good during the Enlightenment paved the way for durational time to be incorporated into liberal democratic thought. The explicit consensus of Enlightenment thinkers was that ethical knowledge can and should be systematized. Philosophers from the Encyclopedists to Mill sought to defend different means for producing and systematizing ethics. Voltaire was keen to find a procedure for weighing evidence that would make decision-making more scientific. It was in many ways a movement whose main thrust was to systematically identify the sources of human progress and excellence while also specifying the means for applying this science. Locke and Leibniz went further, and both claimed that for knowledge to be considered ethical, it must be mathematical.[28] Durational time is one of a few types of goods that could fulfill this mandate.

Objectivity and Impartiality

Implicit in the idea that a quantifiable science of ethics is desirable is the idea that scientifically measured goods impart politics with the kind of objectivity that liberalism seeks and purports to deliver. Time that is measured by scientific instruments is subject to natural laws rather than human laws, and is thus considered objective in comparison with ways of valuing that derive solely from human judgment. Even before calendars, clocks, and watches had realized their potential for associating time with scientific authority and global universalizability, Plato noted the scientific valence of time accorded it an air of objectivity and the potential to organize and control human activity: "The connection between numbering and knowing, the ability to count or measure and the ability to grasp, comprehend, or control, runs very deep in Greek thought about human cognition."[29] This was not solely a Greek preoccupation. Later, Cicero would conceive a similar relationship between deliberation, truth, and

---

[27] He also argued that commensuration was necessary for stabilizing our values in much the way that Condorcet sought to achieve. Nussbaum, *Fragility of Goodness*, 107.

[28] Nussbaum and Hursthouse, "Plato on Commensurability and Desire," 81.

[29] Nussbaum, *Fragility of Goodness*, 107.

time.[30] That which can be quantified is rational, objective, and impartial as opposed to the product of partial, subjective human judgment.

Scientifically measured time is time measured by mechanical instruments and lays claim to "dissociate time from human events."[31] It may not actually dissociate fully from human events, but in some ways we understand it as the product of natural laws, measured by machines that operate according to scientific principles, and free from human-made beliefs. Scientifically measured time cannot be made to pass more quickly or slowly by human intervention. Measured durational time exists apart from human influence and would continue in the absence of any particular human presence. The clock will keep ticking regardless of what an autocrat or a popular resistance says, regardless of whether a boundary is moved, and regardless of the conditions of the market. Property and territorial boundaries are established by people. Scientific time is neither created nor controlled by people. When US legislators created the rules governing who would be entitled to citizenship, they disagreed about the precise quantity of time that was appropriate for the task. But no one questioned whether a temporal procedure was tainted by human bigotry. One's race, one's property, and one's gender were qualitative and subjective measures of character prone to generating at least some argument. Time stands apart from those measures and appears untainted by subjective human origins.

Our knowledge that scientific time operates independent from human influence allows us to infer that procedures using time to represent or measure traits, experiences, relationships, etc., and then to transact over rights, can also be objective. This doesn't mean that the transactions themselves will be objective. It just means that the *use of time* in this way will not automatically compromise the objectivity of the procedure in the same way that the use of one's lineage or one's net worth would. The objectivity of scientifically measured time can cast an aura of objectivity on temporal valuations whether or not such valuations have any claim to objectivity.

Egalitarianism

Because scientifically measured time appears objective, laws and policies that invoke time also often appear to be egalitarian procedures distributing

---

[30] Nadia Urbinati, *Representative Democracy: Principles and Genealogy* (University of Chicago Press, 2006), 2852.

[31] Lewis Mumford and Langdon Winner, *Technics and Civilization* (University of Chicago Press, 2010), 15.

liberal rights. Objectivity has a special place in liberal theory that is intimately connected to egalitarianism. Kantian and neo-Kantian liberalism both require starting from a position of objectivity and reasoning toward egalitarianism.

The most salient attribute of scientifically measured durational time that lends it the appearance of being egalitarian is the fact that, unlike other goods that could be used as proxies in politics, time is available to everyone, and its availability is not directly subject to human decisions or laws. In the language of economics, this view of durational time classifies it as a "free good" in contrast to a "positional good" whose value changes depending on the consumption of others. This classification leads political philosophers such as Michael Sandel to make the assumption that temporal rules are fairer and more egalitarian than other types of rules. Many attributes of time give it a guise of egalitarianism that money and property, among the many other bases for rights, lack. Scientifically measured time passes at the same rate regardless of one's social status or birthright. Scientific time cannot be bequeathed intergenerationally in a way that would preserve a legal class hierarchy. It also cannot be bought. Unlike money, property, aristocratic birth, or even faith, everyone has time. A prison sentence, an age of maturity, or even an electoral cycle uses a metric for measuring value that is universally accessible and a good that is universally available. It would be difficult to appropriate the political time of one group for use by another. If every citizen is allowed a period of deliberation between a political party's primary and the general election, it is hard to imagine that time being taken from one voter or group of citizens for use by another. In this context, time appears incorruptible. Thinking about time and corruption hearkens to Pocock's formulation of *virtu*. He pointed out that in early modern politics a shift occurred in which the converse of *virtu* changed from *fortuna* to corruption.[32] Secular political time is the time of *virtu*. In Pocock's thinking, a temporally ordered republic can ward off corruption, in part because it is not as readily subjected to corrupting practices as is a political system in which birthright or property are used as proxies for political values. I will return to whether this is actually true. However, compared to other goods that might stand in for fitness for citizenship or good judgment, time *appears* to be more equally distributed and less corruptible.

[32] *Machiavellian Moment*, 405.

Furthering the air of egalitarianism that scientific time takes on is the fact that in a state all people exist together in the same time. Much as math is a lingua franca, so too is time itself. We can see the seeds of a common form of political time develop in Enlightenment French politics. In 1792, the recently founded French Republic started political time over, imposing an entirely new calendar and means of measuring time on the population as a way to demarcate the end of the monarchy and the creation of a sovereign citizenry. This made calendrical time an early means with which to transcend laws and practices that establish class, caste, and clan. In some ways the creation of the FRC bears a similarity to *Calvin's Case* insofar as both sovereign states identified a zero-option point at which subjecthood commenced. But the FRC went one step further than *Calvin's Case* and offers insight into how Enlightenment philosophy reshaped temporal law for the purposes of liberal democracy rather than monarchy. *Calvin's Case* predicated subjecthood on allegiance via birthright rather than the consent of equally situated citizens. This placed subjects into a hierarchical relationship between the sovereign above them and those whose time of birth did not qualify for subjecthood below them. Unlike their British forebears, the use of time by the French bore the imprint of burgeoning Enlightenment egalitarian norms that were absent from Coke's jurisprudence.

Sharing a political temporality made it possible for people whose social classes and religious memberships were not equal or identical to have equal political weight.[33] Instead of placing people into a hierarchical relationship with their ancestors, the FRC placed them into horizontal relationships of shared time with their countrymen. Sharing a temporal context held at least as much potential as did sharing a territorial context. This is evident in Sylvain Marechal's influential almanac, whose calendar was a precursor to the FRC, and which the FRC eventually adopted. "Marechal is able to represent this common or lived experience of time as if ... it emanated from the rational measure of time itself."[34] People never inhabit the exact same space, but all living countrymen can inhabit the same moment. For the French, a traditional way of measuring time was exchanged for a modern rational calendar, wiping out the *ancien regime* and paving the way for reason to replace royal authority. Sensory knowledge, including how people sense time, affected thought. Hence,

---

[33] Sanja Perovic, *The Calendar in Revolutionary France: Perceptions of Time in Literature, Culture, Politics* (Cambridge University Press, 2012), 47.

[34] Perovic, *Calendar in Revolutionary France*, 46.

rational measures of time (such as a metric calendar) could produce rational thought and rational citizens. In particular, proportions of time and regular time measurement were significant to this process.[35]

Revolutionary-era French politicians hoped that imposing a new calendar would bolster a political regime whose explicitly stated purpose was to transcend legally established class boundaries and treat all citizens as equals. Whereas in early modern politics a legal class system had been justified by reference to its stabilizing effect, now that the "Machiavellian Moment" had passed and open-ended calendrical time was treated as a medium for stability rather than instability, secular shared temporality could supersede hierarchical legal classes. We can also infer a similar point from Jefferson's insistence that future generations not be governed by past generations. Such despotism recreates hierarchical relations by denying an equal voice to the living and overemphasizing the decisions of the dead. In fact, only people sharing a temporal context, living together in the same time, can be each other's political equal.

The claims that scientifically measured political time is both impartial and egalitarian are enhanced by the fact that this form of political valuation is explicitly secular. The preceding chapter identified a break between politics and non-secular forms of time that allowed secular sovereigns to exist and secular states to develop. This isn't to say that religious power brokers do not engage in power politics on the terms set by scientific time. Indeed, an idea of political time was essential to the conversion of Calvinist theological values into the basis for liberal individualist politics.[36] The key transition required treating a certain portion of non-work and non-worship time as deliberative democratic capital and not as simple leisure, itself anathema to the sober-minded industrious individual. Political time to the Calvinist stands in contrast to Aristotelian leisure. In order for the Calvinist to justify leaving off of worship or productive work, political time had to be demarcated from potentially indolent and materially unproductive leisure. But political time was also decidedly not the time of worship and, even framed in terms that a Calvinist could accommodate, it was secular. It contained no barrier or religious test that would deny access to politics to a non-Calvinist or non-believer, a fact that was important to establishing a politics based on toleration as the US founders sought to do.

---

[35] See William Max Nelson, *The Weapon of Time: Constructing the Future in France, 1750 to Year I* (University of California Press, 2006), esp. 259–60.
[36] Landes, *Revolution in Time*, 92.

The Calvinist adaptation of secular time was important to institutionalizing the rationalist deist commitments of the US founders. Condorcet was a deist, as were Jefferson, Madison, Paine, and Franklin, among others. Scientific time was for them an extension of the laws of nature. In addition to suggesting the analogy of a distant clockmaker god, scientifically measured time was an excellent proxy for the values the founders sought to realize through politics. Jefferson's obsession with time and timekeeping was well known, as was Franklin's concern with the use of time. In each case, to read their discussions of time is to read about industriousness, balance, and proportion, rather than life, death, and salvation. In advocating for an immigrant probationary period, Jefferson and his peers were not invoking divine authority, but rather a secular standard by which the fitness for citizenship of people of any faith, or no faith at all, could be measured. Electoral cycles established to ensure responsive and stable representative government were not superstitious numerology. They were approximations about good decision-making made by political philosophers and social scientists who sought to realize secular and rationalist Enlightenment norms through political institutions.

It is important to not lose sight of the fact that time is only being posited as *appearing* objective and egalitarian. As the next chapter will discuss in detail, temporal laws and policies are often neither objective nor egalitarian. But the assumption that they are both is often enough to enhance their appeal. This intuition, whether correct or incorrect, makes temporal rules far easier to justify and impose than rules that trigger intuitions about unfairness and impartiality.

Time as Janus-faced

The final point to observe about the qualities that make time such an ideal means of representing political value is that the preceding list of attributes – situatedness, quantifiability, universality, egalitarianness – are not traits that many other goods embody. In particular, the idea that something can appear situated and universal at the same time puts time among a very small group of Janus-faced goods whose properties morph along such a wide spectrum. Generally, what is situated is by definition not universal or objective, and what is objective or universal cannot be situated. But one of the paradoxes of political time is that it simultaneously draws on a version of time that is attributed to scientific rather than human-made laws, and on attributes of time that are social creations. Here I blur the distinction between ostensibly "timeless" liberal political structures and those in which time justifies or legitimates, instead showing that time is used for legitimation in both forms of authority.[37]

The omnipresence of durational time in the procedures that address a liberal democracy's most fundamental rights is the outcome of an intuition, often unarticulated, that scientifically measured durational time is a more impartial and egalitarian means to measure and represent processes, values, traits, and relationships than almost any other means. This is only a belief: there are good reasons to question whether scientifically measured durational time is a fair, impartial, or egalitarian means for administering rights. In fact, it would be impossible for political time to be both situated, as we see that it is, and neutral, as a claim of impartiality suggests. However even an assumption of neutrality associated with scientifically measured durational time – facial neutrality – is significant. These two ways of thinking are in tension. I will explore these tensions by asking which of time's Janus faces, the impartial egalitarian or the situated, becomes the face of the political economy of time. But before turning to that, the next chapter elaborates further on how the political economy of time, and in particular the process of commensuration, works.

CONCLUSION

Temporal boundaries carve sovereign borders that bound both states and nations. Inside these boundaries are peoples: groups of persons in political relationships with each other and with the state. Peoplehood itself is created by multiple complex forces including temporality. The time identified by multiple temporal boundaries – durational time – holds even greater potential for enacting political procedures. It becomes a political good by virtue of its relationship to political processes, and in particular those associated with democratic processes of reasoning, deliberation, learning, and development that yield consent.

The institutionalization of procedures that treat durational time as a political good reveal that time has been accorded political value. Individuals' time has been accorded political value just as surely as capitalism vests individuals' time with monetary value. Political time is a good that political theorists can analyze in several ways. Temporal formulae will reveal normative valuation in a political system. And the way in which

[37] Melissa Lane, "Political Theory and Time," in *Time in Contemporary Political Thought*, ed. P.J.N. Baert (1st edn, Amsterdam: Elsevier, 2000), 235–9 (surveying the history of treating time as a universal showing the transition from Plato's).

these formulae are constructed and applied merits serious consideration. Just as many other attributes of procedural justice warrant interrogation, the ways in which politics treats the political time of citizens reveals volumes. In order to evaluate how egalitarian a political system is, we will need to assess how it treats the time of its population. To do this in systematic fashion requires understanding how the temporal side of politics operates. While the topics of equal treatment and what equal treatment entails are among the most well-covered topics in political theory, their relationship to durational time has not received much sustained attention despite the fact that durational time is so ubiquitous in procedures for administering rights. This means that important related questions of political justice are not being raised or discussed as thoroughly as others. In the preceding chapter, territorial sovereignty was shown to vest single moments with authority. The current chapter described a process through which time comes to be valued, and through which power is democratized by spreading it across time – both by pacing decision-making and by vesting the time of individual citizens with authority. In the chapter that follows I pick up the idea that time has a special role in liberal democratic states and explore how that becomes manifest. This will allow further normative analysis of how temporal transactions are structured and what are their consequences.

5

The Political Economy of Time

INTRODUCTION

The claims made in this book thus far have been descriptive. They also fulfill the edict that social science should describe ordinary and even obvious human activity in ways that offer insight into the causes, consequences, and meaning of social and political life. This chapter begins in that vein, by delving more deeply into the nature of temporal formulae and the ways in which procedural justice is effected using time as a medium of exchange. Having established that durational time is a political good with special importance in procedures for distributing rights, and having attributed both intrinsic and representational value to durational time in politics, this chapter looks more closely at how liberal democratic states and their citizens transact over power using precise durations of time. And it explores the normative consequences of expressing qualitative traits, experiences, relationships, etc., in the quantitative terms of measured durational time.

The chapter proceeds in two sections. The first extends the analysis presented in the previous chapter, arguing that if time is a good with political value, then we can call the system of political transactions in which time is a means of exchange through which rights are earned or forfeited a *political economy of time*. The chapter offers a brief genealogy of the mode of thought that produces a political economy of time and identifies the outcome as being forms of commensuration. We can gain insight into the implications of representing various politically relevant processes using quantities of time from this analogy. Time becomes a medium of exchange in politics because durational time is uniquely situated with respect to procedures of commensuration. However, commensuration is regarded by some thinkers as both overly reductive and tethered to a corrosive form of market logic. The chapter evaluates both of these claims and argues that commensuration is vulnerable to some but not all of these critiques. In addition, commensuration is critical to governing in the context of the state because it is efficient and essential to forging agreements among decision-makers with different normative stances. Temporal commensuration in particular is able to wring procedural solutions from contradictory points of view because of the different types of meaning attributed to time discussed in the preceding chapter.

The second part of the chapter pushes on the normative claims alluded to in Chapter 4. Part of the explanation offered for the ubiquity of temporal formulae is the fact that scientifically measured time is quantifiable and has the air of an impartial and even egalitarian means for conducting politics. Yet, it is also true that ideas about time are often deeply embedded in very situated political histories. Time cannot simultaneously be neutral or impartial and situated or embedded. This insight spurs further interrogation of whether temporal procedures, or at least the temporal element of procedures that confer or deny rights, can be fair, impartial, or egalitarian. And, if they can be so, are they actually fair, impartial, or egalitarian in practice? Ultimately, the chapter concludes by questioning two long-standing critiques of commensuration: that commensuration is reductive, and that it introduces normatively corrosive market practices into spheres of politics that ought to remain free from commodification. The discussion points to the unique advantages of temporal formulae. But it also identifies the dark side of temporal commensuration, as evidenced by instances in which some people's political time is devalued or accorded no value at all. This contradicts an implicit belief that scientifically measured durational time is an egalitarian medium of exchange. The devaluation of a group or individual's political time reflects skepticism about their moral worth. Practices that devalue people's time significantly weaken the case for using time rather than money, property, or birthright as a medium of exchange in procedures for according people rights.

THE POLITICAL ECONOMY OF TIME

Durational time is a good that has been accorded political value. The preceding chapter explored the nature of the value that time acquires in procedures that distribute rights in liberal democracies. This value becomes essential to innumerable procedures for determining who is eligible for which rights, and for the administration of those rights in liberal democratic states. Chapter 4 also enumerated the reasons that time works well as a proxy for normative standards that are not quantifiable. Time's political value becomes apparent when one considers the many and varied rights formulae that include a temporal qualification.

Similar to the way Marx showed how wage labor remunerates work based on the quantity of time spent performing work, many political formulae measure fitness for rights based on quantities of time. Just as time acquires an entirely new form of value once it becomes the medium of exchange in a labor-based economy, so too does time acquire a new form of value once it becomes the medium of exchange in a rights-based politics. This political economy of time lends a transaction-like cast to political procedures that normative theorists like Michael Sandel and Michael Walzer would have us believe ought never be transactions.[1] (I explore the transactional nature of the political economy of time in greater detail later in the chapter.) Liberal democratic states create equations that use time and other variables to formulaically confer and deny rights to political subjects. Prison sentences, immigration probationary periods, social security eligibility, abortion requirements, and many other rights-related procedures invoke formulae in which time plays a fundamental role in granting or retracting rights.

Temporal equations are remarkably elastic political tools. Because they can incorporate multiple variables and many kinds of variables, they can make nearly surgical distinctions about rights. For example, for a long time US and Canadian law imposed different ages of consent on penile–vaginal intercourse and homosexual sodomy as a means of privileging heterosexuality.[2] The US privileges immigrants who are married to citizens or perform military service by offering them a temporal "credit" of two years, making their immigration probationary period three rather than five years in total. Immigrants from Cuba, asylees, members of the military, and various other exceptional individuals all benefit from a lower temporal cost for citizenship. Similarly, apportionment in the US is aligned with the decennial schedule for the census but courts have begun to question the wisdom of continuing to count (for the purposes of

---

[1] See Michael J. Sandel, *What Money Can't Buy: The Moral Limits of Markets* (London: Penguin, 2012); Michael Walzer, *Spheres of Justice: A Defense of Pluralism and Equality* (New York: Basic Books, 1983). Debra Satz draws similar conclusions to Walzer and Sandel, albeit on different grounds. See Debra Satz, *Why Some Things Should Not Be for Sale: The Moral Limits of Markets* (Oxford University Press, 2010).

[2] Eugene Volokh, "Statutory Rape Laws and Statutory Consent Laws in the U.S.," *Washington Post* (May 1, 2015), www.washingtonpost.com/news/volokh-conspiracy/wp/2015/05/01/statutory-rape-laws-in-the-u-s/?utm_term=.0b291c845d52. Many other countries impose gendered and sexualized distinctions as well. "Age of Consent Position Statement," Canadian Federation for Sexual Health (archived July 11, 2011), https://web.archive.org/web/20110714075413/www.cfsh.ca/What-We-Do/Archived-Position-Statements/Age-of-Consent.aspx

apportionment) people incarcerated for very short periods of time.[3] And the standard term of service required for participation in the military's Reserve Officer Training Corps (ROTC) program, eight years, can be reduced for members selected for the "Green to Gold" program that trains officers for careers in the military. Different temporal arrangements are made for non-scholarship trainees.[4] These and other formulaic approaches to the distribution of rights among a population offer precision, but also import a set of norms into democratic politics that many find objectionable, or at least worthy of interrogation.

There are temporal equations that use time and circumstance to approximate marriage vows (common-law marriage), the legal transfer of property (adverse possession), the legal adulthood of people accused of heinous crimes, the deterioration of evidence in a criminal case, eligibility for retirement in an array of professions (police, military, teaching), and social security as well as myriad other statuses and rights. Temporal equations are so pervasive that it is difficult not to take them for granted. However, this means of transacting over rights is ubiquitous in modernity. And, although it is not confined to modern politics, it is particularly well suited to modernity.

Time in Governmentality, Political Economy, and Market Logic

Although the idea that time could have political value is pre-modern, governmental logic fuses together the ideas of temporal value and political economy in a distinctly modern sophisticated political economy of time. The political potential of time has been common knowledge since the ancients considered temporality. We see this when we examine the ancient belief that leisure time qualified people for citizenship.[5] What changes in modernity are the means for measuring time and novel means for conducting politics. Governmental and market-based thought intersect with new technologies and the age-old awareness of the political power of time. Time causes none of this nor are the new technologies causal mechanisms. But, as historians such as David Landes and E.P.

[3] New York Times Editorial Board, "The Wrong Way to Count Prisoners," *New York Times* (July 15, 2016), www.nytimes.com/2016/07/16/opinion/the-wrong-way-to-count-prisoners.html?_r=o; *Davidson* v. *City of Cranston*, No. 14-91L (DRI May 24, 2016).
[4] "Army ROTC Service Commitment," US Army, www.goarmy.com/rotc/service-commitment.html
[5] Aristotle, *The Politics*, ed. Stephen Everson (Cambridge University Press, 1996), Books II.11, VII.9.

Thompson have chronicled, modern technologies of timekeeping enable
ideological changes on a scale that was previously inconceivable.[6]

The origins of political economy that Foucault describes in his genealogy of governmentality foreshadow the leakage of the market and market
logic into political structures that pave the way for the development of
a political economy of time.

Foucault's definition of governmentality begins by identifying it as:

> [T]he ensemble formed by the institutions, procedures, analyses and reflections,
> the calculations and tactics that allow the exercise of this very specific albeit
> complex form of power, which has as its target population, as its principle form
> of knowledge, political economy, and as its essential technical means apparatuses
> of security.[7]
>
> The art of government ... is essentially concerned with answering the question
> of how to introduce economy – that is to say, the correct manner of managing
> individuals' goods and wealth within a family ... and of making the family
> fortunes prosper – how to introduce this meticulous attention of the father
> towards his family into the management of the state.[8]
>
> ... The art of government is just the art of exercising power in the form and
> according to the model of the economy.[9]

Foucault deploys the phrase "political economy" to mean a politics in
which efficiency, rationality, and other characteristics of economy are
rescaled and applied to the work of governing. In such a context,
a political economy of time is a logical outgrowth of the drive toward
efficiency and rationality. This is not because it directly accomplishes the
goal of managing politics in the manner of a family; in fact, Foucault says
that eventually the family becomes the object rather than the model for
government. Instead, the political economy of time reflects a move toward
a science of politics in which the exercise of power is modeled on economics whenever possible. As Foucault observes, this translates into governing
in ways that are "convenient," and in which law becomes a multiform
tactic to achieve various means and ends.[10] Foucault is describing the
redefinition of government as a process of rationalizing rule over people in
order to wrest power away from religious authorities.

---

[6] David S. Landes, *Revolution in Time: Clocks and the Making of the Modern World*
(Cambridge, MA: Belknap Press of Harvard University Press, 2000); E.P. Thompson,
"Time, Work–Discipline, and Industrial Capitalism," *Past & Present* 38, no. 1 (1967):
56–97.

[7] Michel Foucault, *The Foucault Effect: Studies in Governmentality*, eds. Graham Burchell,
Colin Gordon, and Peter Miller (University of Chicago Press, 1991), 102.

[8] Ibid., 92.   [9] Ibid.   [10] Ibid., 95.

The process Foucault describes crystallizes in the late sixteenth and early seventeenth centuries, and fully flowers in the eighteenth century, alongside capitalism. English economist and philosopher Sir William Petty is credited with inventing the concept of "political arithmetic" in the seventeenth century. Petty was concerned with reducing risk, budgeting, fiscal policy, and collecting and deploying demographic data: many of the subjects of Foucault's analysis. But the concept of political arithmetic became shorthand for the movement away from determinism and toward the deployment of actuarial sciences that would allow burgeoning states to assess, govern, and ultimately control their populations. It was the realization of what Hobbes had said politics must do: tame the future.[11]

Security came to be located in that which is denumerable. Censuses became more complex and were joined by numerous other forms of studying the population that were geared toward quantifying the phenomena that secured or endangered the population. The idea of a census or a study of public health was not brand new, but each matured during the turn to modernity. So too did some of the most universally recognized temporal equations. For example, Foucault's *Discipline and Punish* chronicles in agonizing detail the transformation of criminal sentences from punishments meted out in pain and exotic forms of death to the development of prisons where inmates served temporal sentences meted out in precise units of time.[12] Historians of imprisonment note that the practice of temporal punishment is so pervasive that it is difficult for many people to even imagine a criminal justice system without the prison at its center.[13] This is despite the fact that, for most of human history, criminal justice meant exile, torture, or death rather than prison time. As Foucault documents, the transformation of punishment occurred in the much larger context of temporal control through which the time of all political subjects, starting with very young school children, was structured by the state with the goal of creating a maximally efficient population.[14] This quantification of human life took place at the same time as the flowering of

---

[11] On the idea of colonizing the future, see William Max Nelson, *The Weapon of Time: Constructing the Future in France, 1750 to Year I* (University of California Press, 2006), 102 and esp. ch. 4, 218–69.

[12] The book opens with a famous description of drawing and quartering but within the first ten pages Foucault has moved to a description of a highly efficient prison where convicted criminals lead orderly lives and are productive workers. *Discipline and Punish: The Birth of the Prison* (New York: Vintage, 1979), 1–9.

[13] Norval Morris and David J. Rothman, *The Oxford History of the Prison: The Practice of Punishment in Western Society* (Oxford University Press, 1998), vii.

[14] See Foucault, *Discipline and Punish*, esp. pt. 3, no. 2 "The Means of Correct Training."

capitalist markets, causing more than one observer to note congruence between the market economy and the political economy.[15]

In this light, it is not difficult to see how or why political economies of time took root and flourished. For the administration of large liberal states whose populations require procedural efficiency, quantification is essential. Liberal states are less bounded than small kingdoms and republics. A modern state requires highly efficient means to punish, naturalize, or to demonstrate the maturity of citizens. This efficiency, in turn, requires quantification and precision. If durational time has value, and can be precisely measured using scientific instruments, its value as a proxy is not just approximate: it is precisely calculated. This was expressly what Plato advocated with his idea of *technē*. The temporal equations described in this book are very efficient, precise procedures for translating ineffable political qualities, processes, and relationships into concrete statuses that can be easily governed. They embody the actuarial spirit that Foucault describes, and that Petty and his peers sought. It is also not difficult to see why the political economy of time became so tightly woven into liberal democracies as they developed. The establishment of citizenship in the US was an opportune moment and context in which to create a political economy of time that operated within a liberal democracy. Using clocks and calendars to make observable measurements of reason and consent dovetailed with the beliefs of the deist and rationalist founding fathers. Like Locke, they were inclined toward empiricism even in the realm of political norms. Furthermore, the founding occurred in a larger context of burgeoning unitization and measurement. During this period both states and individuals were starting to conceive of a secular political time that could shape political relationships.[16] As noted earlier, the eighteenth-century foundation of the National Debt in England marked the transformation that allowed an entire society to start extending credit for future actions based upon actuarial evaluations of the past.[17] Similarly, offering a permanent political status (citizenship) to people willing to demonstrate a personal history of commitment to the country and its

---

[15] The observation is perhaps made at greatest length by Marx but is a staple of studies of the history of political economy. See David McNally, *Political Economy and the Rise of Capitalism: A Reinterpretation* (University of California Press, 1988).

[16] Benedict Anderson, *Imagined Communities: Reflections on the Origin and Spread of Nationalism* (London: Verso, 2006), 46–55.

[17] John Greville Agard Pocock, *Virtue, Commerce, and History: Essays on Political Thought and History, Chiefly in the Eighteenth Century* (Cambridge University Press, 1976), vol. II, 98–9, 112.

political system by living there for a period of years extends rights to people based on an assessment of their past using a quantitative measure.[18] Conversely, a prison sentence demands a person serve time for behavior that renders them unfit for full citizenship rights.

As Chapter 3 has documented, a consensual democracy such as the US, operating within the confines of a large modern state, requires a way to assess and measure consent and fitness for rights, among other elements of democratic citizenship. The judges who established temporal citizenship rules for the US had a plethora of existing means for demonstrating and even documenting consent, several of which were already widely in use. Oaths of allegiance, to take one example, would have been far more direct, concrete, and active expressions of consent for a population that had been divided against itself.[19] While an oath is regarded by some to be an actual transformation of consciousness, there are competing views on whether or not such overt verbal promises are effective predictors of future behavior.[20] More appropriate to the development of large-scale liberal democracies would be forms of political arithmetic that could be applied universally, required no recourse to subjective judgment, and which would work efficiently for large populations. This did not necessarily mean discarding oaths or any other qualitative measures of fitness for rights. But it did mean adopting practices that embodied the new spirit of uniformity and efficiency that had swept both the economies and politics of developing liberal democracies. As late as the twentieth century, while Taylorist principles of scientific management were conceived and honed, temporal schema evolved. Time management and scientific time-study further and further segmented different processes, encouraging people to "act in accordance with their *true* interests."[21] Both supporters and critics of scientific time management saw this as a political and moral practice.[22]

---

[18] The opposite logic applies to sentencing criminal offenders in the US. Prison sentences are calculated using a formula that retracts rights for a precise period of a person's future based on an actuarial assessment of their past behavior. A career criminal with multiple felony offenses will receive a longer sentence than a first-time offender who committed the same act.

[19] Jean Bodin, *Bodin: On Sovereignty*, ed. Julian H. Franklin (Cambridge University Press, 1992).

[20] Sanford Levinson, "Constituting Communities through Words that Bind: Reflections on Loyalty Oaths," *Michigan Law Review* 84 (June 1986): 1448, 1459.

[21] Ruth W. Grant, *Strings Attached: Untangling the Ethics of Incentives* (Princeton University Press, 2011), 19.

[22] Ibid., 20.

Commensuration and Political Time

The political economy of time can claim uniformity and efficiency because it is essentially a process of commensuration. As mentioned in passing in the preceding chapter, commensuration is the means through which qualities are transformed into quantities.[23] Put differently, commensuration begins when something that is qualitative, and possibly intangible, is represented using a quantitative measure. Commensuration allows comparisons of things that in their original form might seem impossible to compare. Choosing rationally requires that different facets of value be transposed onto a single plane in the unique way achieved by commensuration.[24] Wendy Espeland describes this as a process in which "[c]ommensuration renders all forms of difference as a matter of more or less rather than of kind."[25] Commensuration also standardizes comparisons and other procedures by using proxies for things that are difficult to specify.[26] It simplifies things that are intangible and disparate by representing them quantitatively and in a way that uses a common measure.[27] Commensuration occurs in economic markets, when monetary values are placed on goods that would otherwise be impossible to value in comparison with one another. The embodiment of traits, relationships, and processes using a precise duration of time is another instance of commensuration.

The fact that time serves as a metric for acts of commensuration was foreshadowed in Chapter 4's discussion of Marx's observation that time becomes a universal measure of exchange value. In production, a common standard for expressing work is important for circumventing the irregularities of effort, skill, or the other ways one might measure work's value. This is a prime example of commensuration. So too are the uses of durational time that are the subject of this book. An age of maturity or

---

[23] See Wendy Nelson Espeland and Mitchell L. Stevens, "Commensuration as a Social Process," *Annual Review of Sociology* 24 (1998): 316 ("Commensuration transforms qualities into quantities").

[24] Ibid., 323.

[25] Wendy Nelson Espeland and Michael Sauder, *Engines of Anxiety: Academic Rankings, Reputation, and Accountability* (New York: Russell Sage Foundation, 2016), 29.

[26] Espeland and Stevens, "Commensuration as a Social Process," 316.

[27] See ibid. ("[Commensuration] is a way to reduce and simplify disparate information into numbers that can be easily compared. This transformation allows people to quickly grasp, represent, and compare differences. One virtue of commensuration is that is offers standardized ways of constructing proxies for uncertain and elusive qualities. Another virtue is that it condenses and reduces the amount of information people have to process, which is useful for representing value and simplifying decision-making").

a prison sentence treats a quantity of time as commensurate with the lived political experiences and processes that a society decides are important to becoming qualified to hold full rights of citizenship (maturity), or to satisfying an appropriate punishment (prison sentence). It is nearly impossible to imagine a modern state functioning without those kinds of quantitative measures of processes that are, at heart, qualitative. Chapter 4 discussed why time is a likely proxy in liberal democracies. Time has the appearance of universality, impartiality, availability, and quantifiability. These attributes of measured durational time also make it a good tool for commensuration.

The Political Purpose of Commensuration

There are at least three categories of political dilemmas for which commensuration processes are absolutely essential. The first arises because values are generally incommensurable. The normative scaffolding of any polity is riddled with values and ideas that can't readily be measured in political practice. Equality, toleration, and liberty are all normative standards for which there is no obvious single metric. How, then, is a polity to know with any certainty when it is egalitarian, tolerant, or free? One of the most challenging tasks for people thinking about or making policy is to figure out which circumstances signal equality, toleration, liberty, etc., and then forge a path toward achieving those circumstances. In the process of so doing, equality may be defined as the condition of having a decent education, favorable work prospects, and a fair shot at meeting one's basic needs. Or it could be defined as the provision of those basic needs. In either case, those circumstances can be translated into quantitative terms that more abstract notions such as equality cannot. In the US, an education is typically achieved by completing sixteen years of public schooling and passing standardized tests; work prospects are evidenced by a low unemployment rate; a fair shot at meeting one's basic needs requires affordable housing, healthcare, etc. Each of these standards for equality can now be represented using quantitative data. The same kind of translation could be performed for toleration or liberty or any other value. That which cannot be measured is made measurable by representing it using a quantitative metric. The metric may be temporal (sixteen years of public schooling) but it certainly will not always refer to time, as is the case with a general equivalency degree. What is important is that the metric allows the state to create and apply uniform standards for the fulfillment of normative mandates.

The second political dilemma that commensuration addresses is conflict among foundational norms. This was broached briefly in the preceding chapter. Democracy and liberalism are in conflict with one another. The liberal norms that compel us to make decisions in an impartial and egalitarian fashion are directly opposed to the ethical situated democratic norms that demand a bounded *demos*.[28] There is no way to simultaneously be impartial and partial, to be unbounded and bounded. Commensuration cannot solve this problem, but it can facilitate situational compromises. For example, if we decide that the standard for membership in the *demos* can be represented by eighteen years of maturation within a society, and we decide that adults who live in the society for five years have demonstrated adequate citizenliness to overcome their foreign birth, then we have reconciled the imperative to bound the *demos* with the imperative to not consign all foreign-born persons to permanent semi-citizenship. The 18-year-olds who reach membership in the *demos* through maturation will be embedded in the *nomos* of the polity via a quantity of time, just as the people who complete a probationary period prior to naturalizing will have transcended their foreignness via a quantity of time as well. Citizenliness has thus been expressed in a temporal quantitative metric, and a compromise has been forged.

Further exacerbating the consequences of incommensurable values and conflict between different norms is disagreement about which values should govern or take precedence over others. In cases of disagreement about normative hierarchies, commensuration can do more than just pave the way for normative compromises. It can also provide "cover." In thinking back to the deliberations over naturalization procedures in the US, the multiple parties to the discussion held divergent views about which qualities would-be citizens should exhibit. In this case, creating a metric for the purpose of commensuration made it possible for each of the deliberators to associate a different personal quality with the probationary period they were imposing on would-be citizens. Because multiple processes can occur in the same period of time, it is conceivable that one might develop loyalty, shed prejudices, and become civically knowledgeable at the same time. The probationary period sidestepped a discussion of which of those (or other) citizenly traits was most important in a way that a qualitative measure of fitness for citizenship could not.

---

[28] Elizabeth F. Cohen, *Semi-Citizenship in Democratic Politics* (Cambridge University Press, 2009).

Part of the reason that the commensuration exhibited in temporal political formulae can facilitate normative compromise is that political formulae allow the inclusion of multiple standards for determining who can qualify for which rights. It is not just the case that multiple processes can occur in any given period of time, and that different people will believe that different processes are occurring in the same duration of time. It is also the case that time pairs comfortably with other variables that might be included in a political formula. A simple formula, such as an age of maturity, includes only one variable. But a naturalization formula is far more complex, allowing for the inclusion of a loyalty oath, a civics test, the evaluation of someone's character, and even an interview. This isn't unique to time, but it bears mention because the question of whether temporal formulae are overly reductive will be raised in the section that follows the next.

Commensuration and Incompletely Theorized Agreements

Political formulae involving commensuration bear a strong similarity to what Cass Sunstein has labeled, "incompletely theorized agreements" (hereafter ITAs).[29] An ITA allows participants in a deliberation to agree on a practice without necessarily agreeing on the general theory that guides the selection of the practice.[30] For example, people might agree on a probationary period for naturalization without agreeing on the purpose the probationary period is intended to serve. Sunstein writes, "[T]here are special advantages to incompletely theorized agreements in law (and elsewhere). They allow diverse people to agree, live together, avoid error, and render many decisions."[31] Dickering over the quantity of time in a probationary period at least has the advantage of a common unit of measurement. All the better if the person who thinks that loyalty ought to derive from faith in god believes the probationary period exists to develop and test this faith, while the person who thinks that the loyalty ought to derive from political relationships believes the probationary period exists to develop civic ties.

---

[29] "Incompletely Theorized Agreements," *Harvard Law Review* 108, no. 7 (May, 1995): 1737.

[30] Thanks to Adam Cox for helping me explore the congruence between the way I am describing how time figures into compromise and Sunstein's description of ITAs.

[31] "Incompletely Theorized Agreements," 1738.

ITAs rely on the kind of commensuration that temporal formulae (among other types of formulae) enact. Sunstein observes that rules and analogies have a special place for resolving disputes when people disagree on principles:[32]

A key function of social rules is to allow people to agree on the meaning, authority, and even the soundness of a governing legal provision in the face of disagreements about much else. Much the same can be said about other devices found in the legal culture, including standards, factors, and emphatically analogical reasoning. Indeed, all of the lawyer's conventional tools can allow the achievement of incompletely theorized agreements on particular outcomes, though in interestingly different ways.[33]

ITAs use analogical thinking to ease the path toward agreement on practices in the face of disagreement about principles.

Like ITAs, commensuration produces rules from analogical thinking. In the case of the subject of this book, temporal rules have political purchase because time is widely treated as having a form of value that is representational, or to use Sunstein's terms, analogical. Time is endowed with value through the process of creating a political metric that lacks the pitfalls of other potentially valuable political goods such as property, birthright, or cash. The temporal rules that endow time with political value are ubiquitous because rules and metaphor are of great importance to resolving normative disputes and because time is a "building block metaphor" in societies around the world.[34] It is overdetermined that many political formulae for distributing rights use durational time and/or deadlines. Time is an unavoidable circumstance and lends itself easily to both metaphor/analogy and to quantification. Out of this we get rules – waiting periods, prison sentences, deadlines, maturity ages, etc.

Sunstein makes five arguments as to why ITAs are important. These arguments also help explain why the commensuration measures that temporal rules enact are so common and so crucial in liberal democracies.

1. ITAs allow people who disagree to come to a decision and allow norms to coexist without requiring that we rank those norms.
2. ITAs reduce the costs of enduring disagreement by reducing the degree to which people who do not get their way actually lose.
3. ITAs allow for moral evolution.

---

[32] Ibid., 1743.   [33] Ibid., 1741–2.
[34] Mark Johnson and George Lakoff, "Conceptual Metaphor in Everyday Language," *Journal of Philosophy* 77, no. 8 (1980): 453–86.

4. ITAs help when people have limited time and capacity.
5. ITAs are well adapted to systems that must respect precedent.[35]

To these I add a sixth and seventh that are implied by Sunstein but not included in his enumeration.

6. ITAs shore up politics in political systems founded on norms that contradict one another. Liberalism and democracy are linked, but yet each call for different outcomes when norms like liberty and self-determination come into conflict. ITAs gloss over those conflicts. This is related to 2, above, but treats the normative conflict as a political inevitability, rather than an outcome of particular people who may or may not show up and disagree with one another.
7. Without ITAs, a liberal democracy would be mired in disagreement caused by essentially contested concepts.[36] ITAs are the practical outcome of the fact that politics is built on essentially contested concepts. Citizenship, representation, and justice are building block concepts in a liberal democracy, and there is no consensus on what any of them means or entails. Citizenship as a concept is essentially contested.[37] Citizenship as a social contract is an incompletely theorized agreement. Without an ITA, the essentially contested nature of citizenship would stymie any attempt to specify a membership. Similarly, without a formula for apportioning representation and scheduling elections, the essentially contested nature of representation would stymie any attempt at self-government.

It is no coincidence that one of Sunstein's repeated instances of an incompletely theorized agreement is the creation of sentencing guidelines in the US. Sunstein cites Justice Breyer explaining the complexity of the Sentencing Commission (a legislatively appointed body) guidelines with reference to the difficulty of getting a group to agree to a rank ordering of crimes by severity.[38] Indeed, Sunstein points to Breyer's discussion of the dispute over what justifies the assignment of one prison sentence versus another sentence, or even another form of punishment, and observes that different commissioners had divergent views about how different crimes should be ranked, and "a rational system was unlikely to follow ... empirical evidence to link

---

[35] See Sunstein, "Incompletely Theorized Agreements."
[36] W.B. Gallie, "Essentially Contested Concepts," *Proceedings of the Aristotelian Society* 56 (1956): 167–98.
[37] Cohen, *Semi-Citizenship in Democratic Politics*, 13.
[38] Sunstein, "Incompletely Theorized Agreements," 1733.

detailed variations in punishment to prevention of crime."[39] Though Justice Breyer does not stress the point, it seems clear that the seven members of the Commission were unlikely to agree that deterrence provides a full account of the aims of criminal sentencing. In these circumstances, one might wonder how the Sentencing Commission proceeded to justify its sentences. In fact, the Commission adopted no general view about the appropriate aims of criminal sentencing. Instead, the Commission adopted a rule – one founded on precedent: "'It decided to base the Guidelines primarily upon typical, or average, actual past practice.' The commission reached an incompletely theorized agreement on the value of starting (and usually ending) with past averages."[40]

Sunstein's logic could be handily adapted to apply to thorny questions related to the legality of abortion. Like punishment, access to abortion is considered to be a healthcare-related right by some, a requirement for a woman's autonomy by others, and outright murder by its most strident opponents. The abortion trimester system uses time to commensurate in a way that yields political compromise. The trimester system in effect takes a no compromise issue – abortion is or is not murder – and imposes a semi-artificial/arbitrary set of deadlines within the period of the pregnancy. These deadlines are compromises, legalizing some abortions and prohibiting others. So too are waiting periods that have been imposed as prerequisites for abortion in some US states. By using temporal measures to determine when certain features of life exist or when autonomy concerns outweigh other interests, we do not satisfy anyone holding an absolutist position on whether abortion is murder, but we do create a compromise.

ITAs are particularly pervasive in law and in judge-made law, but they are important whenever decisions have to be made by people with strongly held normative principles.[41] We often know x is true without knowing exactly why x is true. "When the convergence on particular outcomes is incompletely theorized, it is because the relevant actors are clear on the result without being clear, either in their own minds or on paper, on the most general theory that accounts for it."[42]

Critiques of Commensuration

There are two main critiques of commensuration that bear on a normative evaluation of a political economy of time. The first has to do with whether

[39] Ibid., 1743.   [40] Ibid., 1743–4 (citing Justice Breyer).   [41] Ibid., 1738.
[42] Ibid., 1737.

commensuration is reductive. The second has to do with the intrusion of market practices into normative arenas that should not be market-based.

The Reductiveness Critique

A long-standing critique of liberalism is that it calls for forms of procedural justice, including but not limited to commensuration, that are reductive. Such reductiveness does damage to the deeply held beliefs of particular peoples. This was the heart of the argument Aristotle launched against Plato's advocacy of commensuration. Comparison is a crucial technique for Plato, even if it is one that receives inadequate scrutiny.[43] "The *Protagoras* saw Socrates arguing that a *technē* in which all values were commensurable on a single quantitative scale was still a way of saving the lives of *human beings.*"[44] In Aristotle's time, commensuration came to be recognized as a scientific method of evaluation.[45] Aristotle pushed for value pluralism and against commensuration.[46] As discussed in Chapter 3, Aristotle thought that injustice resulted from the abstraction and subsequent conflation of distinct norms. Aristotle decried the quest for a science of ethics because its goal is a single common conception of the good.[47] Reducing the idea of the good to a single measure impoverishes the good, conflating or excluding all manner of distinct values. In this view, turning ethics into a science does away with the idea of value altogether. Human beings value many and varied goods and are poorly served when they are asked to trade them in for a single good. Things get lost in the process of standardization and the transformation of the qualitative into the quantitative. Centuries later, Georg Simmel concluded much the same as Aristotle, saying that "objectification of value inserts distance between us and what is valued," which points out how commensuration's abstractions changes human relationships to each other.[48] Michael Walzer's argument that spheres of justice with distinct social meanings should not leak into one another expresses a communitarian version of this view of commensuration.[49] To Walzer, the domination of one social sphere by another renders social meaning, which is the source of

---

[43] Melissa S. Lane, *Method and Politics in Plato's Statesman* (Cambridge University Press, 1998), 18.
[44] Martha Craven Nussbaum, *The Fragility of Goodness: Luck and Ethics in Greek Tragedy and Philosophy* (Cambridge University Press, 2001), vol. II, 294.
[45] Nussbaum, *Fragility of Goodness*, 294.   [46] Ibid.   [47] Ibid., 295.
[48] Espeland and Stevens, "Commensuration as a Social Process," 319.
[49] Michael Walzer, *Spheres of Justice: A Defense of Pluralism and Equality* (New York: Basic Books, 1983), ch. 1.

any good's value, incoherent. Social meanings cannot be transposed without being destroyed in the process.

Whether voiced by Aristotle or contemporary critics of liberalism, the concern that commensuration conflates and impoverishes norms and values is powerful.[50] But it is built on the contestable premise that all forms of commensuration are equally reductive. We can see this most clearly when we compare the Aristotelian critique of commensuration with Sunstein's defense of ITAs. ITAs are basically instances of commensuration. They create concrete outcomes in the absence of normative clarity or agreement. So, to take Sunstein's example, we can decide on a prison sentence for a crime in the absence of certainty or agreement about why we are imposing the sentence in the first place. Out of a very murky discussion of punishment, severity of crime, criminal history, etc. comes a very precise response to the crime: a specific number of years to be spent in prison.

One attribute of ITAs, as Sunstein describes them, directly contradicts the presumption that commensuration is reductive and damaging to moral meaning. Sunstein characterizes ITA's as *less*, rather than *more*, abstract than the principles that stand behind them. In other words, he stands Aristotle's directional arrow of abstraction on its head. To Sunstein, the idea of a five-year prison sentence is concrete, whereas the ideas of punishment, rehabilitation, retribution, separation, etc. that are used to justify incarceration are abstractions. Sunstein believes the reason ITAs are important and common is that people have an easier time agreeing on specifics than they do on norms and principles. Here he turns to Mill for support of his claim that people more readily sign on to a specific outcome than to arguments and norms that suggest the outcome.[51]

Settling the argument between teams Aristotle/Simmel and Mill/Sunstein is important for the following reason. One of remaining claims of this book is that temporal justice and injustice exist and are the outcome of how the political time of various groups and individuals is treated by the state. To Aristotle, injustice is the outcome of conflating and

---

[50] Insightful critiques of commensuration as a mode of valuing are found in Elizabeth Anderson, *Value in Ethics and Economics* (Cambridge, MA: Harvard University Press, 1993); Margaret Jane Radin, *Contested Commodities: The Trouble with Trade in Sex, Children, Body Parts, and Other Things* (Cambridge, MA: Harvard University Press, 1996); and Joseph Raz, *The Morality of Freedom* (Oxford University Press, 1986).

[51] Sunstein, "Incompletely Theorized Agreements," 1733.

abstracting distinct norms, thus damaging their meaning and making it impossible to achieve their ends. But, if Sunstein is correct, Aristotle may not have identified the source of injustices in commensuration regimes.

Temporal Formulae: Rich Not Reductive

Temporal formulae resemble ITAs because they commensurate, and they do so in ways that refer to an array of variables. A formula such as a prison sentence compresses multiple qualitative and quantitative data points (criminal history, severity of crime, good or bad behavior) into one number: the time to be served. People who want to naturalize in the US can have their probationary period reduced by marrying a US citizen or enlisting in the military. Each of these acts is commensurate with a two-year reduction of the naturalization probationary period. The formula for naturalization also includes a qualitative criterion, good moral character, which is assessed in an interview.

Although political formulae can be criticized for oversimplifying very complex decisions, temporal formulae actually accommodate and incorporate a substantial degree of complexity. The number and diversity of the considerations that go into a prison sentence or a probationary period is considerable. Aristotle might dismiss this as reductive because the final outcome, the prison sentence, is a single number. But the richness of meaning that durational time has been shown to have given us reason to question this critique of temporal formulae. As Chapter 3 demonstrated, durational time has an array of normative meanings. In liberal democracies there is a long-standing tradition of associating durational time with processes, relationships, and traits, including consent, social connection, civic education, loyalty, maturity, etc. A five-year prison sentence or probationary period may appear reductive and simple but durational time contains volumes of meaning. Furthermore, a procedure such as a naturalization formula, which includes multiple measures, refers to an array of metrics and qualitative judgments. This potential to refer to multiple norms and multiple standards distinguishes temporal formulae from many other types of commensuration.

Yet evidence abounds that time's richness and elasticity do not guarantee that any given temporal formula will be a just one. Sunstein's preferred case of an ITA, US sentencing guidelines, is widely regarded to be disastrous on a number of levels. People subject to the guidelines have been incarcerated for excessive amounts of time and in ways that exhibit bias.[52] But any effort to understand why a given temporal formula produces an unjust outcome will reveal the diverse normative content as well as political interests and empirical misjudgments that contribute to the formula's failure. In other words, a society that sentences criminals to time in prison using a wide array of variables and inputs may still do so unjustly. If the sentence is deemed unjust, the fact that it is a quantitative sentence rather than a qualitative one is not necessarily, or even likely, the source of the injustice. The norms that went into the formula and the manner in which the formula was structured are the sources of the injustice. In the absence of just normative intentions and just procedures, no response to criminality will be just. And in the presence of just normative intentions and just procedures it seems eminently plausible that the duration of time for which someone is incarcerated could represent a fair outcome for a criminal infraction. Certainly incarceration holds some appeal when compared with either torture or death, which were default responses to crime for most of human history.

Commensuration, Market Logic, and Commodification

If commensuration processes, like sentencing guidelines, can be unjust, but commensuration is not automatically a source of injustice due to its reductiveness, then some other attribute of political formulae must be responsible for unjust outcomes. A second critique of commensuration attacks its processes for their affinity with market logic and commodification. In this line of thought, commensuration is an attribute of market logic. Market logic corrupts politics by commodifying goods that are not, or ought not to be considered commodities. So, for example, a critic landing this charge against commensuration might have taken issue with the comment mentioned in Chapter 3, in which a legislator referred to a short probationary period as making citizenship "too cheap."[53] The problem with commensuration is not that it oversimplifies, but that the conversion of qualitative valuations into quantitative measures encourages politics to become transactional.

The charge that commensuration applies market logic is borne out by the way in which scholars of commodification regard commensuration. Margaret Radin treats commensurability as one of the four indicators that

---

[52] Michelle Alexander, *The New Jim Crow: Mass Incarceration in the Age of Colorblindness* (New York: The New Press, 2012); Naomi Murakawa, *The First Civil Right: How Liberals Built Prison America* (Oxford University Press, 2014).

[53] Annals of Congress 1 (1790): 1148.

something has been commodified.[54] Politics is widely thought by normative political theorists to be an arena of human life in which money and markets ought not hold sway. Put in Walzer's terms, the domination of the political sphere by norms that properly belong to the market renders politics itself meaningless.[55] The reasons for this are manifold, but among them is the concern that money will corrupt politicians and create inegalitarian procedures and outcomes. Michael Sandel's book, *What Money Can't Buy: The Moral Limits of Markets*, critically catalogs the degree to which "market thinking" has come to dominate not just the production and distribution of goods, but also social and political life. Sandel calls for a rethinking of the dominance of market logic in realms of life that have been traditionally governed by nonmarket norms because market logic leaves little room for virtues like fairness and equality. Not only should money not enter politics, but ways of thinking about goods that suit the market are inappropriate in a sphere of society like politics, in which norms of mutual concern, egalitarianism, and fairness should hold sway.

Temporal Formulae: Transactional for Better and for Worse

Forms of commensuration that invoke time rather than money are a mixed political blessing. As was the case with the critique that commensuration is overly reductive, the fact that the political economy of time is transactional is not necessarily a reason to condemn it. Despite the clear connection between commensuration and commodification, as was the case with the reductiveness critique, the idea that commensuration's compatibility with market logic is necessarily unfair and inegalitarian misses the potential of commensuration to exhibit inverse qualities. The market logic of commensuration is necessary, if not sufficient, for many of the formulae that rectify injustice. Identifying and deciding to address inequalities implies an agreement that people's different life circumstances can be compared, and that there is a means of compensating people for disadvantage. Race, gender, age, geography, and innumerable other circumstances create advantaged and disadvantaged classes among differently situated people. In cases such as these, where qualitative differences are at issue, commensuration is necessary to try and address inequalities. First, a qualitative difference is identified, for example a racial or gendered status disparity or disparity in the quality of representation. Next, the qualitative disparity is expressed in quantitative terms, for

---

[54] *Contested Commodities*, 118–22.   [55] Walzer, *Spheres of Justice*.

example the number of minority or female CEOs or elected legislators. That quantitative expression can then be applied in policies and laws that address differences. These are political acts of commensuration involving exchanges. Money and other material resources cannot compensate for all existing disparities, so we apply political power, social opportunity, and other non-monetary and non-material solutions to those that remain.[56]

Special rights of representation, majority–minority districts, and some iterations of affirmative action are examples of this kind of commensuration. They equate representation with a numerically calculated opportunity for a minority group to elect a representative. Majority–minority districts translate representation into a statistical ratio of minority members to non-minority group members in an electoral district. Of course, representation itself is an essentially contested concept.[57] The decision to equate representation with a numerically calculated opportunity for a minority group to elect a representative is only one among a number of possible ways to redress the historical exclusion of that group from electoral politics. Another solution might involve descriptive representation of that group in a legislature. This makes the electoral ratio a means of commensuration in the context of representation and political power.

Other temporal transactions can be structured in ways that compensate people for disadvantages – for example by creating separate queues for people whose use of time is limited by structural inequality. An instance of this is found in the policy for naturalizing refugees and asylees in the US. Unlike economic or family reunification immigrants, refugees and asylees in the US are required to wait only three years, rather than five, before they can naturalize.[58] In addition, once an asylee's application for asylum has been accepted, the time they have lived in the US since arriving is "counted" toward their probationary period. A victim of human rights abuse arriving in 2000 whose asylum application is accepted in 2002 can count all of the months they lived on US soil, even if they arrived without

---

[56] See Iris Marion Young, *Justice and the Politics of Difference* (Princeton University Press, 1990).

[57] See Jane Mansbridge, "Rethinking Representation," *American Political Science Review* 97, no. 4 (Nov. 2003): 515–28; Hanna Fenichel Pitkin, *The Concept of Representation* (University of California Press, 1967); Andrew Rehfeld, *The Concept of Constituency: Political Representation, Democratic Legitimacy, and Institutional Design* (Cambridge University Press, 2005).

[58] US Citizenship and Immigration Services, "Continuous Residence and Physical Presence Requirements for Naturalization," United States Department of Homeland Security, www.uscis.gov/us-citizenship/citizenship-through-naturalization/continuous-residence-and-physical-presence-requirements-naturalization (accessed Aug. 20, 2016).

papers of any kind ("illegally"). If one subscribes to the idea that asylees are entitled to special protection, this temporal formula helps rebalance the scales of justice. Similarly, some have argued for new sentencing procedures that would allow "particularly burdensome" prison time to reduce someone's overall sentence.[59] For example, a person with a medical condition that makes incarceration or solitary confinement more excruciating than it would be for an average person, or people committed to facilities that are overcrowded, might expect a reduction in the overall length of their imprisonment.

But, as existing sentencing guidelines remind us, not all temporal transactions over rights can be so readily justified. The political economy of time deploys commensuration processes that can be fair and just, and egalitarian. However, they are not always all of these things, and on some occasions the intent and the outcome of political formulae are patently unfair, unjust, and inegalitarian. The denouement of the analogy between the market and the political economy of time is the revelation of domination and exploitation within the political economy of time. The section that follows examines this dark side of the political economy of time.

NORMATIVE IMPLICATIONS

The picture that has been painted of political time is the very definition of the term Janus-faced.[60] Superficially, time seems to meet the demands of situated norms (democracy) and, simultaneously, neutral, impartial norms (liberalism). Temporal and other standards for rights supplant the use of birthright and property requirements for citizenship rights because they appear to transcend differences of class and race, among other forms of difference, and instead deploy a universally available currency with widely recognized social meaning. However, upon closer inspection, time is actually a metric that is used to facilitate and veil all manner of normatively ambiguous political compromises. Plenty of these compromises are unremarkable. But others treat the time of some citizens as having more value than that of other citizens, thus disadvantaging those whose time is accorded less or no political value.

[59] Mirko Bagaric, Richard Fred Edney, and Theo Alexander, "(Particularly) Burdensome Prison Time Should Reduce Imprisonment Length – And Not Merely in Theory," *Melbourne University Law Review* 38, no. 2 (2014): 409–43.

[60] The phrase Janus-faced is itself a temporal reference to looking both forward and backward at the same time.

In the political economy of time, an individual or a group of individuals' time can be devalued or made valueless in a way that creates or perpetuates disadvantage. Just as wage theft deprives people of the full value of their labor, unduly depriving people of the value of their political time is a form of political time theft. Prison sentences often inflict excessively lengthy periods of incarceration on vulnerable racial minorities, minors with limited civil rights are tried and sentenced as adults, and some non-citizens wait for indefinite periods of time, never knowing if or when they will be allowed to naturalize or be deported. In these and other instances, the state devalues the time of members of its population in ways that contradict basic notions of fairness and equality. When the time of an individual or group has little or no value, they are not able to acquire or exercise rights using the procedures with which other similarly situated people access rights.

The devaluation of a person or group's political time is a structural obstacle to equality. Fully understanding the nature of this obstacle requires recognizing the larger assault on that person's moral equality underlying the structural obstacle. Time has been posited as having political value because of its relationship to human experiences and social and political processes. The point of agreement between Plato, Aristotle, and Condorcet, was that the kinds of wisdom and political relationships that make us into citizens capable of consent and self-government develop in durational time. Time comes to play an important role in politics not just because it facilitates commensuration, but also because temporal measures have a greater potential to place people into more or less egalitarian relationships than other metrics. To devalue someone's time is to devalue her actual life and lifespan. It is a thoroughgoing means to disenfranchise someone.

As Chapter 4 has demonstrated, time acquires its instrumental political value because it is integral to processes that political subjects experience and undergo. Processes that occur over time can transform children into adults, turn foreigners into countrymen, and even unmake criminality. It is in time that Condorcet saw the production of consent and truth. To say that someone is impervious to the effects of time, or does not experience the effects of time as would an ordinary political subject, is to say that person is a deficient being. If an entire race, gender, or class of persons is ostensibly relatively impervious to the effects of time, this designates them as lesser beings, incapable of consent, truth-seeking, loyalty, etc. A person's political time cannot be devalued without also devaluing the people whose time is in question. To proceed as if no amount of time could transform someone into a rights-bearing citizen is to deny that person's moral equality by implying that she is immune or incapable of the processes that make people political in the first place. Such an action imposes hierarchy and exclusion upon people who ought to be considered equal members.

The moral inferiority claim and its limits are efficiently illustrated by the debate surrounding the status of undocumented immigrants who have been living in the US for extended periods of time. There are three main positions about what should happen to this class of persons. One position holds that they should simply be deported and prevented from returning and/or acquiring legal status. A second position holds that they should go to the back of a figurative line and wait their turn before acquiring legal status. A third position calls for the speedy naturalization of long-time residents who have no papers. The first position is often called an "original sin" argument because it treats the crime of entering the country without papers as irredeemable. No amount of time spent as a law-abiding resident can erase the stain of illegal entry. The second position shares with Michael Sandel the belief that waiting one's turn in a line imparts the quality of fairness to a legalization scheme, regardless of any other mitigating needs, and regardless of the fact that legalizing someone actually does not require any particular amount of time or any substantial amount of time at all. The third position recognizes the time spent in the US by persons here illegally, acting in the way that full citizens act, as legitimizing their claim to citizenship, regardless of the circumstances in which a person entered the country. Position 1 treats the crime of illegal entry as indicative of, or perhaps causing, moral inferiority. In this view, a person who behaves in the same manner as all other aspiring citizens, and for the same amount of time as those aspiring citizens, can never achieve the requisite qualities or undergo the processes that qualify a person with proper documents for citizenship. Position 3 takes the opposite stance, claiming that entering the country without papers has no bearing on the processes that someone undergoes once they live and behave just as does any other foreign-born person. In this view, there is no original sin that makes someone impervious to the effects of time. Those effects, which we recognize as transformative when we naturalize legal permanent residents, act on all similarly situated persons. The key difference between Position 1 (original sin) and either of the other two positions is that Position 1 takes the time of undocumented border crossers to be permanently valueless. Position 2 devalues the time of undocumented immigrants by making them wait longer for citizenship than people who entered the country with papers. Position 3 treats the time of undocumented immigrants as having very similar value to that of other immigrants.

The extremity of Position 1 (original sin) is mirrored in debates about sentencing reform. Mandatory minimum sentencing calculates punishments using formulae for criminal history and classification of crimes. In the US, mandatory minimum sentences yielded overwhelming numbers of extremely long sentences, a fact that was evident by the 1980s.[61] There is now widespread recognition among judges, legislators, and activists that these sentences were disproportionate to the transgressions that triggered them. A society generally enacts lifelong imprisonment for crimes so heinous that it is almost certain that the perpetrator can never again be recognized as the moral equal of a citizen. The processes of punishment and redemption (regardless of which process one believes ought to happen during incarceration) will not occur in someone whose moral character is of such dubious quality. The time of the undocumented immigrant and of the person serving a life sentence for non-heinous crimes is treated as valueless by a state that deems those individuals morally inferior to people who experience the political effects of time.

Harsh prison sentences for minor crimes and the permanent barring of a member of society from legal status are difficult measures to justify in the absence of evidence that someone is truly impervious to the effects of time. Why should it take longer for person X to receive rights than it does for person Y? What is it about person X that causes her to experience processes in different amounts of time than the rest of us do? The same might be said for age-of-consent laws that distinguish people's ability to give consent on the basis of their gender or on the basis of the type of sex (usually homosexual sodomy) in question. We would expect the time of similarly situated persons to be treated as having similar value. The similarity between the moral status of a documented and undocumented immigrant makes the disparity between their political statuses seem out of proportion. And the disparity between the moral status of a remorseless murderer and a non-violent serial drug offender makes the similarity in their sentences seem out of proportion.

Because political time acquires value in a way that has been analogized to the way time acquires value in a market economy, Marx's critique of capitalism provides a framework for analyzing the failings of the political economy of time. Marx's critique focuses on the exploitation that occurs

[61] Marc Mauer, "The Impact of Mandatory Minimum Penalties in Federal Sentencing," *Judicature* 94, no. 1 (2010): 7.

in a market economy. Exploitation transfers the benefits of the time and effort spent laboring from the person performing the labor. As the process of work and exploitation repeats itself, inequality becomes more egregious and more entrenched. Exploitation functions in the political economy of time in a similar way.

Political exploitation occurs when political power, rather than (or in addition to) economic goods, is unjustly transferred from one individual or group to another. Political exploitation in the political economy of time occurs when select, often vulnerable, members of a population experience the devaluation of their time at the hands of the state. In a labor market, the mark of exploitation is the transfer of profit from the person performing work to the owners of the means of production. In a political economy of time, exploitation transfers political power from people and groups who have less power to those people and groups who have more power. A political subject's time is one of their most important political goods. Time is used to transact over all kinds of rights and political power. When a subject's political time is devalued, or has no value, they are deprived of part or all of their political power. They lose political voice, status, and the opportunity to give consent, among other key powers. In a democracy, their disempowerment increases the political power of remaining members of society and increases the likelihood that power differentials will be ossified.

For example, people subject to mandatory minimum sentencing guidelines that impose extremely harsh penalties for relatively minor crimes, and people singled out for harsh penalties on the basis of race, spend long periods of time in prison. During this time, they lose many of their political rights, although they are still counted for the purposes of congressional apportionment.[62] They are also expected to work without any substantial remuneration.[63] In some cases they find themselves permanently imprisoned, and others are permanently disenfranchised. These political subjects' time is devalued by the state the moment they are prosecuted for crimes more frequently than people not in their demographic category. The devaluation and exploitation are then compounded by a harsh sentence. They spend a quantity of time in prison that one could reasonably expect would end in the full reinstatement of their rights, but that

---

[62] Sanford Levinson, "'Who Counts?' 'Sez Who?'" *St. Louis Law Journal* 58 (2014): 937.

[63] Brigette Sarabi, "The Prison Index: Taking the Pulse of the Crime Control Industry," in *Prison Policy Initiative*, ed. Peter Wagner (Springfield, MA: 2003), section III, "Prison Labor: Prison Labor in the Federal Prison; Prison Labor in the States."

reinstatement does not happen in a timely fashion, if at all. And even after they have served their sentence, the exploitation is extended. Some people in the US are imprisoned for non-payment of court fees, fines, and costs associated with their representation and incarceration. This has allowed a practice to flourish in which racial minorities are targeted for abusive treatment by law enforcement agents, fined excessively, and then incarcerated.[64] Once incarcerated, they accrue more debt. Ethnographic and quantitative analyses show that, "[a]s a result of the rise in monetary sanctions – also called legal financial obligations (LFOs) – indigent defendants, who comprise the vast majority of criminal defendants in the United States, remain under criminal justice supervision, paying per-payment and collection costs and interest on the initial sentence for the remainder of their lives."[65] Worse yet, people unable to pay these debts can then be sent back to prison.[66] The act of discharging their debt to society causes them to accrue further debt that is expressed first in monetary and later in temporal terms.

Per Chapter 3's claim that time is a necessary but insufficient condition for processes, including but not limited to the acquisition of experience and knowledge: temporal formulae in which no room is left for other variables besides time will function poorly. Mandatory minimum sentencing rules are widely regarded as a failure because they attempted to reduce all possible inputs into sentencing. The judgment of judges and other ways of meting sentences were prohibited. These sentences exemplify the worry that Aristotle evinced in response to Plato's proposal to create a technē, a science of normative measurement.

Similar exploitation is visited upon people who arrive in the US without documentation. Undocumented Americans, like temporary workers, students, and others who hold non-immigrant visas, may spend extremely long periods of time in residence. But that time can never lead to naturalization. Like incarcerated persons, undocumented immigrants are counted for the

---

[64] *A Pound of Flesh* details the reintroduction of debtors' prisons in the US. Following the shooting death of Michael Brown in Ferguson, Missouri, multiple reports documented the excesses of the fees and fines imposed on African-American residents of the city. And, shortly thereafter, the unexplained death of Sandra Bland in a Texas prison drew attention to the practice of "waiting out" tickets in jail when one could not or chose not to pay them. See Alexes Harris, *A Pound of Flesh* (New York: Russell Sage Foundation, 2016).

[65] Harris, *Pound of Flesh*, 3.

[66] Ibid.; "The Outskirts of Hope: How Ohio's Debtors' Prisons Are Ruining Lives and Costing Communities," American Civil Liberties Union of Ohio (2013). This rampant practice is unconstitutional in the US and has been prohibited by numerous state legislatures as well.

purpose of apportionment. The time of these political subjects has also been devalued. The instances of temporal devaluation cited above show how the devaluation of a group's time transfers political power (among other resources) away from that group and into the hands of others. As their time is devalued, immigrants and incarcerated persons are prevented from participating in electoral politics, receive little formal representation, and experience innumerable other exclusions from the material and political benefits of equal membership. Their time cannot be repaid, nor are there other ways to be compensated for their lost political time. It is a non-recognition that yields permanent disadvantage.

The previous discussion of commensuration identified Aristotle's concern about reductiveness and Sandel's analysis of market logic as two primary critiques of commensuration. I argued that reductiveness was not necessarily a trait of temporal formulae, but that market logic is a feature of temporal formulae, for better and for worse. The dynamic that creates temporal injustice is not the reductiveness that Aristotle identifies. Temporal injustice arises when market style formulae, with their vulnerability to exploitive arrangements, meet inegalitarian norms. Political exploitation occurs after a temporal formula is created that devalues the time of one group and transfers their political power to another.

Sandel sees this dynamic but reverses the directionality, pointing out that "markets leave their mark on social norms."[67] Viviana Zelizer illustrates the opposite relationship in her work on the social meaning of money, making the point that we assign vastly different normative meaning to wages, "pin money," and lottery winnings, among many other types of currency that would seem identical to someone unfamiliar with social context.[68] Each comes with its own set of social statuses and meanings. Established norms leave their mark on markets. Her point applies aptly to political time as well. In every society in which time is assigned a political value, the processes through which this occurs appeals to long-standing traditions. This means that in some cases in which a group of people's time is devalued, long-standing political exploitation creates deep disparities in political power. In the political economy of time, structural inequalities that precede decisions about temporal value and exchange leave their mark on how different people's time is valued, and the terms on which they are able to exchange that time for rights.

---

[67] *What Money Can't Buy*, 64.
[68] *The Social Meaning of Money: Pin Money, Paychecks, Poor Relief, and Other Currencies* (Princeton University Press, 1997).

Sociologists of time have asserted their own version of Zelizer's argument – that norms leave a mark on money – in a way that makes clear why these norms yield exploitive outcomes expressed in the valuation of time. Lynn Hunt, citing Barbara Adam, points out that while universality arrived as soon as a temporal frame of reference encompassed all people, "[it] was and is much harder to stomach the idea that everyone's time, that literally all experience, has the same ontological weight, as it were."[69] Hunt's and Adam's recognition of the relationship between time and ontology expresses a more general formulation of the argument that devaluing someone's time classifies that person as impervious to political processes, incapable of acts like consent, deliberation, reflection, and learning. Just as there are variations on how people's work time is compensated, political economies of time show that not everyone's time actually is treated equally. The free white man arriving in 1791 spent two years qualifying for naturalization because he was a free white man. Thousands of others who were neither free, nor white, nor male, found their time valued quite differently or not at all.[70]

Over time, the disparities in power generated by the selective devaluation of some people's time become more severe and deeply entrenched. Political systems and their normative logics create very stable sets of rules about the political value of time. Ages of maturity, naturalization waiting periods, prison sentences, retirement ages, and so on, all invoke very predictable formulae for determining the rights of people based on temporal equations. These rules are founded on the premise that time has value, and assign it a particular degree of value with respect to the acquisition of rights. Often these rules stay in place for very long periods of time. As described in the preceding section on commensuration, these rules are also the product of compromises among the main normative traditions in a society. Thus, temporal valuations are supported both by the power of normative precedent (long-standing tradition) and the power of consensus. Both the formulae that express these valuations and their consequences can be very difficult to change. Such broad and deep support

[69] Lynn Avery Hunt, *Measuring Time, Making History* (Budapest: Central European University Press, 2008), 26 (quoting Barbara Adam, *Time and Social Theory* (Cambridge, UK: Polity, 1990), 166).

[70] Historian Mae Ngai makes very insightful reference to the different temporal standards that have been applied to racial minorities, and in particular immigrants who were also racial minorities, in US politics. *Impossible Subjects: Illegal Aliens and the Making of Modern America* (Princeton University Press, 2004), 59–64.

can make the political economy of time a powerful and enduring conduit for structural inequality.

Political exploitation that results from objectionable temporal practices is particularly durable because time's political value is often not made explicit. In the absence of recognition that time has a precise political value, it is easy to treat temporal formulae as if they are not transactional when in fact they are. A consequence of ignoring the political value of time in a context of transactions over power is that temporal injustices are very difficult to recognize and very easy to disguise or explain away. Critics of market exchanges in politics often consider temporal commensuration an appealing alternative to letting money bleed into political life. But their focus on money may cause these scholars to overlook the fact that non-monetary transactions can still bring market logic to bear on the realms of social and political life they seek to insulate from commodification. They may not be positioned to notice how integral temporal forms of commensuration can be to their own version of fairness. Sandel's focus on instances of market logic in which people gain access to elusive tickets, congressional face time, high occupancy vehicle lanes, etc., using forms of paid line-standing in which someone is paid to wait on behalf of someone who views their own time as more valuable, illustrates this point. Sandel's first quibble is with the fact that money and the market displace the ideal of "first come first served."[71] His second qualm is that it monetizes things that ought to be free and changes the costs of any experience for which one can purchase line-standing.[72] Sandel argues that the first-come, first-served principle is egalitarian and that paying people in order to jump a queue is unfair. In defending the idea of "waiting one's turn" Sandel believes that he is arguing against the commodification and marketization of goods that ought not be distributed via the market.

What Sandel and other advocates of line-standing do not acknowledge is that waiting periods, waiting one's turn, and being "first come, first served" (FCFS) are each transactional processes in which time has replaced money as the means of exchange. Sandel assumes the first-come, first-served principle is egalitarian and that paying people in order to jump a queue is unfair. Surely Sandel knows that not everyone at the front of a queue got there fairly. But, more significant is that Sandel never defends the claim that appropriating time is fairer than charging money or more appropriate to certain spheres. He never questions whether time is more freely or equally available to people than money, or whether it is

---

[71] *What Money Can't Buy*, 28.   [72] Ibid., 33.

an ethical and egalitarian way to distribute a wide range of goods. Other scholars who have done work more specifically focused on the politics of queues, waiting, and lines tangle with the same assumptions. Katharine G. Young states that "the queue represents two important distributive values: equality and desert."[73] Queues are not supposed to respect irrelevant factors in distributing goods, so people imagine them to be impartial, as per the previous section, and universalistic. Still others note that people think queues are fair and that once a queue is established, the violation of the queue is unfair.[74] Sandel and other queue theorists are hardly alone in these assumptions nor did they pull them from thin air. When surveyed, lots of people will reveal a belief that FCFS is a fair distributive principle and that jumping a queue is unfair.

It is also peculiar for Sandel, who has elsewhere rejected the idea of universalizing principles, to defend line-waiting based on its universal appeal. Indeed, FCFS as a principle of allocative justice seems to contravene not only much of what Sandel has written elsewhere, but almost every other systematic approach to social justice ranging from the radically libertarian to the deeply communitarian and everything in between.[75] One might expect a philosopher of his persuasion to instead rely on an embedded temporality, such as a narrative about which persons have widely recognized claims that ought to prevail. For example, a society might privilege seniority or distribute opportunities based on who has not had that opportunity recently. These are all temporal principles, but they are embedded in contexts in a way that FCFS is not. At best, we might look at Sandel's embrace of FCFS as a version of Nozick's "justice in acquisition" in which someone becomes entitled to a place in line simply by being the first person to claim that place, and acquires the good that is at the front of the line by spending their time waiting for it.

In either case, what is most striking from the perspective of the political economy of time is that Sandel sees no need to explain why the appropriation of time for gatekeeping purposes is ethically preferable to the appropriation of money. This omission is a symptom of his failure to recognize that both paying in time and paying in money to access

[73] "Rights and Queues: On Distributive Contests in the Modern State," *Columbia Journal of Transportation Law* 55 (2016): 78.
[74] Ronan Perry and Tal Zarsky, "Queues in Law," *Iowa Law Review* 99 (2013): 1603–4.
[75] For a comparison of FCFS with other principles of allocation, see Ezekiel J. Emanuel, Govind Persad, and Alan Wertheimer, "Principles for Allocation of Scarce Medical Interventions," *The Lancet* 373, no. 9661 (2009).

a performance or a member of Congress exhibit a market mentality. In either case a unit of measurement has been introduced in order to value the good in question and in order to distribute it. In either case it is also true that a valuable good – either time or money – is levied for the access. People may pay in time for the right to speak to a member of Congress or they may pay in dollars. Regardless of the currency being charged, a price is exacted that will be too high for some to pay. And in either case people will be more or less advantaged in their access to the medium of exchange. It is not even the case that using time as an exchange mechanism upends dominant hierarchies of advantage. A lobbyist is more likely to be able to "spend" their time waiting to see a member of Congress than a part-time worker, with multiple jobs, whose hours are long and unpredictable. And even if this were not true, spending one's time in line is only nominally less transactional than exchanging money for a prized ticket. The member of Congress does not directly profit from the temporal price that is set when constituents must wait in order to gain access to their office. But exacting the temporal price does contribute to making that access valuable and to its scarcity.

Sandel is not the only scholar to assume that relying on time instead of money in commensuration avoids tainting politics with transactional attributes. A number of scholarly arguments stridently critique the idea that someone could buy their way into instant citizenship. Shachar and Hirshl condemn "the new grammar of market-infused valuation" that is implied in the sale of passports and citizenship.[76] To them, the corruption and contagion critiques of markets applies to a requirement of cash payment for citizenship but not in a requirement of a temporal price on citizenship. Again, the political economy of time is hardly identical to an economic market. But it is transactional. Political formulae that involve quantitative dimensions such as temporal formulae are readily understood through the lens of transactions. These procedures are not identical to financial transactions, but they are transactional. A commensuration process that relies on a good that has been assigned a political value lends a transactional cast to the political economy of time. In fact, many political decisions are actually transactional, or transactions thinly veiled to avoid the appearance that marketplace logic could override other political norms. This is particularly true of any process that requires a person to spend a precise quantity of time in

---

[76] Ayelet Shachar and Ran Hirschl, "On Citizenship, States, and Markets," *Journal of Political Philosophy* 22, no. 2 (2014): 247–8.

order to qualify for a right. Once the state has assigned a value to time, the levying of a temporal price for a right takes on a transactional cast. And like transactions in the market economy, temporal formulae run the risk of exploiting vulnerable members of society. However, in the absence of widespread recognition that time is a political good, such forms of political exploitation proliferate and persist.

CONCLUSION

Whether the subjects in question are disenfranchised ex-felons, or long-term residents who are ineligible to naturalize, recognizing the linkage of time with sovereignty, consent, legitimacy, and enfranchisement commits democracies to treating the time of all political subjects in a fair and equal fashion. The state decides on a valuation of time and constructs the formulae that confer and deny rights so that they accord with liberal democratic norms.

Because time is made integral to democratic decision-making it also acquires a relationship to compromise and commensuration. Members of a society hold incommensurate values and beliefs. We try to overcome our differences through time, as we educate, discuss, and reason our way toward decisions. In the preceding chapter, the use of durational time as a means of qualifying people for rights initially appeared egalitarian because time is more widely available than property, money, or aristocratic birthright. But ascriptive hierarchies disrupt even radically egalitarian norms. When this occurs, time ceases to be the great equalizer that one might have imagined it could be, even if it remains a good that is readily and equally available to all, free from the inegalitarianism of property, birthright, and other means of distributing rights.

Treating certain values as incommensurable offers a way to operate strategically in a negotiation. By refusing the terms of an exchange, not based on what one is offering or receiving, but based on the entire mode of value representation, one makes commensuration impossible. Thus, sacred land cannot be bought. Honor cannot be traded. Some circumstances are permanent, and no amount of time can change them. So, while commensuration, and in particular temporal commensuration, is common and important, a society signals something equally important when it refuses to create a temporal formula that might allow someone to change their political status or rights. Some people will be incarcerated for life, some felons will never be able to vote again, and someone who has been denationalized can never be a citizen again.

6

Conclusion

INTRODUCTION

This book began by noting that single moments in time frequently serve to create temporal boundaries around states. These temporal boundaries are no less forceful than the territorial boundaries that are more traditionally associated with the exercise of sovereignty. Dates can carve boundaries between populations, around states, and right through citizenries. Just as a political map shows us the territorial boundaries of a nation-state, a political calendar will show us the temporal boundaries of that same state, including who holds power when, for how long, and who is subject to that power in which ways. A political calendar is actually a temporal map describing the establishment of the state, transfer of power, and various other distributions of power. Recognizing and analyzing the role of time in forming and maintaining political boundaries is critical to evaluating processes of inclusion or exclusion. Thus, a temporal mapping of politics displays important normative information about who is included, how power is distributed, and the bases on which rights are made available.

Temporal boundaries also dissect the population of a sovereign state, dividing regular and irregular immigrants, minors and adults, workers and retirees, and so on. Where a person stands in relation to a single moment in time – a founding, a deadline, or an event such as the conclusion of a war – can often determine their entire political status. The arbitrariness of allowing single moments to have so much power points to the fact that simple deadlines hold very little potential for being democratic. When single moments are made sovereign, they tend to signal authoritarianism and subjecthood rather than democracy and citizenship.

Slowly, with the imposition of multiple sovereign moments, opportunities for lived consent and democratic decision-making are created. Because consent requires the sorts of actions, relationships, and dispositions that unfold during the passage of time, it cannot be given in a single instant. Durational time is not the only prerequisite for consent, but it is an important one. In a specific duration of time, for example the one that early judges in the US identified in the constitutional ratification process, a person is able to choose and consent. These characteristic acts of democratic citizenship exist in the passage of durational time.

A period of ratification, however, is still only one-time event. Constitutions are not usually re-ratified on a periodic or continual basis. They may be slowly reinterpreted, but they are largely static and, as time marches forward, the degree to which citizens can be said to have consented to constitutional terms grows smaller. This runs contra to the spirt of democratic self-government, which lies in decisions that are made and remade, allowing for continual deliberation, learning, the entry of new members, and accountability, among many other democratic goods. For this reason, recurring deadlines are the kind of temporal boundaries best suited to democratic politics. Recurring deadlines allow for political calendars that permit renegotiation without undermining the permanence of the sovereign state. It is in the durations of time that are hardwired into democratic procedures such as elections that the substantive processes required to make democratic politics transpire.

As deadlines proliferate and recur, durations of time acquire special value in democratic politics. Time's value is partly instrumental, because the passage of time is necessary for important political processes to occur. But often, waiting periods and schedules also treat durational time as proxies for a vague or undefined set of processes, rather than just connecting those durations of time to specific processes and benchmarks. We don't know whether these processes are occurring, and we may not even agree on which ones ought to be occurring. But we agree to the idea that the passage of time is an adequate proxy for whatever it is that we hope occurs in between elections, prior to naturalization, while children mature into adults, etc.

It is tempting to take waiting periods and political schedules for granted and assume that they are unavoidable rather than the product of deliberate choices and design. People expect politics to have a rhythm and schedule and they also expect to be asked to wait what they consider to be reasonable periods of time for at least some rights. But the ubiquity of deadlines and waiting periods does not explain their imposition. Waiting periods are not the only way we could measure a person's entitlement for rights. Other qualitative and quantitative measures and proxies for citizenly qualifications exist and sometimes are selected either in place of temporal proxies or alongside them. The fact that time is nearly universally used in political procedures is therefore significant and worth sustained inquiry, no matter how natural and inevitable we might have been inclined to think it is.

Several attributes of time make it uniquely situated to serve as a proxy for the array of qualities, relationships, dispositions, and other things that are regarded as prerequisites for democratic rights and citizenship. First, some conception of time, including scientifically measured time, is embedded in the social and political context from which it springs. The way we produce and deploy calendars, our sense of what time means, and all temporal systems are imbricated with national histories and peoples. The temporal regimes imposed on citizens and all political subjects feel natural in part because they are familiar and connected to other familiar institutions. This lowers the costs required for states to impose temporal laws and policies on their citizens and subjects.

Time is also quantifiable and measurable. For large bureaucratic states – the primary political units of modernity – quantifiable metrics of abstract, intangible, and ineffable qualities are a necessity. The efficiency and regularity of that which is quantifiable is essential to governing large diverse populations. Time offers regularity and the opportunity to commensurate that which we would otherwise only be able to understand as qualitative. Many of the same reasons that time becomes the most common medium through which work is translated into compensation for workers also make time a convenient means through which we translate human actions, relationships, etc. into political terms. Time is an extremely common abstract exchange value that allows processes to be re-expressed in concrete outcomes like rights and political statuses (such as citizen).

Following from observations about time's quantifiability is the fact that we think of time as an impartial means of transacting over rights. Time lacks the subjective qualities possessed by so many of the other means with which we might measure people's fitness for rights and citizenship. Clocks and calendars are as close to impartial judges as anything could come. Our intuitions about time support this conclusion. For example, a default presumption about queues and lines is that they are inherently fair, and that jumping a queue or otherwise imposing personal preferences on a FCFS procedure is unfair.

This leads us to think of time as a more egalitarian form of political exchange value than most other means with which political commensuration could be conducted. Clocks and calendars advance at the same rate, regardless of someone's social status, race, gender, or any other mutable or immutable characteristic. This makes them seem not only impartial, but also egalitarian. Everyone's day has twenty-four hours and everyone's week has seven days. Compared to something like money, blood lineage, or property, time is egalitarian. Not everyone can be well-born or have property, but everyone has time. The appearance of egalitarianism and impartiality may be belied by one's lived experience, but it nonetheless remains the case that time is often treated as being an impartial and egalitarian means of conducting politics. The temporal components of laws and policies frequently escape interrogation.

The combination of time's quantifiability, its embeddedness, its ostensible impartiality, and its egalitarian veneer make it an ideal means with which to commensurate in politics. Commensuration is the translation of abstract, intangible, and incomparable goods into terms on which they can be compared and sometimes even exchanged for one another. Commensuration is an essential political activity, especially in large liberal democratic states. If personal qualities, characteristics, relationships, and dispositions, along with all manner of distinct processes could not be translated into uniform political terms using some kind of regularized measurement, states could not be liberal or democratic. By assigning time political value, polities can achieve the scale of nation-states without having to abandon their stated commitments to liberal and democratic norms.

However, the terms on which temporal commensuration occurs also make clear when political forms of exploitation are occurring. If the time of similarly situated persons is not accorded similar value by the state, we must recognize this disparity as exploitive and unjust on the part of the state. It is through this comparative lens that we can identify the injustices inherent in excessively long prison sentences, dead-end semi-citizenship political statuses, ever later ages of retirement, the trial of children as adults, and any unduly long period in which a person or group waits for political status or rights that other similarly situated persons obtain more readily.

FURTHER DIRECTIONS FOR THOUGHT AND RESEARCH

Most liberal theories and theorists implicitly accept that the state can command the time of its subjects. Some of the ways states do so are evidently legitimate insofar as they comport with the normative foundations of the political system. A range of reasonable schedules generally comports with democratic norms. Others do not appear legitimate because they directly contravene a fundamental norm. Palestinians who have to wait in lengthy queues to pass through spaces that Israelis navigate with ease are being subjected to evidently unfair treatment. Still others, such as US sentencing guidelines, are facially legitimate but have illiberal or undemocratic intentions and consequences that undermine their legitimacy.

However, there is also nothing inherently either exploitative or even conservative about the fact that time has political value or that the state commands the time of its citizens and subjects. One task of political science is to observe different temporal laws and policies, within and between states, and to come to both empirical and normative conclusions about their justifications, functioning, and outcome. On these bases, recommendations may be made in the service of further democratizing politics.

Different regime types and rulers will engender various kinds of temporal ordering. Some will follow more democratic rhythms by using durational time to structure decision-making and deadlines to ensure accountability. Others will do the reverse, using single moment deadlines to impose arbitrary rule and open-ended durations to preclude accountability. Within either framework there are circumstances in which individuals and groups who lack other resources can mobilize time to work in their favor. It is with a discussion of these possibilities for political time that I wish to conclude.

Below I will briefly make two sets of points about how time can be turned in the service of fairness and democratic justice. The first point has to do with how people can work within a relatively democratic temporal regime or existing set of temporal laws in order to effect progressive change. The second addresses how to break rules in a way that could allow for the reappropriation of power by people who are not fully enfranchised by a democratic regime.

In a relatively democratic temporal regime, existing temporal rules and rhythms can be used by citizens in ways that appropriate power for the disempowered. Nadia Urbinati projects from her reading of Condorcet that time can become a political weapon that is held by an electorate that "periodically" passes judgment on its representatives. Instead of using the language of violent conflict, I would temper Urbinati's statement to say that time is just like any other political good (e.g. money, status, education) insofar as it can be deployed in an array of ways by actors – generally citizens – whose time is recognized as having value. Identifying temporal boundaries reveals opportunities for appropriating or reallocating political power or for producing new compromises. Elections are the obvious example of points when almost everyone knows that macro-level balances of power can be renegotiated. But anything, from a census that determines congressional reapportionment, to the extension of a policy or agreement that was temporally limited such as Temporary Protected Status for refugees, can be structured in a way that appropriates power for people who were previously disempowered.

Policymakers can also work within existing temporal frameworks to create entirely new temporal boundaries that redistribute political power. For decades, Germany struggled with their own equivalent of the US undocumented problem. Large numbers of children born to guest-workers were unable to claim German citizenship despite having known no other home. Eventually a law was enacted that created age deadlines at which points children born to non-citizens could elect to become German citizens.[1] This act created a new temporal border that children born to guestworkers could cross in order to acquire a full set of citizenship rights. Replacing other boundary markers with temporal boundaries will have the same sorts of consequences that we associate with other quantitative commensurating representations. Just as we lose the ability to represent certain traits of work once we move to a system in which hours of effort determine dollars, we also lose the ability to represent certain traits of rights-bearingness once we decide that years of residence determine who deserves rights.

Finally, political scientists, judges, and policymakers can also look closely at temporal equations, once the norms at stake have been ascertained, and ask whether they comport with the normatively democratic founding principles and other related standards of justice. We should interrogate which values time is injecting into temporal rules and equations. This can push forward normative and practical progress. Theorists and social scientists will want to expose the normative underpinnings of any temporal law or policy. For example, the creation of the sentencing guidelines in the US was intended to take information about a criminal's past as a means of predicting future behavior. Heavier sentences were imposed on repeat and lifetime offenders because they were deemed at greater risk for recidivism, even though many criminologists believe that other data, such as family structure and age, are better predictors of future behavior.[2] In this case, the temporal equations that overvalue

---

[1] "Law on Nationality," Federal Foreign Office, www.auswaertiges-amt.de/EN/EinreiseUndAufenthalt/Staatsangehoerigkeitsrecht_node.html

[2] Alyse Bertenthal and Mona Lynch, "The Calculus of the Record: Criminal History in the Making of US Federal Sentencing Guidelines," *Theoretical Criminology* 20, no. 2 (2015): 145–64.

past criminal behavior do not reflect the practical goal of the sentences. If the intent to try and sort potential recidivists from non-recidivists remains intact, sentencing reform could be undertaken that would adjust existing formulae. Of course, if critics like Michelle Alexander are correct (as many believe they are), and the intent of sentencing guidelines is to incarcerate and disenfranchise African Americans, then an adjustment will not be undertaken and if it were undertaken it would not be pursued in a way that punishes fairly. In this case, sentencing must be fully renegotiated in order to produce guidelines that are not just facially neutral, but genuinely impartial.

Elsewhere I have made the point that people become semi-citizens when they are incarcerated because they lose important rights of democratic citizenship.[3] When people are not fully enfranchised citizens, they are not always able to work within an existing temporal regime to advocate for adjustments to their status. In these cases, people must work against the deadlines and waiting periods that favor full citizens. Working against existing temporal rules and policies can take at least as many forms as the rules and policies themselves. Here I focus on one category of temporal resistance: disruption.

Radicalism often seeks to disrupt temporal expectations in ways that use time as a means of appropriating power on behalf of those for whom traditional means of exercising power has been foreclosed. Part of what makes Condorcet anti-radical is the degree to which he built into his political tracts protections against radicalism. To be radical in a carefully paced constitutional system that abides by the traditional norms of legal rationality may require exploding the temporality put into place by thinkers such as Condorcet. For example, protests often disrupt temporal norms and expectations for the purpose of lodging demands or imposing a new order. This can happen in the private sector: workers' strikes set calendars for slowing or stopping work in an attempt to use time against negotiating adversaries. Other kinds of protests and strikes deploy similar logic, seeking to disrupt the temporal rhythm of people and events that can be mobilized for support. However, the iconic protest at the Attica prison shows how difficult successful disruption can be for the most profoundly disempowered.[4] Time, in such cases, is

---

[3] Elizabeth F. Cohen, *Semi-Citizenship in Democratic Politics* (Cambridge University Press, 2009).

[4] Adam Gopnik, "Learning From the Slaughter in Attica: What the 1971 Uprising and Massacre Reveal about Our Prison System and the Democratic State," *New Yorker*

frequently on the side of the state and existing power holders even as it may be one of the few "weapons of the weak" to use James Scott's iconic phrase.[5]

The final lesson I take from thinking about how politics intersects with measured time has to do, appropriately, with permanence. One central claim of this book has been that processes are widely recognized as being transformative in ways that allow the transformation of a person's political status. Although the book has examined instances of both the extension and retraction of rights, extensions and retractions are not the moral inverse of one another. The retraction or denial of rights has sometimes devastatingly deleterious consequences for those who are left rightless. Retractions and denials therefore merit special scrutiny. And in cases where people experience the permanent retraction of their citizenship rights, maximal scrutiny may not suffice. Permanent punishments and retractions of rights include actions such as denaturalization, imprisonment for a person's full natural lifespan with no possibility for reconsideration, and capital punishment.

Democracy is predicated on a belief in a non-static conception of human character. This developmental model of character justifies the ongoing need to revisit political decisions of all sorts. In this way of thinking, elections are not just held in order for representatives to be held accountable, but also because people's political positions, needs, ideologies, etc. develop over time along with the rest of their character.

The idea that people's characters change over time as a result of their experiences and accumulated wisdom can be traced back to ancient democratic theory. Aristotle posited that a person could only come to embody *phronesis* (excellence of character and wisdom that is essential to democratic politics) after accumulating sufficient experience and having the chance to reflect upon that experience. As Chapter 3's discussion of presentism determined, Locke and other early modern thinkers also worried about the potential for tyranny that lies in any immutable law or decision.

Rather than seeking a form of government that could project an image of immutability over time, Locke's proposal for a parliamentary regime takes into account that the future will bring the unexpected and that the process of legislation

---

(Aug. 29, 2016), www.newyorker.com/magazine/2016/08/29/learning-from-the-slaughter-in-attica ("But the powerful waited out the powerless, and the affair ended with minimal violence").

[5] *Weapons of the Weak: Everyday Forms of Peasant Resistance* (New Haven, CT: Yale University Press, 2008).

and execution of governmental tasks therefore has to be designed so as to be able to cope with what cannot be anticipated.[6]

A compatible sort of developmental democracy is integral to contemporary democratic theories such as Seyla Benhabib's "iterative democracy" which relies on the repetition of deliberative and decision-making procedures as a means of building knowledge and moving toward accord. But for the purposes of this conclusion, one of the most useful perspectives on the processive nature of human character comes from Hannah Arendt. Arendt writes of the self that it is only truly knowable once a life has been led to its conclusion.[7] Patchen Markell characterizes Arendt as believing that our identities are the results of actions rather than antecedent to them.[8]

The non-static nature of both politics and human character has implications for the politics of recognition and also for democratic norms more generally. Indeed, there are very few attributes of democratic politics that imply that a person – even a fully mature adult – is a static being with views and characteristics and needs that never change. All kinds of character development processes can be expected to occur in difficult-to-predict ways as people go about their lives. If we can never assume the current state of a person's character to be permanent, then the idea that a state could impose a permanent disability that denies the possibility of transformation, such as an inalterable restriction on rights, is based on a fundamentally flawed view of human nature. Any permanent denial of rights is objectionable to a democratic theorist if one accepts the premise that no person's character can be assumed to be static. Policy analysts and philosophers who specialize in questions of punishment have been moved to express dismay at the idea that punishments for serious crimes can be imposed in ways that fail to account for the fact that the perpetrators of said crimes will be subject to processes that inevitably change their characters.[9]

---

[6] Jose Brunner, "Modern Times: Law, Temporality and Happiness in Hobbes, Locke and Bentham," *Theoretical Inquiries in Law* 8, no. 1 (2007).
[7] *The Origins of Totalitarianism* (New York: Harcourt, Brace, Jovanovich, 1973).
[8] *Bound by Recognition* (Princeton University Press, 2003), 13.
[9] Leonard Noisette, "The Risks of Permanent Punishment," *New York Times* (Nov. 15, 2011), www.nytimes.com/roomfordebate/2011/11/14/taking-and-restoring-the-rights-of-felons/the-risks-of-permanent-punishment; Jennifer Lackey, "The Irrationality of Life Sentences," *New York Times* (Feb. 1, 2016), http://opinionator.blogs.nytimes.com/2016/02/01/the-irrationality-of-natural-life-sentences

Change also occurs in the individuals that compose a society responsible for punishing an offender. McCarthyism was a high-water mark in US anti-communist prosecutions, many of which have now been reconsidered. The wartime internment of Japanese Americans is now a source of national shame. What now appears to many to be treasonous behavior on the part of Edward Snowden may later come to be seen as far less malign or even noble. The change could be the result of new information that triggers a public retrial. But it could also come about because norms for security, government spying, and related subjects change. For these reasons, it makes sense for any democracy to leave open avenues for periodically revisiting highly consequential punishments like denationalization or incarceration. And this reasoning also advises against permanent punishments that cannot be revisited, such as execution. Permanence and finality run contra to the temporal premises upon which democracy is predicated.

CONCLUSION

The main arguments of this this book have focused attention on subjects that are often taken for granted: the schedules, deadlines, and waiting periods that contribute to the structure of democratic citizenship. The approach has been analytic, insofar as the political value of time is a concept that exists primarily outside of the view of most social scientists. A great deal remains to be said about time's value: one might attempt to quantify and compare the value, to further specify its sources in specific instances, or argue about whether time ought to have the role that it does in any specific transaction over rights. The approach has also been normative insofar as it provides a means to identify and characterize a particular and important form of exploitive injustice.

Much has also been omitted on the way. The book contains little discussion about the tempo of politics or phenomenological experiences of waiting periods and deadlines. It also does not discuss the many forms of waiting that are imposed not by explicit rules but by the unintentional or intentional imposition of circumstances that result in waiting. These and many other attributes of political time are highly significant and deserve extended independent treatment of their own.

Despite the tendency to ignore durational time in politics, its roles in the political lives of democratic citizens and subjects can only proliferate as quantitative measures of every imaginable facet of individual and collective lives gain ever more traction. What Foucault trained his eye on – the significance of the clock and calendar for the imposition of political discipline – is no less pervasive today than it was in early modern capitalism. Each new deadline, waiting period, and temporary extension of a temporary measure creates boundaries within which people must exercise their sovereignty and a means for extending, denying, or retracting rights associated with citizenship. Such boundaries can be both legitimate and entirely consistent with the underpinnings of liberalism and democratic theory. Using time as a means to make concrete that which is intangible and make commensurate those things which are incommensurate is neither inherently oppressive or liberating. But, assuming that time is an egalitarian measure, or, alternately, assuming that temporal constraints are illegitimate, distracts from analyzing the intention and results of temporally defined laws and policies. In particular, the wholesale rejection of commensuration shortchanges the way in which commensuration, especially temporal commensuration, can serve democratic ends in politics. In the case of something such as time, which serves as a fundamental metaphor for a multitude of human experience and action, commensuration can be performed in ways that are not reductive and do not render human experiences and qualities unrecognizable. This does not mean that all forms of temporal commensuration will serve just and democratic purposes. But temporal commensuration contains the potential to express a multitude of rich meanings in terms that are legible to the state. Few other things could be deployed successfully toward such diametrically opposed ends and, for this reason, few other variables deserve more focused attention from analysts of politics.

Bibliography

Abizadeh, Arash, "On the Demos and Its Kin: Nationalism, Democracy, and the Boundary Problem," *American Political Science Review* 106, no. 4 (2012): 867–82.

Achen, Christopher H. and Larry M. Bartels, *Democracy for Realists: Why Elections Do Not Produce Responsive Government* (Princeton University Press, 2016).

Adam, Barbara *Time* (Cambridge, UK: Polity, 2004).

Time Watch: The Social Analysis of Time (Chichester, UK: Wiley, 2013).

Time and Social Theory (Chichester, UK: Wiley, 2013).

"Age of Consent Position Statement," Canadian Federation for Sexual Health (archived July 11, 2011), https://web.archive.org/web/20110714075413/ www.cfsh.ca/What-We-Do/Archived-Position-Statements/Age-of-Consent .aspx

Alexander, Michelle *The New Jim Crow: Mass Incarceration in the Age of Colorblindness* (New York: The New Press, 2010).

Allen, Thomas M. *A Republic in Time: Temporality and Social Imagination in Nineteenth-Century America* (University of North Carolina Press, 2008).

Ambrosio, Thomas *Irredentism: Ethnic Conflict and International Politics* (Westport, CT: Praeger, 2001).

Aminzade, Ronald, "Historical Sociology and Time," *Sociological Methods and Research* 20, no. 4 (1992): 456–80.

Anderson, Benedict, *Imagined Communities: Reflections on the Origin and Spread of Nationalism* (New York: Verso, 2006).

Value in Ethics and Economics (Cambridge, MA: Harvard University Press, 1993).

Annals of Congress 1 (1790).

Ansart, Guillaume, *Condorcet: Writings on the United States* (University Park, PA: Pennsylvania State University Press, 2012).

Arendt, Hannah, *The Origins of Totalitarianism* (New York: Houghton, Mifflin, Harcourt, 1973).

Aristotle, *The Politics*, ed. Stephen Everson (Cambridge University Press, 1996).

"Army ROTC Service Commitment," US Army, www.goarmy.com/rotc/service-commitment.html

Bagaric, Mirko, Richard Fred Edney, and Theo Alexander, "(Particularly) Burdensome Prison Time Should Reduce Imprisonment Length – and not merely in theory," *Melbourne University Law Review* 38, no. 2 (2014): 409–42.

Barshack, Lior, "Time and the Constitution," *International Journal of Constitutional Law* 7, no. 4 (2009): 553–76.

Bartelson, Jens, *A Genealogy of Sovereignty* (Cambridge University Press, 1995), vol. XXXIX.

Basic Law for the Federal Republic of Germany in the revised version published in the Federal Law Gazette Part III, classification number 100–1, as last amended by the Act of 11 July 2012 (Federal Law Gazette I p. 1478).

Baubock, Rainier, "Sharing History and Future?" *Constellations* 4, no. 3 (1998): 320–45.

  Migration and Citizenship: Legal Status Rights, and Political Participation (Amsterdam University Press, 2006).

Beers, Thomas M., "Flexible Schedules and Shift Work: Replacing the '9-to-5' Workday?" *Monthly Labor Review* 123 (2000): 33–40.

Benveniste, Emile, "Le langage et l'expérience humaine," in *Problèmes du langage*, ed. Emile Benveniste (Paris: Gallimard, 1966).

Bergson, Henri, *Time and Free Will: An Essay on the Immediate Data of Consciousness* (New York: Dover Publications, 2001).

Bertenthal Alyse and Mona Lynch, "The Calculus of the Record: Criminal History in the Making of US Federal Sentencing Guidelines," *Theoretical Criminology* 20, no. 2 (2015): 145–64.

Bilder, Mary Sarah, "The Struggle Over Immigration: Indentured Servants, Slaves, and Articles of Commerce," *Missouri Law Review* 61 (Fall 1996): 3–84.

  The Transatlantic Constitution: Colonial Legal Culture and the Empire (Cambridge, MA: Harvard University Press, 2004).

Bittman, Michael and Judy Wajcman, "The Rush Hour: The Character of Leisure Time and Gender Equality," *Social Forces* 79, no. 1 (2000): 165–89.

Bobo, Kim, *Wage Theft in America: Why Millions of Americans Are Not Getting Paid – And What We Can Do About It* (New York: The New Press, 2011).

Bodin, Jean, *Bodin: On Sovereignty*, ed. Julian H. Franklin (Cambridge University Press, 1992).

Boscarino, Jessica E., Rogan T. Kersh, and Jeffrey M. Stonecash, "Congressional Intrusion to Specify Specific Voting Dates for National Office," *Publius* 38, no. 1 (2008): 137–51.

Boyd, Julian P. ed., *The Papers of Thomas Jefferson* (Princeton University Press, 1958), vol. XV.

Braudel, Fernand, *On History*, trans. Sarah Matthews (University of Chicago Press, 1980).

Brendese, P. J., "Black Noise in White Time: Segregated Temporality and Mass Incarceration," in *Radical Future Pasts: Untimely Political Theory*, eds. Romand Coles, Mark Reinhardt, and George Shulman (University Press of Kentucky, 2014).

Brennan, Jason, *Against Democracy* (Princeton University Press, 2016).

Brickner, Mike, "The Outskirts of Hope: How Ohio's Debtors' Prisons Are Ruining Lives and Costing Communities," *American Civil Liberties Union of Ohio* (2013).

Brockmann, Stephen, "German Culture at the Zero Hour," Dietrich College of Humanities and Social Sciences (Research Showcase at Carnegie Mellon University, 1996).

Brunner, Jose, "Modern Times: Law, Temporality and Happiness in Hobbes, Locke and Bentham," *Theoretical Inquiries in Law* 8, no. 1 (2007): 277–310.

Busse, Anna Grzymala, "Time Will Tell? Temporality and the Analysis of Causal Mechanisms and Processes," *Comparative Political Studies* (2010): 1–31.

Calvin v. Smith, 77 Eng. Rep. 377 (KB 1608).

Carens, Joseph H., "Aliens and Citizens: The Case for Open Borders," *Review of Politics* 49, no. 2 (Spring 1987): 251–73.

Immigrants and the Right to Stay (Cambridge, MA: MIT Press, 2010).

Casella, Alessandra, Thomas Palfrey, and Raymond G. Reizman, "Minorities and Storable Votes," *Quarterly Journal of Political Science* 3, no 2 (2005): 165–200.

Casper, Gerhard, "Forswearing Allegiance" (University of Chicago, Maurice and Muriel Fulton Lecture Series, 2008).

Chinn, Jeff and Lise A. Truex, "The Question of Citizenship in the Baltics," *Journal of Democracy* 7, no. 1 (1996): 133–47.

Clawson, Dan and Naomi Gerstel, *Unequal Time: Gender, Class, and Family in Employment Schedules* (New York: Russell Sage Foundation, 2014).

Cohen, Elizabeth F., *Semi-Citizenship in Democratic Politics* (Cambridge University Press, 2009).

"Jus Tempus in the Magna Carta: The Sovereignty of Time in Modern Politics and Citizenship," *PS: Political Science & Politics* 43, no. 3 (2010): 463–6.

"Reconsidering US Immigration Reform: The Temporal Principle of Citizenship," *Perspectives on Politics* 9, no. 3 (2011): 575–83.

Cohen, Ira J., *Solitary Action: Acting on Our Own in Everyday Life* (Oxford University Press, 2015).

Cohen, Joshua, "Deliberation and Democratic Legitimacy," in *Debates in Contemporary Political Philosophy: An Anthology*, eds. Derek Matravers and Jon Pike (Abingdon, UK: Routledge, 2003).

Colbern, Allan, "Regulating Movement in a Federalist System: Slavery's Connection to Immigration Law in the United States" (unpublished manuscript) (on file with the author).

Conca, James, "Children Win Another Climate Change Legal Case in Mass Supreme Court," *Forbes: Opinion* (May 19, 2016), www.forbes.com/sites/j amesconca/2016/05/19/children-win-another-climate-change-legal-case-in-mass-supreme-court/%235dc9412c556b

de Condorcet, Le Marquis, "On the Constitution and Function of Provisional Assemblies," in *Condorcet: Foundations of Social Choice and Political Theory*, trans. and eds. Iain McLean and Fiona Hewitt (Aldershot, UK: Edward Elgar, 1994).

"On the Forms of Elections," in *Condorcet: Foundations of Social Choice and Political Theory*, trans. and eds. Iain McLean and Fiona Hewitt (Aldershot, UK: Edward Elgar, 1994).

"A Survey of the Principles Underlying the Draft Constitution (1793)," in *Condorcet: Foundations of Social Choice and Political Theory*, trans. and eds. Iain McLean and Fiona Hewitt (Aldershot, UK: Edward Elgar, 1994).

"The Theory of Voting," in *Condorcet: Foundations of Social Choice and Political Theory*, trans. and eds. Iain McLean and Fiona Hewitt (Aldershot, UK: Edward Elgar, 1994).

Connolly, William E., *Neuropolitics: Thinking, Culture, and Speed* (University of Minnesota Press, 2002).

A World of Becoming (Durham, NC: Duke University Press, 2011).

Cox, Adam B., "The Temporal Dimension of Voting Rights," *Virginia Law Review* 93, no. 2 (2007): 361–413.

Dahl, Robert A., *Democracy and Its Critics* (New Haven, CT: Yale University Press, 1989).

A Preface to Democratic Theory (University of Chicago Press, 2013).

Davidson v. City of Cranston, No. 14–91 L (DRI May 24, 2016).

Davis, Kathleen, *Periodization and Sovereignty* (Philadelphia, PA: Pennsylvania University Press, 2008).

Desjardins, Lisa: interview by Diane Rehm, PBS Newshour, *Diane Rehm Show*, National Public Radio (April 1, 2016, 10 AM), http://thedianerehmshow.org/shows/2016–04–01/friday-news-roundup-domestic

Diskant, Gregory L., "Obama Can Appoint Merrick Garland to the Supreme Court If the Senate Does Nothing," *Washington Post: Opinion* (Apr. 8, 2016), www.washingtonpost.com/opinions/obama-can-appoint-merrick-garland-to-the-supreme-court-if-the-senate-does-nothing/2016/04/08/4a69670 0-fcf1-11e5-886f-a037dba38301_story.html.

Dodds, Graham G. and Stephen Skowronek, "Presidential Leadership in Political Time: Reprise and Reappraisal," *Canadian Journal of Political Science* 41, no. 4 (2008): 1033–4.

Elster, Jon, "Ethical Individualism and Presentism," *The Monist* 76, no. 3 (1993): 333–48.

Emanuel, Ezekiel J., Govind Persad, and Alan Wertheimer, "Principles for Allocation of Scarce Medical Interventions," *The Lancet* 373, no. 9661 (2009).

Espejo, Paulina Ochoa, "The Time of Popular Sovereignty: Political Theology and the Democratic State" (PhD diss., Johns Hopkins University, 2006).

The Time of Popular Sovereignty (University Park, PA: Pennsylvania State University Press, 2011).

"People, Territory, and Legitimacy in Democratic States," *American Journal of Political Science* 58, no. 2 (2014): 466–78.

"Taking Place Seriously: Territorial Presence and the Rights of Immigrants," *Journal of Political Philosophy* 24, no. 1 (2016): 67–87.

Espeland, Wendy Nelson and Michael Sauder, *Engines of Anxiety: Academic Rankings, Reputation, and Accountability* (New York: Russell Sage Foundation, 2016).

Espeland, Wendy Nelson and Mitchell L. Stevens, "Commensuration as a Social Process," *Annual Review of Sociology* 24 (1998): 313–43.

Feldman, Leonard C., "The Banality of Emergency: On the Time and Space of 'Political Necessity,'" in *Sovereignty, Emergency, Legality*, ed. Austin Sarat (Cambridge University Press, 2010).

Fishkin, James, *Democracy and Deliberation: New Directions for Democratic Reform* (New Haven, CT: Yale University Press, 1991).

Forde, Steven, *Locke, Science and Politics* (Cambridge University Press, 2013).

Foucault,Michel, *Discipline and Punish: The Birth of the Prison* (New York: Vintage, 1979).

  The Foucault Effect: Studies in Governmentality, eds. Graham Burchell, Colin Gordon and Peter Miller (University of Chicago Press, 1991).

  Security, Territory, and Population: Lectures at the Collège de France, 1977–78, ed. Arnold I. Davidson (Basingstoke, UK: Palgrave Macmillan, 2009).

Franklin, Frank George, *Legislative History of Naturalization in the United States* (New York: Arno Press, 1906).

French, Rebecca R., "Time in the Law," *University of Colorado Law Review* 72 (2001): 663–748.

Fritzsche, Peter, *Stranded in the Present: Modern Time and the Melancholy of History* (Cambridge, MA: Harvard University Press, 2004).

Frymer, Paul, "'A Rush and a Push and the Land Is Ours,': Territorial Land Expansion, Land Policy, and U.S. State Formation," *Perspectives on Politics* 12, no. 1 (2014): 119–44.

Gallie, W. B., "Essentially Contested Concepts," *Proceedings of the Aristotelian Society* 56 (1956): 167–98.

Giddens, Anthony, *A Contemporary Critique of Historical Materialism* (Berkeley and Los Angeles: University of California Press, 1981).

  The Consequences of Modernity (Cambridge, UK: Polity, 1990).

Goetz, Klaus H., "How Does the EU Tick? Five Propositions on Political Time," *Journal of European Public Policy* 16, no. 2 (2009): 202–20.

Goetz, Klaus H. and Jan-Hinrik Meyer-Sahling, "The EU Timescape: From Notion to Research Agenda," *Journal of European Public Policy* 16, no. 2 (2009): 325–36.

  "Political Time in the EU: Dimensions, Perspectives, Theories," *Journal of European Public Policy* 16, no. 2 (2009): 180–201.

Goodin, Robert E., "Enfranchising All Affected Interests, and Its Alternatives," *Philosophy & Public Affairs* 35, no. 2 (2007): 40–68.

  "Temporal Justice," *Journal of Social Policy* 39, no. 1 (2010): 1–16.

Goodin, Robert E., James Mahmud Rice, Michael Bittman, and Peter Saunders, "The Time–Pressure Illusion: Discretionary Time vs. Free Time," *Social Indicators Research* 73, no. 1 (2005): 43–70.

Goodin, Robert E., James Mahmud Rice, Antti Parpo, and Lina Eriksson, *Discretionary Time: A New Measure of Freedom* (Cambridge University Press, 2008).

Gopnik, Adam, "Learning From the Slaughter in Attica: What the 1971 Uprising and Massacre Reveal about Our Prison System and the Democratic State," *New Yorker* (Aug. 29, 2016), www.newyorker.com/magazine/2016/08/29/l earning-from-the-slaughter-in-attica

Gould, Joe and Leo Shane III, "U.S. Congress Passes Waiver for Mattis to Lead Pentagon," *DefenseNews* (Jan. 13, 2017), www.defensenews.com/articles/u s-congress-passes-waiver-for-mattis-to-lead-pentagon

Grant, Ruth W., *Strings Attached: Untangling the Ethics of Incentives* (Princeton University Press, 2011).

Greene, David, "Crimean Tatars Pressured to Become Russian Citizens," National Public Radio (Oct. 28, 2014, 4:39 AM ET), www.npr.org/2014/10/ 28/359512062/crimean-tatars-pressured-to-become-russian-citizens

Greenhouse, Carol J., "Just in Time: Temporality and the Cultural Legitimation of Law," *Yale Law Journal* 98, no. 8 (1989): 1631–51.

A Moment's Notice: Time Politics Across Cultures (Ithaca, NY: Cornell University Press, 1996).

Greenstein, Theodore N., "Economic Dependence, Gender, and the Division of Labor in the Home: A Replication and Extension," *Journal of Marriage and Family* 62, no. 2 (2000): 322–35.

Gronke, Paul, Eva Galanes-Rosenbaum, and Peter A. Miller, "Symposium: Early Voting and Turnout," *PS: Political Science and Politics* 40, no. 4 (2007): 639–45.

Gronke, Paul, Eva Galanes-Rosenblum, Peter A. Miller, and Daniel Toffey, "Convenience Voting," *Annual Review of Political Science* 11 (2008): 437–55.

Habermas, Jurgen, *Between Facts and Norms: Contributions to a Discourse Theory of Law and Democracy* (Cambridge, MA: MIT Press, 1996).

Habermas, Jurgen and William Rehg, "Constitutional Democracy: A Contradictory Union of Contradictory Principles?" *Political Theory* 29, no. 6 (2001): 766–81.

Hacking, Ian, *The Taming of Chance* (Cambridge University Press, 1990).

Hager, Eli, "The Willie Bosket Case: How Children Became Adults in the Eyes of the Law," *Marshall Project* (Dec. 29, 2014), www.themarshallproject.org/ 2014/12/29/the-willie-bosket-case

Harris, Alexes, *A Pound of Flesh* (New York: Russell Sage Foundation, 2016).

Harvey, David, "Time–Space Compression and the Postmodern Condition," in *Modernity: Critical Concepts in Sociology*, ed. Malcolm Waters (London: Routledge, 1999), vol. IX.

Hawkins Homer and Richard Thomas, "White Policing of Black Populations: A History of Race and Social Control in America," in *Out of Order? Policing Black People*, eds. Ellis Cashmore and Eugene McLaughlin (New York: Routledge, 1991).

Hayduk, Ronald, *Democracy for All: Restoring Immigrant Voting Rights in the United States* (New York: Routledge, 2006).

"Noncitizen Voting Rights: Extending the Franchise in the United States," *National Civic Review* 92, no. 4 (2003): 57–62.

Healy, Patrick, "Early Voting Limits Donald Trump's Time to Turn Campaign Around," *New York Times: Election 2016* (Aug. 16,2016), www.nytimes .com/2016/08/17/us/politics/early-voting-limits-donald-trumps-time-to-turn-c ampaign-around.html

Hewitt Fiona and Iain McLean, trans. and eds., *Condorcet: Foundations of Social Choice and Political Theory* (Aldershot, UK: Edward Elgar, 1994).

Higgins, Rosalyn, "Time and the Law: International Perspectives on an Old Problem," *International and Comparative Law Quarterly* 46, no. 3 (1997): 501–20.

Hirschl Ran and Ayelet Shachar, "On Citizenship, States, and Markets," *Journal of Political Philosophy* 22, no. 2 (2014): 231–57.

Hoffman, Peter B., "Twenty Years of Operational Use of a Risk Prediction Instrument: The United States Parole Commission's Salient Factor Score," *Journal of Criminal Justice* 22, no. 6 (1994): 477–94.

Howarth, Randall S., *The Origins of Roman Citizenship* (Edwin Mellen Press, 2006).

Hunt, Lynn Avery, *Measuring Time, Making History* (Budapest: Central European University Press, 2008).

Immigration and Nationality Act, 8 USCA § 1407 (West 2015).

Inglis v. Trustees of Sailor's Snug Harbor, 28 US 99 (1830).

Jacobs, Jerry A. and Kathleen Gerson, "Overworked Individuals, or Overworked Families? Explaining Trends in Work, Leisure, and Family Time," *Work and Occupations* 28, no. 1 (2001): 40–63.

Jefferson, Thomas, Letter to James Madison (Paris, Sept. 6, 1789), www.let .rug.nl/usa/presidents/thomas-jefferson/letters-of-thomas-jefferson/jefl81.php

Jehlen, Myra, *American Incarnation: The Individual, the Nation, and the Continent* (Cambridge, MA: Harvard University Press, 1986).

Jessop, Bob, *State Power* (Cambridge, UK: Polity, 2007).

"Time and Space in the Globalization of Capital and Their Implications for State Power," in *Rethinking Marxism* 14, no. 1 (2002): 97–117.

Johnson, Mark and George Lakoff, "Conceptual Metaphor in Everyday Language," *Journal of Philosophy* 77, no. 8 (1980): 453–86.

Kant, Immanuel et al., *Toward Perpetual Peace and Other Writings on Politics, Peace, and History* (New Haven, CT: Yale University Press, 2006).

Kaprielian-Churchill, Isabel, "Rejecting 'Misfits': Canada and the Nansen Passport," *International Migration Review* 28 (1994): 281–306.

Kettner, James, *The Development of American Citizenship, 1608–1870* (Chapel Hill, NC: University of North Carolina Press, 1978).

Khan, Liaquat Ali, "Jurodynamics of Islamic Law," *Rutgers Law Review* 61 (2008): 263–93.

Koselleck, Reinhart, *The Practice of Conceptual History: Timing History, Space Concepts*, trans. Todd Samuel Presner (Stanford University Press, 2002).

Krotoszynski, Ronald J., Jr., "A Poll Tax By Another Name," *New York Times: Opinion* (Nov. 14, 2016), www.nytimes.com/2016/11/14/opinion/a-poll-tax-by-another-name.html?_r=1.

Kryder, Daniel and Sarah Staszak, "Constitution as Clockwork: The Temporal Foundations of American Politics" (prepared for annual meeting, American Political Science Association, working paper, 2006).

Kutner, Jenny, "Louisiana Is Imposing a 3-Day 'Reflection' Period on Women Seeking Abortions," *Mic* (May 23, 2016), https://mic.com/articles/144150/l ouisiana-will-force-women-to-spend-three-days-thinking-about-if-they-want-abortions#.THpgCu9nr

Kuwait: Ministerial Decree No. 15 of 1959 promulgating the Nationality Law, http://gulfmigration.eu/kuwait-ministerial-decree-no-15-of-1959-promulgat ing-the-nationality-law

Lackey, Jennifer, "The Irrationality of Life Sentences," *New York Times* (Feb. 1, 2016), http://opinionator.blogs.nytimes.com/2016/02/01/the-irrationality-of-natural-life-sentences

LaCroix, Alison L., "Temporal Imperialism," *University of Pennsylvania Law Review* 158 (2010): 1329–73.

Landemore, Hélène, *Democratic Reason: Politics, Collective Intelligence, and the Rule of the Many* (Princeton University Press, 2013).

Landes, David S., *Revolution in Time: Clocks and Making of the Modern World* (Cambridge, MA: Belknap Press of Harvard University Press, 1983).

Lane, Melissa S., *Method and Politics in Plato's Statesman* (Cambridge University Press, 1998).

"Political Theory and Time," in *Time in Contemporary Political Thought*, ed. P.J.N. Baert (1st edn, Amsterdam: Elsevier, 2000).

Law, Anna O., "Lunatics, Idiots, Paupers, and Negro Seamen – Immigration Federalism and the Early American State," *Studies in American Political Development* 28, no. 02 (2014): 107–28.

Law on Nationality, Federal Foreign Office, www.auswaertiges-amt.de/EN/ EinreiseUndAufenthalt/Staatsangehoerigkeitsrecht_node.html

Lee, Jaeah, "Why Cops Are Told to Keep Quiet After a Shooting: The Controversial Science Between the 48-Hour Rule," *Mother Jones* (Aug. 12, 2015), www.motherjones.com/politics/2015/08/why-do-police-depart ments-delay-interviewing-officers-involved-shootings

Levinson, Sanford, "Constituting Communities through Words that Bind: Reflections on Loyalty Oaths," *Michigan Law Review* 84 (June 1986): 1440–70.

"'WHO COUNTS?' 'SEZ WHO?,'" *St. Louis Law Journal* 58 (2014), 937–1189.

Lindahl, Hans, "Breaking Promises to Keep Them: Immigration and the Bounds of Distributive Justice," in *A Right to Inclusion and Exclusion? Normative Fault Lines of the EU's Area of Freedom, Security and Justice*, ed. Hans Lindahl (Oxford: Hart, 2009).

Linstead, Stephen and John Malarkey, "Time, Creativity, and Culture: Introducing Bergson," *Culture and Organization* 9, no. 1 (2010): 3–13.

Lister, Matthew J., "Citizenship, in the Immigration Context," *Maryland Law Review* 70 (2011): 175–233.

Locke, John, *1690. Two Treatises of Government*, ed. Peter Laslett (Cambridge University Press, 1988).

Luhmann, Niklas, *Social Systems* (Stanford University Press, 1995).

Lukes, Steven and Nadia Urbinati, *Condorcet: Political Writings* (Cambridge University Press, 2012).

Maas, Willem, "Freedom of Movement Inside 'Fortress Europe,'" in *Global Surveillance and Policing: Borders, Security, Identity*, eds. Elia Zureik and Mark B. Salter (Cullompton, UK: Willan, 2005).

McFarland, Andrew S., "Interest Groups and Political Time: Cycles in America," *British Journal of Political Science* 21, no. 3 (1991): 257–84.

McIlvaine v. *Coxe's Lessee*, 6 US 280 (1804).

McLean, Iain and Arnold B. Urken, "Did Jefferson Or Madison Understand Condorcet's Theory of Social Choice?" *Public Choice* 73, no. 4 (1992): 445–7.

McNally, David, *Political Economy and the Rise of Capitalism: A Reinterpretation* (University of California Press, 1988).

Madison, James, *Notes of Debates in the Federal Convention of 1787* (Ohio University Press, 1966).

Mansbridge, Jane, "Rethinking Representation," *American Political Science Review* 97, no. 4 (Nov. 2003): 515–28.

Markell, Patchen, *Bound by Recognition* (Princeton University Press, 2003).

Mauer, Marc, "The Impact of Mandatory Minimum Penalties in Federal Sentencing," *Judicature* 94, no. 1 (2010): 6–9.

Meyer-Sahling, Jan-Hinrik, "Time and European Governance: An Inventory," *Archive of European Integration* (paper presented at the Biennial Conference of the European Studies Association, Panel 'The Temporality of Europeanisation and Enlargement,' Montreal, Canada, May 17–20, 2007).

Meyler, Bernadette, "The Gestation of Birthright Citizenship, 1868–1898: States' Rights, the Law of Nations, and Mutual Consent," *Georgetown Immigration Law Journal* 15 (2001): 519–62.

Michelman, Frank, "Morality, Identity, and Constitutional Patriotism," *University of Colorado Law Review* 76 (1998): 399–427.

Milkman, Ruth, Anna Luz Gonzalez, and Victor Narro, *Wage Theft and Workplace Violations in Los Angeles* (Los Angeles, CA: Institute for Research on Labor and Employment, 2010).

Miller, David, "Territorial Rights: Concept and Justification," *Political Studies* 60, no. 2 (2012): 252–68.

Moore, Margaret, *A Political Theory of Territory* (Oxford University Press, 2015).

Morris, Norval and David J. Rothman, *The Oxford History of the Prison: The Practice of Punishment in Western Society* (Oxford University Press, 1998).

Muller, J.C., *The Temporality of Political Obligation* (Abingdon, UK: Routledge, 2015).

Mumford, Lewis and Langdon Winner, *Technics and Civilization* (University of Chicago Press, 2010).

Munz, Rainer and Rainer Ohliger eds. *Diasporas and Ethnic Migrants: Germany, Israel and Russia in Comparative Perspective* (Abingdon, UK: Routledge, 2004).

Murakawa, Naomi, *The First Civil Right: How Liberals Built Prison America* (Oxford University Press, 2014).

"Nation's Historians Warn the Past is Expanding at an Alarming Rate," *The Onion* 51, no. 3 (Jan. 22, 2015), www.theonion.com/articles/nations-historians-warn-the-past-is-expanding-at-a,37827

Nelson, William Max, "The Weapon of Time: Constructing the Future in France, 1750 to Year I" (PhD diss., University of California, Los Angeles, 2006).
  The Weapon of Time: Constructing the Future in France, 1750 to Year I (University of California Press, 2006).

New York Times Editorial Board, "The Wrong Way to Count Prisoners," *New York Times* (July 15, 2016), www.nytimes.com/2016/07/16/opinion/the-wrong-way-to-count-prisoners.html?_r=0

Ngai, Mae M., *Impossible Subjects: Illegal Aliens and the Making of Modern America* (Princeton University Press, 2004).

Nix, Simon, "Elections, Parties, and Institutional Design: A Comparative Perspective on European Union Democracy," *West European Politics* 21, no. 3 (1998): 19–52.

Noble, David W., *Death of a Nation: American Culture and the End of Exceptionalism* (University of Minnesota Press, 2002).

Noisette, Leonard, "The Risks of Permanent Punishment," *New York Times* (Nov. 15, 2011), www.nytimes.com/roomfordebate/2011/11/14/taking-and-restoring-the-rights-of-felons/the-risks-of-permanent-punishment

Noonan, Jeff, "Free Time as a Necessary Condition of Free Life," *Contemporary Political Theory* 8, no. 4 (2009): 377–93.

Nussbaum, Martha C., *The Fragility of Goodness: Luck and Ethics in Greek Tragedy and Philosophy* (Cambridge University Press, 2001), vol. II.

Nussbaum, Martha C. and Rosalind Hursthouse, "Plato on Commensurability and Desire," *Proceedings of the Aristotelian Society, Supplementary Volumes* 58 (1984): 55–96.

Ogle, Vanessa, *The Global Transformation of Time: 1870–1950* (Cambridge, MA: Harvard University Press, 2015).

O'Kane, Rosemary H.T., "Cambodia in the Zero Years: Rudimentary Totalitarianism," *Third World Quarterly* 14, no. 4 (1993): 735–48.

Orren, Karen and Stephen Skowronek, "Order and Time in Institutional Study: A Brief for the Historical Approach," in *Political Science in History: Research Programs and Political Traditions*, eds. James Farr, John S. Dryzek, and Stephen T. Leonard (Cambridge University Press, 1995).
  The Search for American Political Development (Cambridge University Press, 2004).

Parsons, Talcott, "On the Concept of Political Power," *Proceedings of the American Philosophical Society* 107, no. 3 (1963): 232–62.

Perovic, Sanja, *The Calendar in Revolutionary France: Perceptions of Time in Literature, Culture, Politics* (Cambridge University Press, 2012).

Perry, Ronan and Tal Zarsky, "Queues in Law," *Iowa Law Review* 99 (2013): 1595–1658.

Pierson, Paul, *Politics in Time: History, Institutions, and Social Analysis* (Princeton University Press, 2004).

Pinfari, Marco, *Peace Negotiations and Time: Deadline Diplomacy in Territorial Disputes* (Abingdon, UK: Routledge, 2012).

Pitkin, Hanna Fenichel, *The Concept of Representation* (University of California Press, 1967).

Planas, Roque, "Thousands of Dominicans Woke Up This Week without Citizenship in Any Country," *Huffington Post* (Feb. 3, 2015), www.huffing tonpost.com/2015/02/03/dominicans-citizenship_n_6606336.html

Pocock, John Greville Agard, *Virtue, Commerce, and History* (Cambridge University Press, 1985).

The Ancient Constitution and the Feudal Law: A Study of English Historical Thought in the Seventeenth Century (Cambridge University Press, 1987).

The Machiavellian Moment: Florentine Political Thought and the Atlantic Republican Tradition (Princeton University Press, 2009).

Pogge, Thomas, *World Poverty and Human Rights: Cosmopolitan Responsibilities and Reforms* (Cambridge: Polity, 2002).

Porter, Theodore M., *Trust in Numbers: The Pursuit of Objectivity in Science and Public Life* (Princeton University Press, 1996).

Price, Polly, "Natural Law and Birthright Citizenship in *Calvin's Case (1608)*," *Yale Journal of Law and Humanities* 9, no. 1 (1997): 73–146.

Rabinow, Paul, *Marking Time: On the Anthropology of the Contemporary* (Princeton University Press, 2009).

Radin, Margaret Jane, *Contested Commodities: The Trouble with Trade in Sex, Children, Body Parts, and Other Things* (Cambridge, MA: Harvard University Press, 1996).

Rae, Douglas, *Equalities* (Cambridge, MA: Harvard University Press, 1981).

Rakoff, Todd D., *A Time for Every Purpose: Law and the Balance of Life* (Cambridge, MA: Harvard University Press, 2002).

Raskin, Jamin B., "Legal Aliens, Local Citizens: The Historical, Constitutional and Theoretical Meanings of Alien Suffrage," *University of Pennsylvania Law Review* 141, no. 4 (1993): 1391–470.

Raz, Joseph, *The Morality of Freedom* (Oxford University Press, 1986).

Rehfeld, Andrew, *The Concept of Constituency: Political Representation, Democratic Legitimacy, and Institutional Design* (Cambridge University Press, 2005).

Rogers, Brishen, "Passion and Reason in Labor Law," *Harvard Civil Rights–Civil Liberties Law Review* 47 (Summer 2012): 314–69.

Roland, Driadonna, "Sovereign Law Made Cliven Bundy a 'Patriot' But Korryn Gaines 'Crazy': An Explainer on the Controversial Beliefs Gaines May Have Held," *Revolt* (Aug. 8, 2016), https://revolt.tv/stories/2016/08/10/sovereign-law-made-cliven-bundy-patriot-korryn-gaines-crazy-3517d33d30

Rosa, Hartmut, "Social Acceleration: Ethical and Political Consequences of a Desynchronized High-Speed Society," *Constellations* 10, no. 1 (2003): 3–33.

Social Acceleration: A New Theory of Modernity (Columbia University Press, 2013).

Rosa, Hartmut and William E. Scheuerman eds., *High-Speed Society: Social Acceleration, Power, and Modernity* (University Park, PA: Pennsylvania State University Press, 2009).

Rossiter, Clinton ed., "Federalist no. 70," *The Federalist Papers* (New York: Penguin Putnam, 1961).

"Federalist no. 71," *The Federalist Papers* (New York: Penguin Putnam, 1961).

Rowland, Kate Mason, *The Life of George Mason, 1725–1792* (New York: Putnam's, 1892), vol. II.

Rubenfeld, Jed, *Freedom and Time: A Theory of Constitutional Self-Government* (New Haven, CT: Yale University Press, 2001).

St. John, Rachel, *Line in the Sand: A History of the Western US–Mexico Border* (Princeton University Press, 2011).

Sanchez, Laura and Elizabeth Thomson, "Becoming Mothers and Fathers: Parenthood, Gender, and the Division of Labor," *Gender & Society* 11, no. 6 (1997): 757.

Sandel, Michael J., *What Money Can't Buy: The Moral Limits of Markets* (London: Penguin, 2012).

Santiso, Javier and Andreas Schedler, "Democracy and Time: An Invitation," *International Political Science Review* 19, no. 1 (1998): 5–18.

Sarabi, Brigette, "The Prison Index: Taking the Pulse of the Crime Control Industry," ed. Peter Wagner, *The Prison Index* (Springfield, MA: Prison Policy Initiative, 2003), section III, "Prison Labor: Prison Labor in the Federal Prison; Prison Labor in the States."

Satz, Debra, *Why Some Things Should Not Be for Sale: The Moral Limits of Markets* (Oxford University Press, 2010).

Sayer, Linda C., "Gender, Time, and Inequality: Trends in Women's and Men's Paid Work, Unpaid Work, and Free Time," *Social Forces* 84, no. 1 (2005): 285–303.

Scheuerman, William E., *Liberal Democracy and the Social Acceleration of Time* (Baltimore, MD and London: Johns Hopkins University Press, 2004).

"Emergency Powers," *Annual Review of Law and Social Science* 2 (2006): 257–77.

Schuck, Peter H. and Rogers M. Smith, *Citizenship Without Consent* (New Haven, CT: Yale University Press, 1985).

Schuster, Justin and Eric Stern, *Diplomatic Discourse* (The Politic, 2015).

Scott, James C., *Seeing Like a State: How Certain Schemes to Improve the Human Condition Have Failed* (New Haven, CT: Yale University Press, 1998).

Weapons of the Weak: Everyday Forms of Peasant Resistance (New Haven, CT: Yale University Press, 2008).

Shapiro, Ian, *Democracy's Place* (Ithaca, NY: Cornell University Press, 1996).

Shelby County, Alabama v. Holder, 133 S. Ct. 2612 (2013).

Sherwin-White, A.N. *The Roman Citizenship* (Oxford University Press, 1973).

Shropshire, Terry, "Mayor Kasim Reed Considers Curfew in Atlanta," *Atlanta Daily World* (July 15, 2016), http://atlantadailyworld.com/2016/07/15/mayor-kasim-reed-considers-curfew-in-atlanta

Simmons, John A., "Tacit Consent and Political Obligation," *Philosophy & Public Affairs* (1976): 274–91.

Simon, Herbert A., "Theories of Bounded Rationality," in *Decision and Organization*, eds. C.B. McGuire and Roy Radner (London/Amsterdam: North-Holland, 1972).

Skowronek, Stephen, *The Politics Presidents Make: Leadership from John Adams to Bill Clinton* (Cambridge, MA: Harvard University Press, 1993).

Presidential Leadership in Political Time: Reprise and Reappraisal (University Press of Kansas Press, 2008).

Smith, Daniel Scott, "Population and Political Ethics: Thomas Jefferson's Demography of Generations," *William and Mary Quarterly*, no. 3 (1999): 591–612.

Smith, Rogers M., *Civic Ideals: Conflicting Visions of Citizenship in US History* (New Haven, CT: Yale University Press, 1997).

Somers, Margaret R., "Where is Sociology after the Historic Turn? Knowledge Cultures, Narrativity, and Historical Epistemologies," in *The Historic Turn in the Human Sciences*, ed. Terrence J. McDonald (University of Michigan Press, 1996).

Genealogies of Citizenship: Markets, Statelessness, and the Right to Have Rights (Cambridge University Press, 2008).

Song, Sarah, "The Significance of Territorial Presence and the Rights of Immigrants," in *Migration in Political Theory: The Ethics of Movement and Membership*, eds. Sarah Fine and Lea Ypi (Oxford University Press, 2014).

"Democracy and Noncitizen Voting Rights," *Citizenship Studies* 13, no. 6 (2009): 607–20.

Southwick, Katherine and Maureen Lynch, "Nationality Rights for All: A Progress Report and Global Survey on Statelessness," *Refugees International* (March 2009).

State Water Resources Control Board, "The Water Rights Process," California Environmental Protection Agency, www.waterboards.ca.gov/waterrights/board_info/water_rights_process.shtml (last visited Aug. 8, 2016)

Stevens, Jacqueline, *States Without Nations: Citizenship for Mortals* (Columbia University Press, 2010).

Stilz, Anna, *Liberal Loyalty: Freedom, Obligation, and the State* (Princeton University Press, 2009).

Stimson, Shannon, "Rethinking the State: Perspective on the Legibility and Reproduction of Political Societies," *Political Theory* 28, no. 6 (2000): 822–34.

Sunstein, Cass R., "Incompletely Theorized Agreements in Constitutional Law," *Social Research* 74, no. 1 (2007): 1733–72.

Thompson, Dennis F., "Democracy in Time: Popular Sovereignty and Temporal Representation," *Constellations* 12, no. 2 (2005): 245–61.

Thompson, E.P., "Time, Work–Discipline, and Industrial Capitalism," *Past & Present* 38 (1967): 56–97.

Tichenor, Daniel J., *Dividing Lines: The Politics of Immigration Control in America* (Princeton University Press, 2002).

United States v. Windsor, 133 S. Ct. 2675 (2013).

Urbinati, Nadia, *Representative Democracy: Principles and Genealogy* (University of Chicago Press, 2006).

Urry, John, "Time, Leisure, and Social Identity," *Time & Society* 3, no. 2 (1994): 131–49.

US Citizenship and Immigration Services, "Continuous Residence and Physical Presence Requirements for Naturalization," United States Department

Homeland Security, www.uscis.gov/us-citizenship/citizenship-through-naturalization/continuous-residence-and-physical-presence-requirements-naturalization (accessed Aug. 20, 2016).

Vohs, Kathleen D., Roy F. Baumeister, Brandon J. Schmeichel, Jean M. Twenge, Noelle M. Nelson, and Dianne M. Tice, "Making Choices Impairs Subsequent Self-Control: A Limited-Resource Account of Decision Making," *Motivation Science* 1 (2014): 19–42.

Volokh, Eugene, "Statutory Rape Laws and Statutory Consent Laws in the U.S.," *Washington Post* (May 1, 2015), www.washingtonpost.com /news/volokh-conspiracy/wp/2015/05/01/statutory-rape-laws-in-the-u-s/ ?utm_term=.0b291c845d52

Walzer, Michael, *Spheres of Justice: A Defense of Pluralism and Equality* (New York: Basic Books, 1983).

Wardle, Lynn D., "*Loving v. Virginia* and the Constitutional Right to Marry, 1790–1990," *Howard Law Journal* 41 (1998): 289–347.

Warren, Tracey, "Class and Gender-Based Working Time? Time Poverty and the Division of Domestic Labor," *Sociology* 37, no. 4 (2003): 733–52.

Young, Iris Marion, *Justice and the Politics of Difference* (Princeton University Press, 1990).

Young, Katharine, "Rights and Queues: On Distributive Contests in the Modern State," *Columbia Journal of Transportation Law* 55 (2016): 65–137.

Rotman Zelizer, Viviana A., *The Social Meaning of Money: Pin Money, Paychecks, Poor Relief, and Other Currencies* (Princeton University Press, 1997).

Zerubavel, Eviatar, "The Standardization of Time: A Sociohistorical Perspective," *American Journal of Sociology* 88, no. 1 (1982): 1–23.

  Time Maps: Collective Memory and the Social Shape of the Past (University of Chicago Press, 2012).

Zolberg, Aristide, *A Nation by Design* (New York: Russell Sage Foundation, 2006).

Index

Abizadeh, Arash, 29, 39
abortion, 5, 93, 97, 122, 134
Adam, Barbara, 111, 148
adverse possession, 102, 123
age
  age of maturity, 101, 109, 114
  citizenship and, 49, 101, 148
  retirement, 27, 49, 123, 148, 156
  sexual consent, 57
Akhtar, Ayad, 43
Alexander, Michelle, 159
Allen, Thomas, 21, 104, 106
Anderson, Benedict, 105, 106
Anderson, Elizabeth, 64
Annales School, 21
Arendt, Hannah, 22, 161
Aristotle
  commensuration and, 135–7, 146, 147
  Condorcet on, 80
  kairos and *chronos*, 25
  time and context, 63
  value of experience, 142, 160
  value of political time, 66–7, 100
asylum seekers, 140–1
Augustine of Hippo, 10

Bartelson, Jens, 36
Baubock, Rainer, 105
Bede, 34
Benhabib, Seyla, 161
Benveniste, Emile, 22
Bergson, Henri, 18, 22, 65
Blackstone, William, 89

Breyer, Justice, 133–4
Brunner, Jose, 76–7, 160–1
Burke, Edmund, 78

Calvinism, 116–17
Calvin's Case, 6, 40–2, 51, 54, 84–5,
  88–9, 115
Cambodia, "year zero," 34
Canada, age of sexual consent, 122
censuses, 1, 31, 44–5, 50–1, 58, 69, 110,
  122, 125, 157
children
  age of maturity, 27, 101, 109, 114
  criminal justice, 57–8
  sexual consent, 57
  voting rights and, 58
Cicero, Marcus Tullius, 112
citizenship, *see also* naturalization; voting
  rights
  age of maturity, 27, 49, 101, 109, 114,
    148
  Calvin's Case, 6, 40–2, 51, 54, 84–5,
    88–9, 115
  contested concept, 133
  Cyprus, 44
  Dominican Republic, 46
  Estonia, 43
  Germany, 42
  Kuwait, 44
  Latvia, 43
  leisure time and, 123
  lived consent, 85–9
  Locke, 67–8

probationary periods, 27, 90–4
  property and, 84
  Soviet Union, 42
  temporal boundaries, 49–53
  Ukraine, 44
  United States, *see* United States
  vote storage, 17
Coke, Edward, 40–2, 51, 83, 85, 88–9,
    91, 115
commensuration
  critiques, 120–1, 134–41, 163
    market logic and commodification,
      138–9, 147, 149–50
    reductiveness, 135–8, 147
    transactionality, 139–41
  egalitarianism and, 113–17
  impartiality, 104, 121, 156, 159
  incompletely theorized agreements and,
      131–4, 136–8
  liberalism and, 110, 117–18, 126–7
  normative implications, 141–52
  objectivity, 104, 112–13
  pitfalls, 13–15
  political purpose, 129–31
  political time, 128–9
  qualitative judgments and, 14, 137
  quantifiable good, 104, 107–12, 121,
      155–6
  scientific measurement, 104, 107–12
  situatedness, 104–7
  standardization, 106, 107
  territorial variations, 106
common law marriage, 102, 123
Condorcet, Nicolas de Caritat, Marquis de
  anti-radicalism, 159
  citizenship, 87
  deism, 117
  democracy, 8, 68–9, 95
  on presentism, 76–9
  time as a good, 82–3
  value of political time, 71–82, 142, 157
    instrumental value, 100–1
  voting rights, 70–1, 72–3, 76, 80
Connolly, William, 74
consequentialism, 39,
constitutions
  Condorcet, 68, 71–82
  democracy and, 69–71, 154
  political value of time, 71–82
cooling-off periods, 2, 79–80
corruption, 73, 79, 114, 151

cosmopolitanism, 39,
countdown deadlines, 6, 31, 56–8, 61
Cox, Adam, 51, 52
critical theory, 29
curfews, 6, 30, 45, 48
Cyprus, citizenship, 44

Davis, Kathleen, 34–5, 36, 37, 106
democracy, *see also* citizenship; political
    value of time
  command of time, 59, 156–7
  commensuration and, 15
  constitutions, 69–71, 154
  deadlines, 7–8
  democratic justice and time, 157–62
  developmental democracy, 160–2
  electoral cycles, 117
  iterative democracy, 161
  liberal democracy, 117–18
    political economy of time, 122
    time as a good, 82–5
  liberalism and, 130, 133
  normativity of time, 62–4
  presentism, 76–9
  repeating deadlines, 62
  territoriality, 38–40
  theorists, 22–3
  time and, 11–12, 62–96
    Condorcet, 8, 68–9, 71–82, 95
    democratic process, 89–94
    temporal boundaries of sovereign
      states, 49–53
    time as a good, 82–5
  voting and, 72–3, 80
denaturalization, 160
deterrence, 134
developmental democracy, 160–2
Dominican Republic, citizenship, 46
durational time, 25, 26–7
Durkheim, Emile, 18, 19

education time, 129
egalitarianism
  political value of time, 104, 113–17,
      155–6
  queues, 149, 150
  time and equality, 63
Einstein, Albert, 18
electoral cycles, 69, 117, 157–8, 160
electoral systems, 50–2
Enlightenment, 68, 71, 77, 112, 115–16

Espeland, Wendy Nelson, 110, 111, 128
Estonia, citizenship, 43

Federalist Papers, 72, 73–4
felons, voting rights, 50
feudalism, 106
filibusters, 17, 79
fixed-single moment boundaries, *see* single moment deadlines
Foucault, Michel, 124–6, 162
France
   Republican Calendar, 6, 33, 115–16
   Revolution, 21–2, 81, 106
Franklin, Benjamin, 63, 117,
freedom of movement, restrictions, 45–9
French, Rebecca, 3
Fritzsche, Peter, 106

Garland, Merrick, 69
Germany
   citizenship, 42
   Nazism, 33, 54–5
   undocumented immigrants, 158
   "zero hour," 33
Giddens, Anthony, 74
Goodin, Robert, 29, 39
governmentality, definition, 124–6
Greece, undocumented population, 47

Habermas, Jürgen, 23
Hacking, Ian, 9, 107,
Hamilton, Alexander, 73–4
historiography, 21, 34–5
Hobbes, Thomas, 36, 37, 77, 125
Hunt, Lynn, 105, 148
Hursthouse, Rosalind, 13

immigration, *see* migration
incompletely theorized agreements, 131–4, 136–8
Israel, 156
Italy, undocumented population, 47

James I, 40, 41
Japanese Americans, 162
Jefferson, Thomas, 77, 78, 116, 117
Jessop, Bob, 74
justice, *see* social justice

Kant, Immanuel, 74, 114
Kettner, James, 83, 89

Khmer Rouge, 34
Koselleck, Reinhart, 21
Kryder, Daniel, 71
Kuwait, citizenship, 44

Landemore, Hélène, 78
Landes, David, 37, 106, 124
Latvia, citizenship, 43
Leibniz, Gottfried Wilhelm, 112
leisure time, 19, 21, 123
liberalism
   command of time and, 59, 156–7
   commensuration and, 110, 117–18, 126–7
   democracy and, 130, 133
   reductiveness, 135–7
Lindahl, Hans, 22
Locke, John
   consensual citizenship, 33, 67–8, 85
   empiricism, 126
   mathematics and ethics, 112
   parliamentary government and, 160–1
   presentism and, 76–7
   social contract, 89
Lol Non, General, 34
longue durée, 21

McCarthyism, 162
Madison, James, 90, 91, 117
Magna Carta, 40–2
Maréchal, Sylvain, 115
Markell, Patchen, 161
Marx, Karl
   capitalist exploitation, 144–5
   measuring time, 110, 128
   working time, 12, 15, 20, 64, 93, 122
Mason, George, 90
mentally ill persons, voting rights, 50
Michelman, Frank, 23
migration, *see also* naturalization
   asylum seekers, 140–1
   probationary periods, 122–3
   undocumented population, 47, 143–4, 146–7, 158
military service, 2, 13, 97, 103, 122–3, 137
Mill, John Stuart, 77, 112, 136
Morris, Gouverneur, 90

nation states, *see* sovereign states
naturalization, *see also* citizenship
   denaturalization, 160

formulae, 97, 131
injustices, 16
probationary periods, 27, 90–4, 97, 103,
    108, 122–3, 130, 138, 140–1
qualitative judgments, 13, 14, 137
representational value of time, 102
time and, 5, 8
United States, *see* United States
Nazism, 33, 54–5
Negri, Antonio, 35
Nelson, William Max, 21–2
new territorialists, 29
Nozik, Robert, 150
Nussbaum, Martha, 9, 13, 107

Ochoa Espejo, Paulina, 22
Orren, Karen, 2, 82
Ortega Y Grasset, José, 22

Paine, Thomas, 117
parole restrictions, 46, 48
permanence, 160–2
Petty, William, 125, 126
Pierson, Paul, 24
Plato
    on attributes of time, 108
    commensuration, 66, 108–9, 110, 111,
        135
    Condorcet and, 80, 95
    objectivity of time, 112
    Protagoras, 107, 135
    technē, 66, 71, 95, 108–9, 126,
        135, 146
    time and context, 63
    value of political time, 142
Pocock, John, 22, 35, 36, 52, 65, 75, 114,
    126
political economy
    Foucault, 124–6
    meaning, 124
    origins, 124
    time, *see* political economy of time
political economy of time
    governmentality and market logic, 123–7
    meaning, 120, 121–3
    measurement. *See* commensuration
    normative implications, 141–52
    overview, 12–18, 120–52
    political exploitation, 145–52, 156
political exploitation, 145–52, 156
political statistics, 107, 108

political value of time
    ancient history, 65–7
    Condorcet, 68–9, 71–82
    constitutional road, 71–82
    democratic process, 89–94
    egalitarianism, 104, 113–17, 155–6
    impartiality, 104
    instrumental value, 99–101, 154–5
    Janus-faced time, 104, 117–18, 141
    modern theory, 67–71
    objectivity and impartiality, 104, 112–13
    overview, 2–5, 97–119
    quantifiable good, 104, 107–12, 155–6
    reasons, 8–12
    representational value, 99, 101–3
    road to constitutions, 71–82
    scientific measurement, 104, 107–12
    situatedness, 104–7
    time as a good in liberal democracy, 82–5
    types of value, 98–9
    why time, 104–18, 155–6
Polybius, 22, 75
Portugal, undocumented population, 47
presentism, 73, 76–9
prison sentences
    Attica protests, 159
    deterrence, 134
    discrimination, 5
    egalitarianism and, 114
    factors, 97
    fitness for citizenship and, 127
    focus on, 27
    formulae, 122
    Foucault on, 125–6
    life sentences, 160
    mitigating factors, 141
    punishment and, 8–9, 16–17
    purpose, 103
    qualitative and quantitative judgments,
        13, 137
    quantitative approaches, 109
    racialized justice, 5, 146, 158–9
    reform, 144
    relativity, 16
    sentencing guidelines, 133–4, 137–8
        illiberalism, 157
        mandatory minimums, 145–6
        racial minorities and, 158–9
    vulnerable minorities, 142
probationary periods
    immigration, 122–3

probationary periods (*cont.*)
 incompletely theorized agreements, 131–4
 naturalization, 27, 90–4, 97, 103, 108,
  130, 137, 138, 140–1
property ownership, 84
punishment, *see also* prison sentences
 character development and, 161
 deterrence, 134
 factors, 97
 objectives, 103
 permanent punishment, 160

quarantines, 30, 46
queues, 5, 27, 140, 149–50, 155, 156

racial minorities
 prison sentences and, 5, 146, 158–9
 restrictions on free movement, 46–7, 49
 temporal boundaries and, 53
Radin, Margaret, 138
Rawls, John, 24–5
refugees, 140–1, 158
repeating deadlines, 31, 58–60, 61, 62
representation
 contested concept, 140
 representational value of time, 99, 101–3
retirement age, 27, 49, 123, 148, 156
Roman law, 92
Rosa, Hartmut, 20, 74
Rousseau, Jean-Jacques, 71–2, 80, 100
Rubenfeld, Jed, 77, 78
Russia, annexation of Crimea, 44

Sandel, Michael, 122, 139, 143, 147,
  149–50
Santiso, Javier, 24
Scalia, Antonin, 69
Schedler, Andreas, 24
Schmitt, Carl, 34
Scott, James, 160
Sedgwick, Theodore, 91
sentence, *see* prison sentences
Simmel, Georg, 135, 136
single moment deadlines, 6, 31, 53–5, 61,
  94, 101
Skowronek, Stephen, 2, 71, 82
slavery, 46
Snowden, Edward, 162
social justice
 permanence and, 160–2
 theorists, 24

time and, 4–5, 12–18, 157–62
social sciences, time and, 18–25
social welfare rights, 2, 110, 122, 123
Socrates, 13, 135
Somers, Margaret, 2, 33, 67
South Africa, 48
sovereign states
 bounding population of political subjects,
  37–45
 constitutions, 30
 sovereign political borders, 32–7
 temporal boundaries, 5–7, 31–2,
  153–4
 countdown deadlines, 6, 31, 56–8, 61
 democracy and, 49–53
 interior boundaries, 45–9
 repeating deadlines, 31, 58–60,
  61, 62
 single moment deadlines, 6, 31, 53–5,
  61, 94, 101
 types, 31, 53
Soviet Union
 breakup, 43, 44
 citizenship, 42, 43
 restrictions on freedom of movement,
  47–8
Staszak, Sarah, 71
states, *see* sovereign states
statutes of limitations, 6, 30, 31, 53,
  56, 57, 101
Stevens, Mitchell, 110, 111
structuration theory, 20
Sunstein, Cass, 15, 131–4, 136–8

Taylorism, 127
Thompson, Dennis, 75, 77
Thompson, E.P., 124
time
 categories, 25
 democracy and, *see* democracy
 durational time, 25, 26–7
 meanings, 25–7
 measurement, *see* commensuration
 political economy, *see* political economy
  of time
 political value, *see* political value of time
 social justice and, 4–5, 12–18,
  157–62
 social sciences and, 18–25
 sovereignty and, *see* sovereign states
 ubiquity, 1–2

Ukraine, citizenship, 44
undocumented immigrants, 47, 143–4,
    146–7, 158
United Kingdom
    Calvin's Case, 6, 40–2, 51, 54, 84–5,
        88–9, 115
    National Debt, 36, 126
    naturalization, 92
    political statistics, 107
    union of the crowns, 40
United States
    abortion, 134
    age of sexual consent, 57, 122
    borders, 38
    California water rights, 48
    censuses, 44–5, 122
    Chinese Exclusion Act (1882), 47, 55
    citizenship, 8, 43, 44–5,
        82, 83–9
        Inglis, 87–8, 89
        lived consent, 85–9
        McIlvaine, 85–6, 87, 89
    Constitutional Convention, 90–1
    Constitutional model, 68
    cooling-off periods, 79–80
    education time, 129
    eighteenth-century nationalism, 106
    founders' deism, 117
    free movement restrictions, 46–7
    internment of Japanese Americans, 162
    juvenile offenders, 57
    McCarthyism, 162
    National Origins Quota Act (1925), 55
    naturalization, 13
        debates, 100, 102, 113, 130, 143
        liberalism, 126, 127

probationary periods, 90–4, 103,
    122–3, 130, 137, 140–1
political ages, 1
prison sentences
    Attica protests, 159
    guidelines, 133–4, 137–8, 157, 158–9
    harshness, 144
    mandatory minimums, 145–6
    racial minorities, 146, 158–9
restrictions on freedom of movement, 48
slavery, 46
standardization of time, 106
Supreme Court, 69–70
undocumented population, 47, 146–7
voting rights, 50, 52–3
Urbinati, Nadia, 71, 80, 157

Voltaire, 70, 112
vote storage, 17
voting rights
    Condorcet, 70–1, 72–3, 76, 80
    democracy and, 72–3, 80
    temporal boundaries, 49–53, 58

wage theft, 5, 19, 142
Walzer, Michael, 122, 135–6
water rights, 48
Westphalia, Treaty of (1648), 36
Whitehead, Alfred, 65
working time, 12, 15, 19, 20, 64, 93, 122

Young, Katharine, 150

Zeliger, Viviana, 147
zero hours, 33
zero option rules, 6, 42–3, 44, 54, 115

Printed in the United States
By Bookmasters